RUDOLF
STEINER

ALSO BY GARY LACHMAN

Into the Interior: Discovering Swedenborg

The Dedalus Occult Reader: The Garden of Hermetic Dreams

A Dark Muse: A History of the Occult

In Search of P. D. Ouspensky:
The Genius in the Shadow of Gurdjieff

A Secret History of Consciousness

Turn Off Your Mind: The Mystic Sixties and
the Dark Side of the Age of Aquarius

WRITTEN AS GARY VALENTINE

New York Rocker: My Life in the Blank Generation
with Blondie, Iggy Pop and Others, 1974–1981

RUDOLF STEINER

An Introduction to His Life and Work

GARY LACHMAN

JEREMY P. TARCHER/PENGUIN

a member of Penguin Group (USA) Inc. *New York*

JEREMY P. TARCHER/PENGUIN
Published by the Penguin Group
Penguin Group (USA) Inc., 375 Hudson Street, New York, New York 10014, USA • Penguin
Group (Canada), 90 Eglinton Avenue East, Suite 700, Toronto, Ontario M4P 2Y3,
Canada (a division of Pearson Penguin Canada Inc.) • Penguin Books Ltd, 80 Strand,
London WC2R 0RL, England • Penguin Ireland, 25 St Stephen's Green, Dublin 2, Ireland
(a division of Penguin Books Ltd) • Penguin Group (Australia), 250 Camberwell Road,
Camberwell, Victoria 3124, Australia (a division of Pearson Australia Group Pty Ltd) • Penguin
Books India Pvt Ltd, 11 Community Centre, Panchsheel Park, New Delhi–110 017,
India • Penguin Group (NZ), 67 Apollo Drive, Mairangi Bay, Auckland 1311,
New Zealand (a division of Pearson New Zealand Ltd) • Penguin Books (South Africa) (Pty)
Ltd, 24 Sturdee Avenue, Rosebank, Johannesburg 2196, South Africa

Penguin Books Ltd, Registered Offices:
80 Strand, London WC2R 0RL, England

Most Tarcher/Penguin books are available at special quantity discounts for bulk purchase for sales
promotions, premiums, fund-raising, and education needs. Special books or book excerpts also
can be created to fit specific needs. For details, write Penguin Group (USA) Inc. Special Markets,
375 Hudson Street, New York, NY 10014.

Library of Congress Cataloging-in-Publication Data

Lachman, Gary, date.
Rudolf Steiner: an introduction to his life and work / Gary Lachman.
p.   cm.
Includes bibliographical references and index.
ISBN: 978-1-58542-543-3
1. Steiner, Rudolf, 1861–1925.   2. Anthroposophy.   I. Title.
BP595.S895L32   2007   2006037302
299'.935092—dc22
[B]

Printed in the United States of America

3   5   7   9   10   8   6   4   2

BOOK DESIGN BY NICOLE LAROCHE

While the author has made every effort to provide accurate telephone numbers and Internet
addresses at the time of publication, neither the publisher nor the author assumes any responsibility for errors, or for changes that occur after publication. Further, the publisher does not have any
control over and does not assume any responsibility for author or third-party websites or their
content.

For Alfred Lachman, 1924–2004, who taught me
things I am only just beginning to learn

Those who go their own way, as I do,
will certainly be subjected to many misunderstandings.
—Rudolf Steiner

CONTENTS

ACKNOWLEDGMENTS

Many people helped in the making of this book. My special thanks go to the kind people at Rudolf Steiner House, London, for the generous use of their excellent library. I am also indebted to the Rudolf Steiner Library in Ghent, New York, for answering many questions. I would like to thank Mitch Horowitz, my editor, for his enthusiasm about the project, and for the encouragement he has given both me and other writers in the field. My good friends Lisa Persky and Andy Zax were of inestimable assistance in the early stages of the work. And as always, I want to give great thanks to my sons Joshua and Maximilian, for their frequent and indispensable inspiration.

INTRODUCTION:
RUDOLF STEINER'S ROSE

I first became seriously interested in Rudolf Steiner's ideas in the late 1980s. I was then finishing a degree in philosophy, and supporting myself by working at a well-known New Age bookshop in Los Angeles. I had heard of Steiner before, but in a different context. I had always been interested in German Expressionism, the art and literary movement that flourished in the years before World War I, and years earlier had come across a photograph of Steiner's first Goetheanum in a book on Expressionist architecture. The flowing, organic forms, the strange curves and, to me, slightly eerie shadows caught my attention, and I noted that the man who had designed and built this remarkable structure was the founder of a spiritual movement, anthroposophy, which at the time I knew absolutely nothing about and even found difficult to pronounce; *Goetheanum* itself was something of a jawbreaker. But a few years later, in the midst of the various fads for crystals, past lives, and the Harmonic Convergence, I decided to investigate Steiner in earnest. At the bookshop there was a well-stocked Steiner section, and standing before it I had the experience that many who are interested in learning more about Steiner have: discouragement at the sheer number of volumes. An entire bookcase and part of another were given over either to Steiner's own works or to books about him. Along with the number of books, the fact that nearly all of them were published by anthroposophical publishers also raised doubts. This suggested a cult of some kind. I thought that if his books were as important as they were said to be, surely a commercial publisher would issue them; although I am open to all sorts of ideas, I have an aversion to groups or teachings that form a kind of spiritual or cultural ghetto. They also seemed weighted with a great deal of theosophical matter; and although I had read about Madame Blavatsky and found her adventures fascinating, I was less enthused about the content of her teaching.

Nevertheless, as I paged through a few volumes, I saw references to names I was very familiar with. Kant, Hegel, Nietzsche— Steiner had even written a book on Nietzsche. How, I wondered, could thinkers like these have anything to do with ideas about reincarnation or the astral plane? Nietzsche certainly had no patience with anything to do with higher or spiritual worlds. I also remembered that people like the Russian artist Wassily Kandinsky, credited with creating the first abstract painting, had been influenced by Steiner. I decided that I would have to put aside my reservations, take a deep breath, and dive in.

I tried one of Steiner's own books first, *Knowledge of the Higher Worlds and Its Attainment* (since translated as *How to Know Higher Worlds*). Although I was studying Western philosophy, I was familiar with a great deal of occult and esoteric literature and, a few years earlier, had been involved in the Gurdjieff work.[1] So the idea of "higher consciousness" wasn't unfamiliar to me, although, sad to say, I knew more about it from reading than from actual experience.

Steiner's prose had an effect on me similar to that reported by earlier writers, sympathetic but critical biographers like Colin Wilson, but also convinced devotees like Friedrich Rittelmeyer. Of one of Steiner's most important books, *Outline of Occult Science,* Rittelmeyer, who became one of Steiner's closest followers, complained that "if I read for any length of time, a feeling of nausea came over me." I knew how Rittelmeyer felt. To put it bluntly, I found Steiner tough going. I had read difficult books before, but this wasn't the problem. Hegel and Heidegger were notoriously difficult philosophers, but I had mastered large portions of them, and I had spent a great many months making my way through Gurdjieff's willfully obscure epic *Beelzebub's Tales to His Grandson.* This was different. Hegel is difficult not—or not only—because he is a poor stylist; if that was the case, no one would bother reading him at all. He's difficult because the thoughts he is trying to express are complex. But there was just something dull about Steiner. Nevertheless, I was bitten and was determined to assimilate at least the basics of Steiner's thought.

In this I was assisted immeasurably by two books. I am a great fan of Colin Wilson's work and his little book on Steiner introduced him to me in the context of Wilson's own ideas about consciousness.[2] Steiner purists might find Wilson's book flawed; a more recent study of Steiner refers to Wilson as someone who is sympathetic to Steiner, but unable to enter into the true meaning of his work. I can understand how a follower of Steiner might feel this, but Wilson writes as someone interested in alternative accounts of human consciousness and history, and his short study put Steiner into the context of other similar thinkers, and relates him to Wilson's own work. This was important, as it gave me a means of placing Steiner in regard to my own concerns. The other invaluable work was Robert McDermott's anthology *The Essential Steiner.* That McDermott was a philosophy professor suggested that thought and ideas, rather than well-meaning but fuzzy spirituality, common to new age literature, would be important to him. His insightful introductions and linking essays made Steiner's vast and complex system available to me, and they showed how Steiner's ideas—often weird, strange, and downright bizarre— grow out of the central themes of German Idealism and Romanticism, two areas of intellectual history I had some grounding in, not to mention much sympathy with.

Accompanied by these two guides, I persevered. It wasn't long before I recognized that I had made the right choice: Steiner was an important thinker, and it would have been a loss had I allowed my misgivings to deter me from coming to grips with him. It was clear that he had many important and fruitful insights about a wide range of subjects. To say "Renaissance man" sounds clichéd, but in this instance it's appropriate. Like his hero and mentor Goethe, Steiner was a "universal man," a creative thinker who was one of the last to apply his considerable mind and remarkable intuitive powers to the whole spectrum of human experience. This kind of all-round intellect is frowned upon today, and given our climate of specialization, it isn't surprising that, even without his unusual ideas, Steiner's polymath approach would have made him suspect. After finding my anthroposophical feet, I started on Steiner's basic books, *Theosophy, An Outline of Occult Science,* and *Knowledge of the Higher Worlds,* which I went back to. Steiner certainly wasn't a page-turner, but a window had been opened into his vision and the sheer vitality of his imagination was captivating. I also found that the difficulty in Steiner's prose proved beneficial:

I had to work at absorbing what he was saying, and the additional effort more often than not paid off. Soon I was collecting his lectures, reading at random almost, finding my way into some fascinating and admittedly strange waters: reincarnation, the life between death and rebirth, our four bodies, the occult history of the world, but also education, art, farming, architecture, social theory, and epistemology. The initial dissonance hadn't disappeared, but now the contrast between, say, Steiner the philosopher and Steiner the occult seer, rather than putting me off, only added to the mystery.

I formulated the cognitive challenge I was presenting myself with in this way: How can I account for the fact that, on one page, Steiner can make a powerful and original critique of Kantian epistemology—basically, the idea that there are limits to knowledge—yet on another make, with all due respect, absolutely outlandish and, more to the point, seemingly unverifiable statements about life in ancient Atlantis? I found myself in the position that the Nobel Prize–winning playwright Maurice Maeterlinck had occupied some seventy years earlier. In 1922 he published a book about the occult called *The Great Secret*. Commenting on one of Steiner's books, Maeterlinck remarks that "having followed him with interest through preliminaries which denote an extremely well-balanced, logical and comprehensive mind," he suddenly comes across a passage that makes him ask whether Steiner "has suddenly gone mad, or if we are dealing with a hoaxer or with a genuine clairvoyant."[3] Colin Wilson himself, who is wholly sympathetic to Steiner, had many reservations about writing a book about him, and at one point had to admit defeat and inform his publisher that he couldn't go through with it. Steiner's claims, Wilson wrote, created such a sense of frustration that "even the most open-minded reader" would soon "give up in disgust." I knew how Maeterlinck and Wilson felt. Steiner's ideas about consciousness, the nature of thought, and the relationship between the mind and the external world were, quite literally, revolutionary, and they had me rethinking the history of Western philosophy. Yet I could turn to another lecture and there Steiner would tell me about reading to the dead, or about the work of the Buddha on Mars, and my response would be either patient acceptance, in which I gave him the benefit of the doubt, or a kind of "Tilt" sign would light up somewhere in my brain. What bothered me more than the truth or accuracy of what he said was how he could possibly verify it. How could he, or anyone, possibly *know* these things? Yet when the frustration became too much, I remembered what I found important in his other insights and I would try to find a way to have it all make sense. In many ways the situation resembled a dysfunctional relationship: I could put the lectures down and walk away, but sooner or later I would be back and the process would start again.

Yet there was something more than my growing acceptance of the essentials of Steiner's philosophy of mind—what I would call, in a book I wrote years later, "participatory epistemology"—that kept me coming back to him, even with all the difficulties in making sense of some of his more unorthodox statements.[4] I had begun to practice, in a desultory way, some of the exercises that Steiner provides in *Knowledge of the Higher Worlds.* I can't say that I pursued these with great diligence, but when I remembered and when an opportunity arose, I would sit quietly, try to cut out distractions, and, as he suggests, try to become aware of my interior world. Steiner's basic insight, the one from which all his other work develops, is the autonomy of the mind, the recognition that consciousness and the I are irreducible realities, spiritual realities, and that our inner world has the power to grasp experience, as he says in one lecture, "in the same way that we can grasp tables and chairs."[5] Steiner calls this "active thinking," and if there is one thing that he wanted to convey it's the importance of making our thoughts and our thinking come alive.

Like many writers and, for sake of a better word, intellectuals, I am often a dull, left-brain type, not frequently given to anything like mystical experience. Yet on at least one occasion I did experience something along the lines of what Steiner is talking about. I found myself with some free time one day, and taking a walk in the warm California sun—a distant memory now from gray London—I wound up in a garden, looking at a rosebush. What made me linger I no longer remember; perhaps at the time I didn't even know. But I found myself looking at a rose and thinking of how the poet Rilke once described a peculiar meditative state that came over him as being silent, like "the interior of a rose." I looked at the rose and thought of Rilke's words, and of Steiner's suggestion that in order to make our thoughts more mobile, we should meditate on processes of becoming, like that of a plant going through its life cycle, from seed to flower. Not much time passed, but at some point I felt that my perception of the rose had shifted from simply seeing it to somehow holding it with my mind. It was an unusual sensation, as if my thoughts, my consciousness, cradled the rose, rather than merely reflected it. Since Descartes and the rise of modern science, our consciousness has generally been thought of as a kind of mirror, reflecting the images of the external world. Essentially passive, our minds are blank slates, waiting for experience to make an impression. But in this moment, it was as though my consciousness reached out and held the rose, as if I were touching it just as I would with my fingers. The sensation was delicate, the experience fleeting. But it was sufficiently real to convince me of its significance. Steiner himself was born with this capacity, although, unlike many natural seers, he trained and disciplined his powers and did not rely on their unconscious, involuntary appearance. It is to his realization that in our segment of history, human beings must learn to develop their "active thinking" through their own efforts, that I, and I suspect others like me, owe our brief experience of this other way of being in the world. This passing moment in which my outer and inner worlds participated in each other convinced me that, for all the strangeness, Steiner was really onto something, and my interest in him deepened. And when I went on to write and publish articles on the Western esoteric tradition, one of the first was on Steiner.[6] It is with this in mind that I invite the reader to engage in a little active thinking of his or her own, and discover the life and work of Rudolf Steiner.

RUDOLF
STEINER

1. THE DWELLER ON THE THRESHOLD

Our main source of information about Rudolf Steiner's life (until his early forties, when he became a public figure and others wrote about him) is his *Autobiography*, written in his last years at the request of his followers and published in serial form in the house periodical of the General Anthroposophical Society, *Das Goetheanum*. Unlike his other books, the autobiography (whose original title, *The Course of My Life*, is still used in one translation) has an ease and gentle rambling flow that suggests that, contrary to what he may have said, Steiner enjoyed writing it and appreciated the chance to reminisce about his past, his friendships, and other relations. Indeed, the book was left unfinished at the time of Steiner's death, and the more than four hundred pages that he did complete only deal with his life up to 1907.

At the outset, Steiner states that he is "little inclined"[1] to write the book, but the chapters that follow tell us otherwise. The last chapters, written in his sickbed while Steiner was suffering from the ailment that would kill him—its exact nature still remains unclear—are rushed and abbreviated compared to the first part, and it's a shame that Steiner wasn't allowed to complete the book at the pace he started it (although, if the first part is any indication, the completed tome may have been twice the size of the book we now have). Part of the training involved in Steiner's "spiritual science" is a kind of life review, a looking back over your past with an eye to locating significant moments when your karma or fate set your life on a particular course. Karma, the Eastern idea that the actions of a past life affect the conditions of a future one, was a central concern of Steiner's throughout his career, but especially in the last years of his life; one of his most important lecture cycles, transcribed and published as the eight volumes making up *Karmic Relationships,* focuses on the strange and, to the uninitiated, often baffling ways in which different "individualities" reincarnate as different historical figures. In these lectures, given in Prague, Breslau, London, and other European cities in 1924, Steiner speaks of the karmic relationships involving significant figures like Ignatius Loyola, the founder of the Jesuits; the philosopher Nietzsche; the playwright August Strindberg; the poet Novalis; the spiritual thinker Emanuel Swedenborg; and many others, including people who played an important role in Steiner's own life. Given Steiner's own belief in the centrality of karma and in his destiny as an agent of spiritual renewal in the West, we can assume that, in reviewing his own life, he was also examining the ways in which his own karma manifested.

Generally, most books about Steiner portray him as someone who, from an early age, was aware of his mission and who accepted his calling without hesitation, striking out toward his goal with unswerving directness. That Steiner recognized he was unlike other people early on is clear, as is his commitment to his destiny. But Steiner's path, like that of most of us, had its detours, dead ends, and wrong turnings and in many ways, the first two thirds of his life were occupied with the need to find himself.

Steiner was, as one writer put it, a very slow developer.[2] The poet William Blake once remarked that while "improvement" makes straight roads, the path of genius is crooked. Steiner's life is a good example of how genius won't be rushed and how it takes its time getting to where it has to go.

It's curious that Steiner's own reason for writing his life story, one he gives in the opening pages of the autobiography, is that the need to answer allegations of inconsistency against him became clear. Others, as we've seen, recognized the "crooked" character of his life, even if they were less understanding about it than they might have been. Although to Steiner the manifold activities and pursuits, the seemingly contradictory positions that were required of him by his fate, were all connected and flowed from one to the other almost seamlessly, to others this was not so clear. Steiner hoped that by spelling out the contours of his path, the notion that he had at different times and for less than noble reasons changed horses in midstream, might be laid to rest. It has to be admitted that Steiner did often find himself in the company of people with whom he basically had little in common, and that even to the sympathetic reader, his frequent turnarounds seem puzzling. Steiner may even have felt this himself, and in his last days, made an enormous effort to see his life as a whole.

Another curious aspect of Steiner's autobiography is that, at the point where it leaves off, there's good reason to argue that Steiner's life as a separate individual had indeed ended. Although nearly twenty years is missing from the story, there's a good argument that, at that point in his life, Steiner the man had more or less disappeared, and Steiner the leader of an international spiritual movement had taken his place. At that point Steiner's story, and the story of anthroposophy, become more or less indistinguishable.

The man and his work became one. The words that begin the last chapter of the book say as much. "In what follows," Steiner tells us, "it will be difficult to separate this account of my life from the history of the Anthroposophical Movement."[3] As one of his biographers remarks, "When he had finished writing this chapter, indeed, he knew that he had reached the end of his life also." The same writer suggests that "the unfinished autobiography in fact did not need to be finished; the purpose for which it had been started had now been fulfilled, and quite possibly nothing could have been added that would have been significant for posterity."[4] This may be a case of making a virtue of necessity, but in many ways these remarks have a ring of truth.

Given this, a reader unfamiliar with Steiner's autobiography might be excused for thinking that prior to his emergence as one of the most significant spiritual leaders of the early twentieth century, his life story would contain at least some insight into his personal life and feelings. This isn't the case; where the issue is his personal life, Steiner's autobiography is frustratingly reticent. Steiner tells us that his aim in writing the book was to set the record about him straight, and to trace the course of his thought and to show how it evolved over time. The book does this, to be sure. Like the story of most philosophers' lives, it's about ideas and intuitions, thoughts and concepts. But along with fulfilling Steiner's aim, in the story of his life, Steiner the man and human being does make a few appearances.

Rudolf Steiner was born on February 27, 1861, in Kraljevec, in a part of Eastern Europe that has changed hands frequently in the last century and a half. When Rudolf was born, the town was in Hungary. Later it became part of Yugoslavia, and with the dissolution of Yugoslavia in 1989, it became part of Croatia. Even in Steiner's own life, the notion that his home was in different lands was central. His parents both came from what was known as the Forest District, the towns of Geras and Horn in Lower Austria, and the fact that they were both German-speaking later caused young Rudolf some difficulties with his Hungarian peers. Steiner always spoke German with an Austrian accent, and throughout his life his roots in Austria were clear in his sociability, what used to be known as *Gemütlichkeit,* a kind of personal warmth, what we today might even call, in the popular sense, soul. But in his early days this quality worked against him, and the quiet, dreamy boy was often considered an outsider.

The Europe that Steiner was born into and in which he grew up is now a kind of fairyland. When he was born, the dual monarchy of Austria-Hungary was just beginning; although still powerful, the old Austrian empire was starting to deteriorate, caught between pressure from Germany and Bismarck from without, and nationalist sentiment from within. It would end, along with much else, in 1918, when the close of World War I left the once long and glorious reign of Emperor Franz Joseph in ruins. The world that Steiner was born into was what we would call today a multicultural society, made up of a rich mix of different ethnic groups that were held together in what seems to us like a remarkable stability. Nationalism and the urge for self-determination by one of these groups, the Serbs, led to the assassination in Sarajevo of Archduke Franz Ferdinand on June 28, 1914. This set in motion the series of events that would start the First World War and change the face of Europe. Some, like the writer and journalist Joseph Roth, whose novel *The Radetzky March* is a marvelous re-creation of this lost age, regretted the passing, and looked back to the old regime with nostalgia. Others documented the era's contradictions. Robert Musil's unfinished masterpiece *The Man Without Qualities* is an almost clinical dissection of the absurdities which led to the collapse of the Hapsburgs. The world that both write about is the world of Steiner's childhood, youth, and early manhood and those interested in a broader background to Steiner's life would profit by reading them. Although decidedly Germanic, Steiner later believed that the mix of cultures and nationalities that surrounded his early life primed him for part of his spiritual mission: to act as a kind of meeting ground between the mysticism of the East and the materialism of the West.

Steiner's parents had met while working on the estate of a Count Hoyos; his father was a gamekeeper, his mother in domestic service. Prior to this, Steiner's father had spent his early years working for and being educated by the monks of a monastery in Geras. Steiner tells us that his father often spoke with great warmth of his years with the monks, and although his father displayed little religious zeal, his stories of life in the monastery may have made a strong impression on Rudolf; Steiner's own vision of Christ was highly unorthodox, but of his commitment to the spiritual life there is no doubt.

When Steiner's parents told the count of their desire to marry, he rejected it—employers had an astonishing authority in those days—and so Johann Steiner and Franziska Blie left the count's employ in order to start a family. Steiner's father took a job as a telegraph operator with the Southern Austrian Railway. He was first assigned to a post in South Styria; later he was moved to Kraljevec. Although determined to make the best of their new life, Steiner recalls that throughout their lives both his parents remained nostalgic for the forests of Lower Austria, and later, when his father retired, they returned there to live.

The picture Steiner gives us of his father is of a dutiful but unfulfilled man. He had no real liking for his work on the railway although, at a time when both the railway and the telegraph were still in their infancy, one might expect some sense of interest in the new, modern world opening around him. The work must have been dull and demanding; Johann would often have to be on duty for seventy-two hours consecutively. The only source of interest for Steiner's father was politics, and when he was old enough to follow it, the young Steiner would often listen to the conversations his father had with another railway employee. Steiner had no interest in the topics, but was amused by the form of the arguments. If one said "Yes," the other said "No," regardless of what they were talking about. Sometimes the exchanges grew heated but the vehemence never exceeded Johann's basic ami-ability, a character trait that Steiner seems to have inherited. The picture Steiner gives us of his mother is somewhat less three dimensional. Although poor, Franziska did her best to make a decent home, and we can assume she had her hands full with her domestic duties; a few years after Rudolf was born she bore two other children, a daughter and another son. Aside from an early mention, Steiner tells us next to nothing about his siblings; an editorial note in the autobiography informs us that their names were Leopoldine and Gustav.

The fact that in his first marriage, Steiner formed a union of convenience with an older woman, and that in his early twenties he developed a strong bond with the mother of four boys he tutored, prompts some questions about his relationship with his own mother. These will have to wait until an enterprising researcher unearths the relevant material, because in this, and other aspects of his personal life, Steiner is less than forthcoming. We can respect and appreciate his statement that "a person's private life does not belong to the public." But interest in the details of Steiner's life needn't stem from prurient curiosity. It's precisely because of his genius that one wants to know as much about him as possible. As with other brilliant men or women, their genius and their life form a unity. Steiner's own researches into the karmic relations of many well-known figures suggest that often what may strike some as trivial or insignificant is precisely the very item upon which more obviously important matters hinge. In any case, Steiner's relationships with women, at least as recounted in his autobiography, tended to be of the platonic type and, to put it bluntly, it's unclear when or if he ever lost his virginity.[5]

About a year after Steiner's birth, the family moved to Mölding, near Vienna. Six months later they moved again, this time to Pottschach, in Lower Austria, where Steiner's father was put in charge of a small Southern Railway station. Steiner lived here until he was eight years old. The landscape was stunning, and the toddler grew into a boy surrounded by magnificent mountain peaks. The Schneeberg (Snow Mountain) in particular was a favorite. The early sunlight hitting the bare peak on summer mornings reflected back to the little railway station and delighted the young boy. The years spent here were an important influence on Steiner, the beauty of nature opened to him and stimulated what would become a profound power of reflection. It was also important that his father worked on the railway. Again Steiner found himself between two worlds, that of nature and science— or at least the results of science. In *Knowledge of the Higher Worlds*, Steiner tells the reader that part of the initiation into the spiritual worlds involves a confrontation with what he calls "the Guardian of the Threshold," a "truly terrible spectral being"[6] who represents the aspirant's unredeemed karma.[7] Yet even in his earliest years, Steiner himself was a kind of dweller on the threshold, occupying the space between two different realms, whether national, cultural, or, in this case, between the natural world within which he would perceive the spirit and the scientific world which would provide him with the method that would allow him to perceive it.

Steiner's portrait of Pottschach presents a picture of a small, sleepy village, where the arrival of the infrequent train was a major event; the schoolmaster, the priest, even the burgomaster would turn out to greet their one regular contact with the larger world. Life for his family was simple, but from Steiner's account we get the impression that he had a happy childhood. The priest from the neighboring village often visited his house, and on one occasion informed Steiner's father that he was fortunate to have so many acacia trees nearby. When his father was puzzled by this, the priest told him that acacia blossoms could be baked like elder flowers, and that they tasted even better. From then on, baked acacia blossoms formed part of the family's diet. Steiner also tells us of a curious habit he had at this time. As soon as he was able to feed himself, Rudolf developed the idea that a cup or plate was to be used only once, and if not observed, he would smash his things after a meal. We can imagine his mother's dismay, and one suspects that a close eye was kept on the boy until he was convinced that these items could be used repeatedly. His odd habit, however, didn't stem from a destructive character, as he was very attentive and careful with his toys. One toy in particular he was very fond of, and the impression it made on him may have influenced some of his later ideas. Steiner was captivated by a kind of picture book whose figures could be moved by pulling a string. He tells us that he and his sister spent many hours with these, and that through them he took his first steps toward reading. In later life, Steiner would argue that a kind of "picture consciousness" formed the type of consciousness of human beings during their "Old Moon" incarnation in the distant past, and that in the future, this would return and be integrated with our current rational consciousness to form a new state, what he called our Jupiter incarnation. One area his childhood toys certainly did influence was Steiner's system of education, which employs similar picture books in its kindergartens.

After an argument with the schoolmaster, Steiner's father decided that he would educate his son himself. Steiner soon found himself sitting next to his father's desk at the railway station, attending to his studies, while his father went about his work. Steiner admits that he was bored by his lessons; like most people of genius, he had a passion for anything that aroused his curiosity, but no time for things that didn't. Steiner was fascinated, however, by what his father had to do; like most young boys, he was interested in his father's work and took to imitating him, becoming absorbed in everything to do with running the station. Later, this insight into how much imitation makes up part of early education would form a central theme in his pedagogical philosophy. Steiner dutifully practiced his writing, with, however, little result, if we go by his later account: Steiner admitted that he could neither spell nor write grammatically until the age of ten. Again, one wonders how much this earlier experience informed his later educational ideas, as it is a standard procedure in the Steiner Waldorf schools to put off teaching reading and writing until the age of seven. For early readers like me, this seems an odd notion, as being able to read is for most of us the first step in broadening our world and moving beyond the limits of our immediate environment.

Steiner tells us that although his early efforts at writing were less than excellent, the practice stimulated his interest in "the laws of nature in their simpler manifestations."[8] He was particularly fascinated in watching how the sand his father poured over his writing dried the ink, and Steiner would often get through his lesson quickly so that he too could engage in this remarkable process. His empirical bent was making an early appearance, and Steiner was often called a "smudger" by his father because of his habit of touching the letters too soon, to test if they were dry. Steiner was also interested in determining the elasticity of the quill he used in his lessons. Forcing his father's paper knife into the slit, he could test this to his satisfaction. Such early science projects, however, did little to improve his penmanship.

These and other early excursions into understanding his world presented Steiner with two themes that would stay with him for the rest of his life. One was to determine how everything was connected; the other, perhaps most significant, was determining the limits of knowledge. To the young boy these certainly didn't appear to him in abstract terms, but again in a kind of picture. Near to Steiner's house was a mill; the miller and his wife were close friends of the family, godparents to Steiner's siblings. Steiner visited the mill often and, as he tells us, took to studying the milling industry intently. Here he found himself at the "inner core of reality." Also close to his home was a textile factory, and Steiner watched as the raw material for the factory arrived at the railway station; later he would see the finished products depart the same way. But what actually happened in the factory itself was a mystery, as he was never allowed to enter it. Here he encountered the "limits of knowledge," and he became obsessed with transcending them. The manager of the factory was a part of this mystery, and Steiner would see him often at the station. His clothes would be covered with a kind of white fluff, his eyes had a fixed gaze, and his voice was mechanical—an effect, Steiner suggests, of working with machines constantly. How was this strange man connected to what went on inside the factory, he asked himself? Although Steiner was determined to crack the mystery, he never asked anyone about it. He developed the odd notion that it is useless to ask about something you can't see, and so the transformation of raw materials into product remained a hidden process to him.

Strangely, although the physical reality of the textile factory remained hidden from him, at around this time, another reality, one that remains hidden from most of us, became available to the young Steiner. In his autobiography, Steiner makes no mention of the event that made him aware of the reality of the spiritual world, and given its importance in his later life, one has to wonder about its omission. But in a lecture given in Berlin on February 4, 1913, Steiner spoke of the experience. Yet even here, he refers to it in the third person, distancing himself from it. At some point, when Steiner was between five and seven years old, he had what we would call a paranormal experience. Sitting in the waiting room of the railway station, he saw a woman he didn't know open the door and enter. Walking to the middle of the room, the woman gestured to the boy. Although he hadn't met her before, Steiner could tell that she looked like people in his family. She then spoke to him, saying, "Try now, and later in life, to help me as much as you can." She remained in the room for a while longer, then walked toward a stove on the other side of the room and disappeared.

Steiner tells us that he was afraid to speak of this experience to anyone, fearing that he might be punished for being superstitious; perhaps more likely, he would have been severely scolded for lying. (Other visionaries had similar reservations; William Blake earned a beating from his father for telling him that he saw angels in a tree; from then on he thought twice about mentioning such things.) But it affected Steiner deeply and later that day he noticed that his father, who was generally amiable, seemed sad. It eventually came out that a close relative had committed suicide on the same day that Steiner had his vision. As mentioned, Steiner had never met the woman, nor had he heard much about her, but in speaking of the event in his lecture, he remarks that it was clearly the spirit of the departed woman who came to him that day and who asked him for help in the time following death. Steiner goes on to say that from then on he had access to a world in which "not only external trees or external mountains speak to the human soul, but also the Beings that live behind them." From then on, the young Steiner lived with the Creative Beings behind the world.

This was Steiner's first conscious experience of the spiritual world and to say it was the determining event of his childhood, if not his life, is no exaggeration. It's also important to recognize that it was an experience involving the dead. Strange to say, Steiner would have much contact with the dead in later life, and a great part of his system involves the experiences the dead undergo prior to incarnating again. Aside from the obvious strangeness of the experience, there are a couple of questions that pique curiosity. Steiner tells us that he hadn't met the unfortunate woman nor did he know much about her, and in any case, as a child of between five and seven, he really couldn't be expected to know about her in any great detail. Yet she appeared to him and asked him for help. But what kind of help could a young boy have given her? Steiner doesn't tell us; all we can assume is that his general attitude toward the spiritual world, his belief, may have been of some help to her and later to the other individuals who had passed into the next world and with whom Steiner had an intimate connection. And here it seems relevant to mention that in the two other significant contexts in which Steiner had some contact with the dead, he again didn't know the people personally.

Another possibility is that somehow this experience was arranged so that Steiner would indeed devote his life and energies to bridging the gap between the physical and spiritual worlds. This begs the question of who could have arranged it, although, given Steiner's ideas about karma, it's possible that before incarnating again—in the time "between death and rebirth," as Steiner speaks of it—he could have arranged it himself. It's unfortunate that we have no information about the woman, other than that she was a relative—one assumes from his father's side, as Steiner speaks of his father's sadness—and that she was obviously troubled by something profoundly enough to commit suicide over it. Did she have any beliefs about life after death or the spiritual world, and did she have some inkling that the young Steiner had a remarkable ability to see into it?

Sadly, these questions more than likely will never be answered. All we know for certain is that after this experience, the young Rudolf Steiner accepted the reality of the spiritual world as unquestioningly as he accepted that of the physical one. Indeed, going by what he tells us, he had a firmer grip on the world of spirits than on the external reality around him. As he grew older, Steiner experienced difficulty dealing with the outer world, and he soon realized that not everyone saw the same world that he did. He also grew to feel lonely; many questions he had about the world were left unanswered. Everyone else seemed unconcerned about this, and was puzzled by his determination to answer them. Steiner had a tenacious need to get to the bottom of things, a preoccupation that some may have considered obsessive. Such unhealthy pursuits—at least from the point of view of the average person—may indeed be the start of what Anthony Storr calls a "schizotypic" personality, a type of person who, while not experiencing full-blown schizophrenia, does share some character traits with schizophrenics. One of these is a tendency toward hallucination. On the other hand, Steiner's preoccupations may have been the first signs of a genius for spiritual science.

When Steiner was eight, the family moved once again; even in his youth, Steiner led something of a nomadic existence, a presage of his later life, traveling across Europe on innumerable lecture tours. Neudörfl is a small Hungarian village near the border of Lower Austria. The Alps were now not as close as they were in Pottschach, but the neighbouring lower mountains had their own charm. In the other direction, toward Hungary, the boy could see a vast even countryside of forests and open fields. One mountain became dear to Steiner; at its top was a chapel with an image of Saint Rosalie, and he often went there with his parents on a family walk. The woods had other delights; they were full of black-berries, strawberries, and raspberries, and Steiner often collected as many of these as he could carry, bringing his offering to the simple evening meal, which was more often than not a hunk of bread and cheese. During his summer holidays, on early mornings

Steiner would also take the thirty-minute walk to a spring near the town of Sauerbrunn, to collect some of the sparkling water for the noon meal.

In 1928 a plaque dedicated to Steiner was put over the door of the railway station at Neudörfl, commemorating his years there, and telling the visitor that "in this house there grew up in the child the foundations of his spiritual world." Certainly the young Steiner's questions had increased. On his walks he often came across a group of monks from a nearby monastery. Steiner wanted very much for the monks to speak with him—perhaps they could have answered some of his questions. They never did, but their presence produced in him a feeling of solemnity, and the sense that there was something very important involved in their activities.

In Neudörfl, Steiner's father seemed to give up the idea of teaching him himself, and the boy was sent to the local school. It sounds to us like a recipe for chaos: the school consisted of one classroom in which five different classes, boys and girls of different ages, were taught at the same time. Steiner admits that it was impossible to do more than endure the boredom of writing his letters on the blackboard, but it was at this school that the second definitive moment in his life occurred. An assistant teacher, a man for whom Steiner felt much affection, lent him a book on geometry. Steiner by this time could read fairly well, although his writing was still deplorable, correct grammar and spelling still far beyond him. It may seem an odd thing to say about a nine-year-old, but Steiner's enthusiasm for the book was boundless. Triangles, polygons, quadrilaterals, parallel lines, the Pythagorean theorem, all captured his attention like nothing before. Steiner's reaction to the book is similar to that of another esoteric philosopher's first encounter with physics; as it would for P. D. Ouspensky after his discovery of the properties of a lever a decade or so later, a door into another world had opened for Steiner.[9] This passion for geometry—a requirement, we recall, of Plato's academy—tells us that in essence Steiner really was a scientist, and that his claims for discovering the outlines of a "spiritual science" were well founded. Perhaps in another context Steiner would have developed into another Newton, but here, in the figures and formulae that crowded the book, his young mind found some comfort for all the deep questions that continued to trouble him. What was important for Steiner about the book was not so much the geometry per se, but the fact that through it he could work out "forms which are seen purely inwardly, independent of the outer senses."[10]

Steiner tells us that "through geometry I first experienced happiness," and that working out the various problems gave him a feeling of "deep contentment."[11] This may seem an extreme statement, but other precocious children have found the pastimes of their peers less than captivating; the philosopher Bertrand Russell, a rationalist far removed from anything like Steiner's spiritual concerns, shared precisely the same experience as Steiner's in his first encounter with mathematics. Einstein did as well.[12] Steiner was clearly a serious child, and he himself tells us that it wasn't until his mid-twenties, when he was a tutor to children, that he learned how to play. But what captured the young Steiner was less a rare but understandable intellectual satisfaction than an unusual confirmation of his experience of the spiritual world. Steiner related his discovery of geometry to his vision of his dead relative. He had an intuition that both were in essence the same, and in later life he would argue this point using the often daunting terminology of epistemology, the study of what we know and how we can know it. But now, the sense that he had crossed yet another threshold manifested in the simple yet accurate dictum that there were two kinds of things: those that were "seen" and those that were "not seen." Both were real, and for Steiner the things that were "not seen" were often more real than those that were. The things "not seen," meaning not grasped by the senses, weren't fantasies or what we'd call "mere imagination." They were inner events, taking place on a kind of interior stage, the soul.

Years later, Steiner would tell his students that although no perfect triangle (or circle, or square) exists in nature, the *idea* of a triangle has as much existence as any physical thing of a triangular shape. What is more, when you or I think of a triangle, it's not as if we each had our own, subjective triangle lodged in our minds. We both observe mentally the *same* triangle. And in doing so we each encounter a real, spiritual world. Because for Steiner, the outskirts of the spiritual world, so to speak, begin in *our own minds.* It is important to grasp this point as it is the essence of Steiner's later philosophy, although at first sight it seems to have little to do with his extraordinary statements about ancient Atlantis or life after death. Steiner recognized that while physical things exist in a physical space outside of us, there is another kind of space, an interior space that we metaphorically say exists "in our heads." I say "metaphorically" because, were we to open our heads and take a look, we wouldn't find this space there, precisely because it isn't a physical but a *mental,* or, as Steiner calls it, a *spiritual* space. (And as our language is geared to describing our physical world, we are forced to use wholly inappropriate terms in trying to articulate the characteristics of this spiritual space.) Steiner found it impossible to think of ideas as mere pictures we make of things—which is, more or less, the general notion of what ideas are. For Steiner, ideas were the "shadows" of spiritual realities; meaning that ideas were realities in themselves. When we look out at the world we see various things: trees, clouds, mountains, and so on. Steiner is saying that when we look *into* ourselves we also see things, and these things are our ideas, which have as objective an existence as trees and mountains. Geometry so affected the young Steiner because it seemed to give confirmation of this: the triangles and other forms he was discovering had a real *objective* existence, but not a physical one, not one that could be grasped by the senses. (And we need to remember that while a triangular shaped object can certainly be grasped by the senses, the pure triangle, the triangle-in-itself, as it were, cannot.)

So, thought young Steiner, the spiritual world (which we must assume he continued to have experiences of) actually exists *within* the soul, in the same way that geometric forms do. And if we can, through a certain inner effort, grasp the reality of an ideal triangle, then we should, he thought, be able to grasp the reality of the other inhabitants of our soul space—like the spirit of his dead relative. And that, in a nutshell, is the core of Steiner's philosophy. It is through our own minds and our power of thought that we gain access to the spiritual world. Steiner would later tell his students that if they wanted to have a conscious experience of the spirit world, they first must learn how to think. For readers who associate spirituality with vague feelings and well-meaning but mushy sentimentality, Steiner's message can seem austere and unattractive. But of all the spiritual thinkers of the twentieth century—or many other centuries as well—his vision is one of the few founded on a firm philosophical basis. If Steiner did nothing more than work out the implications of this childhood insight, he would still remain an important and valuable thinker.

Steiner's discovery of geometry lessened his loneliness. It also compensated for the oppression that he often felt when dealing with "things that were seen." It was perhaps fortunate in more ways than one that Steiner came across geometry when he did. His aversion to the physical world and his preoccupation with the spiritual one may have taken a morbid turn, and what developed into a profound theory of knowledge may have stagnated into a less profitable introversion. Geometry, for all his unusual appreciation of it, helped the young, dreamy boy make a firm contact with a world outside himself, albeit a world that not many understood in the way he did. But this hardly matters. The taste of a real world beyond ourselves is always a tonic, and in Steiner's case it lead to many valuable developments.

Other important experiences came from Steiner's stay in Neudörfl. Although at ten he was still unable to spell correctly or write grammatically, his passion for science grew appreciably. A priest came to the school one day and gathered a group of the "more mature" students, of whom Steiner was one. The priest had brought a drawing of the solar system and he spent an afternoon explaining the Copernican system of astronomy. On another occasion he gave a lesson on solar and lunar eclipses. Steiner spent days making drawings based on these new revelations; his appetite for knowing how things were connected must have felt some gratification. Yet along with his plunge into science, Steiner also experienced a profound connection to the church. Although his father was a freethinker and had no sympathy for the church, the young Steiner felt deeply at home in the rituals and acted as a server or chorister during the Mass. He was impressed by the aura of mystery around the Latin Mass, and his participation in the services allowed him a close contact with the priest who had introduced him to the wonders of astronomy, and who he revered. The importance of having strong role models and figures who inspire reverence in childhood would later become a central theme in Steiner's educational philosophy.

The music and ritual of the church services affected Steiner deeply. He tells us that they "caused the riddles of existence to rise with impelling power" before his spirit. He was less enthused about his catechism classes, however. Steiner's burgeoning religious sense made him feel something of an outsider in his own home, and he developed a kind of doublethink in order to deal with the pressures of once again living in two worlds. He participated in all the outward duties of family life, yet within him, the feelings stimulated by the church services gave a new meaning to his existence.

But aside from geometry, perhaps the most important influence on Steiner at this time was his encounter with a doctor who visited from Wiener-Neustadt. Through him Steiner was introduced to German literature. Lessing, Schiller, and a name that would become very familiar to Steiner in years to come, Goethe, were first made known to Steiner through this visitor. Steiner's family never discussed literature, nor was it ever brought up at school. It was an undiscovered country for Steiner; the doctor from Wiener-Neustadt opened up yet another new world to the precocious boy. Steiner recalls fondly how the doctor would walk with him along the linden trees near the station, discussing the greats of German literature with passion and enthusiasm. Steiner also recalls an important image: the tall, slim doctor striding gracefully, with his umbrella always hanging at his side. Years later, when he was well established, Steiner would be known as the Doctor to his close followers, and in many photographs he could be seen striding up the hill to the Goetheanum in Dornach, an umbrella dangling at his side.

Science, literature, religion: it was a heady brew for the young boy, but its effect was undeniable. Yet the demands of the world of "things seen" were present as well. Steiner's father had to decide whether young Rudolf would go on to the Gymnasium, where the focus was on the humanities, or to the Realschule, a kind of technical institute. For all his new interest in literature—and the work he would do in years to come—the Gymnasium would seem the right choice. But his father felt that a position in the railway would offer a good future for the boy, and he decided that Steiner should study to be an engineer. Thus Steiner was set on a course that would make dealing with the world of "things seen" unavoidable.

2. THE RUSTIC SCHOLAR

Between the ages of eleven and eighteen, Steiner attended the Realschule in neighboring Wiener-Neustadt. His home was in Hungary, but now his school was in Lower Austria, so once again Steiner found himself crossing borders. Normally this would mean a short train journey in the morning, and a long walk back to Neudörfl in the evening, as then there were no trains going back at the right time. But often the trains weren't running, even during the day, and then Steiner would have to make the hour-long journey on foot each way. In the spring and summer, it was a pleasant hike, but in winter things were different. The paths would often be snowed over and the boy would have to plow through, knee-deep, and then the journey took much longer. The idea of walking alone, at night, in an area known for its Gypsies, caused the young boy some concern as well. When we realize how often he would have had to make this demanding trek, we get an idea of how strenuous life was during Steiner's childhood, and how our own lives seem somewhat pampered by comparison.

Sometimes his sister would meet him at the outskirts of the village and help carry his books, but the real challenge facing Steiner at this point wasn't the rigors of braving the elements. City life, with its noise, hustle, and sheer distraction confronted him with a welter of things seen, and just as often heard. Steiner's roots were in nature, in the gentle countryside or in the towering mountains. Now he had to deal with a world that had little time for his poetic, reflective character. Though not huge, Wiener-Neustadt was the largest place Steiner had ever seen—in fact, it was his first real city, everywhere else he knew were villages—and the experience was disorienting. The rows of houses and apartment blocks over-whelmed him; Steiner couldn't conceive of anyone really living like that. If Steiner had difficulty dealing with the external world in the relatively undemanding atmosphere of nature, he now had what must have seemed like a threatening chaos thrust upon him.[1] He found it impossible to find any kind of relationship with his new environment. The only places he felt any connection with were, understandably, the many bookshops, something he hadn't seen before. Often he would linger in front of their show windows, regarding enviously the many volumes on display.

Although in his examination on leaving Neudörfl Steiner did exceptionally well, his examination for entering the Realschule did not go as brilliantly; he passed, but he admits that he cared little for his father's plans for his future. What concerned him were the questions that had occupied him ever since he began to think about the world around him. If attending the Realschule would help him answer them, that was fine; otherwise, he had no real interest in it. This lack of application was evident in his first years at the Realschule, where his performance didn't improve until late in his second year; after that, his work was uniformly considered excellent. Again, like many men of genius, the young Steiner found it difficult to take any interest in the boring necessities he was forced to learn, and he drudged through them only out of a sense of duty.

Steiner admits that at this time he felt a deep need to find an inspiring role model, an adult figure who could elicit a feeling of reverence in him. None of the teachers of his first years did this. Steiner was beginning to feel what the playwright Bernard Shaw calls the "awakening of the moral conscience," and a hunger to find some definite figure in whom to anchor his burgeoning idealism emerged in him. He may seem an unlikely candidate, but at the end of his second year, Steiner's headmaster filled the position. A paper he had written, "The Force of Attraction Considered as an Effect of Motion," which was published in the school annual report, captured Steiner's attention. He understood practically nothing in it, but the little he could decipher seemed to relate to what he had learned from the priest in Neudörfl about the solar system. The paper mentioned a book by the headmaster, with the less than appetizing title *The General Motion of Matter as the Fundamental Cause of All Physical Phenomenon*. Instead of using it to buy toys, a knife, or some other adolescent delight, Steiner saved his allowance in order to get a copy of the book; he then set out to learn everything he could to help him to make sense of it.

The headmaster's argument, put briefly, was that there was no such thing as "gravity," in the sense of some invisible "action at a distance," which he considered a "mystical" idea; and if we recall the original meaning of the term *occult*—"hidden" or "unseen"— then Newton's explanation for why the moon doesn't fall onto the earth but why an apple does, does seem somewhat mystical. Rather than these "unscientific" unseen forces, the headmaster put forth the idea that there are innumerable small bodies in between larger ones, and these in some way push the larger bodies closer to each other. (The idea, to some extent, is similar to that of the ancient Greek philosopher Democritus, who argued that the universe and everything in it is made up of tiny bodies, what he called atoms: everything that takes place in the universe, Democritus argued, is a result of these tiny bodies bumping into each other.) Steiner admits that he saw no reason to accept the headmaster's view, yet he felt it crucial that he *understand* it. And here is an early example of a character trait that is in many ways admirable, but which was also the source of many misunderstandings about Steiner himself. From this point on, Steiner will make it a habit never to simply dismiss an idea or philosophy that he doesn't agree with, but will go out of his way—often bending over backward—to follow it and, if possible, to gather some profit from it. This tendency—one might even say absolute need—to try to see the point of view of another thinker, even when in powerful opposition to it (and to the young boy conversant with nature spirits and other immaterial beings, the notion that matter, was the sole cause of all physical phenomenon must have seemed flat wrong), is testament to Steiner's powers of objectivity, but it also led to much confusion. It's a source of the charges of inconsistency and opportunism that plagued Steiner in later life. Even at an early age, Steiner seemed incapable of simply ignoring an idea that he thought wrong; he had to grasp it thoroughly and be able to *show* that he had. Only then could he reject it. This habit would show up in his encounter with well-known thinkers like Friedrich Nietzsche, and also with others who, very well known in Steiner's time, have since faded to intellectual obscurity. It often led to Steiner's being labeled a follower of a thinker whom he merely took infinite pains to comprehend.

Two other teachers during this time were strong influences on Steiner. In one he felt he had met his ideal. This teacher taught him arithmetic, geometry, and physics. Steiner was impressed by the lucid and exceptionally ordered style of his instruction, a characteristic that Steiner himself would emulate in his own career, both as a lecturer and as a spiritual scientist. This teacher, too, had published a paper in the school's annual report; as in the case of the headmaster, Steiner pored over it relentlessly. He knew nothing about the subject, the theory of probabilities and calculation in life insurance, but this didn't deter him. Soon he could make sense of it. In his third year, he developed a similar relationship with the teacher who taught geometrical drawing. Under his guidance, Steiner's favorite pastime became drawing with a compass and ruler. Between these, and his experience of coming to grips with his headmaster's book, Steiner was beginning to grasp something about the scientific understanding of nature.

Yet the major encounter at this time was with a philosopher who had been dead for more than half a century.

Steiner's windowshopping at Wiener-Neustadt's bookstores paid off one day when he noticed a copy of *Critique of Pure Reason* by Immanuel Kant on display. Again he marshaled his savings and in a short while he bought a copy. Steiner tells us that he was convinced that he could understand the spiritual world of his inner experience only if he was able to fully comprehend the true nature of the physical one. All he was absorbing at this time was directed at this goal. Years earlier, Steiner had encountered the limits of knowledge in the form of a textile factory, and he had vowed to transcend them. Now he was about to meet their most formidable defender.

Steiner remarks that he knew nothing about Kant at the time, although the sage of Königsberg had, with George Friedrich Hegel (whose work Steiner would encounter later on), claim to being Germany's greatest philosopher. Steiner was attracted by the phrase "pure reason" in the book's title; it was, he felt, something along these lines that he was groping toward in his work in geometry, and he was eager to find out what his new discovery had to say about the matter.

When we remember that Steiner had an enormous workload of his own, and that his long treks to and from school left him little time for anything else, we can appreciate the passion that had a fifteen-year-old giving up whatever free time he had to delve into one of the most difficult works of human thought. Kant's dry, pedantic style is legendary, and one wonders how much the young Steiner's study of his work influenced his own style when he came to write his books on spiritual science. Yet even with devoting his free time to philosophical study, Steiner made little headway with Kant, until he hit upon an eminently practical, if somewhat surreptitious expedient. Steiner's history class was a bore, but it offered a way to allow more time with Kant when he realized that the teacher was too lazy to prepare lectures, and that he simply read to the class from the textbook. Steiner read the textbook on his own in a few days, and taking apart his copy of Kant, pasted sections of it into the history book, so that while it would appear to anyone who noticed that he was following the text, he was really grappling with unwieldy items like the antinomies of reason, or the possibility of a priori synthetic statements.

In this way, he said, he slowly came to understand what Kant was saying. And when it came time for his history exam, he got a grade of "excellent."[2]

Steiner tells us that what he wanted then was to establish the relation between the phenomena of nature and human thinking. To this end he often read and reread a page in Kant some twenty times, until he could follow the train of thought clearly. He wanted, he said, to develop his thought so that it was "completely clear and surveyable, unswayed by all arbitrary feelings."[3] But he also wanted to secure that his thought was in harmony with all he was learning about religion; as it was earlier in Neudörfl, religion was still a powerful influence on Steiner. The central need now, however, and for the rest of his life, was to make clear how "the spiritual world was within the sphere accessible to man's perception."[4] Yet what he was learning from Kant argued the exact opposite.

Steiner believed that thinking itself could be developed in such a way that it could "take hold" of things, in the same way that we can in the physical world. That there might remain something "outside" thinking, that one could only "reflect upon," was for him "unbearable." Thought for Steiner must be able to encounter the actual *reality* of things, and the need for him to think through to this reality became a kind of obsession. He talks about sitting quietly during his summer holidays and going through the process of how this takes place "over and over again" in his mind.

Kant's philosophy argues the exact opposite. Thought, for Kant, cannot lead to reality in the way that Steiner would like it to. Kant's central thesis is that rather than *reveal* reality, our thought *imposes* certain "categories" on our experience, and that without these, we would have no experience, no world, at all. Space is one category; time is another. A third is the law of cause and effect. For Kant, our minds, in a much-used simile, are like a pair of spectacles that we need to wear in order to see the world at all. So it is no mere habit of thought to expect the sun to rise tomorrow, as the philosopher David Hume argued; barring any major disruption to celestial mechanics, it will continue to do so for millennia to come—or it will at least *appear* to us that it will.

But this immediately raises the question of what the universe is *really* like. What is it like when we aren't perceiving it through our spectacles? And the answer to that, according to Kant, is that we don't know, and, more important, we can *never* know.[5] We can't see the world without our spectacles (the categories), nor can we ever catch the world when we aren't looking at it. To experience the world at all we need the categories, so it's no good thinking we can slip them off and sneak a peek at a category-less world. There would be *no world for us to see*—at least according to Kant. This notion, that we can never know the world as it really is, was anathema to Steiner.

Kant argued that our *knowledge* can strictly be only of the world perceived through our senses, through, that is, the categories. We can truthfully consider knowledge only that which we can experience through the senses, and what science elaborates on by its measuring and experiments. The "thing in itself," the *Ding an sich,* as Kant called it, is off-limits. We may *intuit* a spiritual world of values, and Kant tried hard to find a rational basis for doing this, but in all honesty we can't consider this knowing it.

For some, like the playwright Heinrich von Kleist, a contemporary of Kant, the upshot of Kant's philosophy was unbearable, and his case may be the only one in history in which a theory of knowledge lead to a suicide. The idea that we can never be certain about what we know drove Kleist to despair, and in a dual suicide pact with a terminally ill woman, he blew his brains out.

The fifteen-year-old Rudolf Steiner was somewhat less excitable than Kleist, and once again, although he disagreed with Kant's conclusions, he profited by coming to grips with them. His belief in the power of thinking to transcend any so-called limits of knowledge, however, was unshaken. He rejected Kant's conclusions precisely because they left something "outside" thinking, which we could only "reflect on," but never *know*. Steiner knew this was untrue, and he was determined to find a way to communicate his knowledge to others.

In an "Autobiographical Sketch" that is known as the Barr Document—because it was written at Barr, in Alsace, at the request of the writer Edouard Schuré—Steiner tells us that after his study of Kant he went on to read his major followers, and after them the philosophers Johann Gottlieb Fichte and Friedrich Wilhelm Joseph von Schelling, two important figures in German Idealism, the philosophical school that Steiner's own ideas have the most in common with. He then makes the curious remark that in this period he experienced "full clarity about the conception of time." This, he says, "belongs already to the external occult influence." What Steiner experienced was "the knowledge that there is an evolution going in a backwards direction, interfering with that which goes forwards; the first is the occult, astral evolution." "This knowledge," he adds, "is the condition for spiritual perception."[6] This seems to suggest that already, at an early age, Steiner had some inkling of what he would later call the Akashic Record, or Akasha Chronicle, a kind of astral recording of the history of the cosmos, and also of the experiences of the dead in between death and rebirth. Yet what does he mean when he says that this knowledge "belongs already to the external occult influence"? Earlier I half-speculated that Steiner's experience of seeing the spirit of his dead relative may have somehow been arranged, so that he would become aware of his power of supersensible perception. What Steiner told Schuré in his sketch was something similar. By his mid-teens, Steiner believed that occult forces were in some way guiding him, leading him to experiences necessary for his development.

Steiner's plunge into the deep waters of philosophy didn't prevent him from developing his practical skills. Around the same time he was wrestling with Kant, he learned bookbinding from one of his father's workmates, taught himself stenography, and, with his sister and brother, tended fruit trees near the station that his parents had been assigned. Another important influence at this time was the doctor from Wiener-Neustadt who had visited Steiner's family in Neudörfl. Steiner met him again, and the doctor invited him to his home. There Steiner was impressed by his enormous library. The doctor lent him books of poetry, and in this way Steiner received classes in literature, along with all his other studies, to which at this point chemistry had been added. Steiner also came upon a series of self-instruction books in mathematics; soon he had taught himself analytical geometry, trigonometry, and differential and integral calculus, subjects he wouldn't be taught at school for some time. And if this wasn't enough, for a diversion he read a huge tome titled *The History of the World*. Steiner explains that although he received high marks in history, until then he hadn't developed an "inner relationship" with the subject; reading this book helped achieve this.

All of this self-motivated study was put to practical use when, at fifteen, Steiner began his lifelong career as a teacher by tutoring his fellow pupils. Steiner was glad to be able to contribute something toward the expense his education was costing his parents. And he gained something from tutoring in other ways as well. Steiner tells us that having to teach his fellow students what he learned in class, forced him to "awaken" from a kind of "dream." "I received the knowledge imparted to me at school as if in a dream," he says. He was awake to "whatever I discovered for myself or obtained from a spiritual benefactor"—such as the doctor from Wiener-Neustadt—but everything else "passed over me like pictures in a dream."[7] Yet in the process of transmitting it to his students, the knowledge, taken in only half-consciously, became truly his.[8]

It's interesting that Steiner speaks of having his school lessons "pass over him like pictures in a dream." This is precisely how he speaks of what he calls our ancient "Old Moon" consciousness, and one gets the impression from this that Steiner must have appeared a trifle odd to his teachers and fellow students—distant, perhaps, with a sense of his mind being elsewhere. (Again the similarity with William Blake.) Years later, speaking of his early twenties, Steiner would refer to himself as the "*unerfahren[er] Büchermensch,*" the "inexperienced bookman." The teenage Steiner was certainly moving in that direction. Yet it's clear he was no ineffectual dreamer, as not only his academic work but his success as a tutor shows. This success wasn't limited to the time at hand, as through his early experiences with his first students, Steiner had to concern himself with learning some "practical psychology" that would come in handy in the future. Through his first students,

Steiner confronted the difficulties and challenges of human development, lessons he would profit from in years to come.[9]

In 1879, Steiner graduated from the Realschule, passing his examinations with honors. The railway had promised to transfer Steiner's father to a station near Vienna when his son was ready to carry on his studies at the Institute of Technology, the equivalent of MIT today. Transferring to Inzersdorf, a small town south of Vienna—since absorbed into its urban sprawl—made it easy for Rudolf to travel from home to school by train. If Wiener-Neustadt had been a challenge for the rustic scholar, the capital must have been an even greater one. Again, the bookstores were a consolation. Steiner spent his first visit to Vienna buying books on philosophy; his aim at that point was to understand the work of Kant's follower, Fichte. Steiner wanted to find ways of expressing with utmost clarity what he called the "living activity of the human spirit."[10] He felt that the only valid starting point for the knowledge he wished to secure was a real grasp of the human "I," the ego. Observing its own activity, Steiner believed that the ego experiences a real spiritual content immediately available to its own consciousness. Fichte had made the human ego the center of his philosophy, and Steiner was at pains to understand this. Little read today outside of classes in the history of philosophy, Fichte grasped an essential insight that was to be of great influence in twentieth-century schools of thought like existentialism. Fichte argued that philosophers have been wrong to think that when they sit, contemplating existence with their minds—as they are prone to do—they are in a position to come to any real understanding of it. Reality is not revealed through contemplation, but through *action*. Armchair philosophers—René Descartes is the prime example—make the mistake of believing that their *passive* approach to the world provides them with an accurate picture of it. The philosopher thus observing the world is only half a man; his other half lies dormant, until some stimulus sparks his *activity*. David Hume once remarked that when he looked inside himself to find his essential I, all he saw was a jumble of thoughts and images. Hume concluded from this that there was no essential I. Fichte argues that Hume didn't see any I because in the passive state in which he looked for it, it didn't exist, or, at best, was asleep. But let Hume—or any of us—throw ourselves into some purposeful action, and our I appears unmistakably. The moral of this is that reality isn't something to contemplate—such passive contemplation often leading to contradictory ideas about its nonexistence—but to be *lived*. In Fichte's ideas, Steiner saw an inkling of the kind of "living activity of the human spirit" he was anxious to articulate. As in the case of Kant, Steiner's peasant common sense made it clear to him that when philosophers go around saying the I does not exist, they have lost themselves in abstract web-spinning, something that not only the philosophers of Steiner's time were prone to do.

To understand Steiner's situation and his powerful need to anchor thinking in spiritual reality, we have to remember that at this time, the most powerful intellectual force in the world was materialism, not the materialism associated with consumerism and our seemingly endless need for more things, although this is an outcome of it, but the belief that everything in the universe could be explained in terms of matter or physical forces. It is still the dominant paradigm today, although since Steiner's time many thinkers have pointed out the inconsistencies in such a claim and have advanced alternative views. Yet since the rise of science as the sole criterion of truth, most of us have tended to accept that, at bottom, *everything* can be explained by the effect of either molecules, atoms, or other bits of matter interacting with each other. The explanations today may be more subtle and complex, but we can see the legacy of materialism in contemporary science's attempts to explain what strikes us as the most immaterial thing of all, our consciousness. The inner world that Steiner was seeking to establish as an autonomous, irreducible *spiritual* reality is, for most neuroscientists and philosophers of mind, really only an effect of purely physical and chemical operations taking place in the brain. The I itself, the center around which our awareness of the world revolves is, as one popular book on the subject put it, only a "user illusion," a device created by our brains to give us the illusion that we are somehow in control—although such an idea prompts endless questions about how we can then talk about brains being ours at all; according to this view, we are really something that belongs to our brains. Another influential book of the late twentieth century made bold claims to have explained consciousness, showing that in reality, it doesn't exist; another, by the Nobel Prize–winning scientist Francis Crick, argued that our "joys and sorrows, memories, ambitions, sense of personal identity and free will" are "nothing more than the behaviour of a vast assembly of nerve cells and their associated molecules."[11] The "nothing more," of course, affirming that while the nerve cells and molecules really exist, our joys, sorrows, personal identity, and free will do not. Several other books have made similar claims.

For our day-to-day lives, the abstruse ideas of philosophers and scientists may be largely ignored. But for someone like Steiner this isn't an option. Why should it make a difference whether consciousness can be explained by material processes or not? Because such mechanical explanations reduce something higher to the effect of something lower. When we think of values like freedom, love, beauty, compassion—none of which, we remember, are material (we can't have a pound of freedom)—we tend to believe that these are somehow more important than the purely physical claims made upon us by our experience. If I haven't had my lunch, gastric juices begin to flow in my stomach, creating the sensation of hunger, and I normally react to this by getting something to eat. But if I am engaged in some activity that I value more than simply satisfying my hunger—like writing this book—I can choose to ignore my hunger and carry on with my work. The different material explanations for my sense of "importance," however, argue in essence that the feeling of value I place on my work is really a product of chemical operations no different than those that produce my feeling of hunger. I normally believe that I can in some way override the commands of my body if I feel it is important to do so. The material explanations of consciousness say that this is an illusion, and that this is true of any other examples I may care to consider, from altruism to falling in love. From evolutionary biology to the ubiquitous "social forces," in today's explained world, the I is little more than an empty stage on which a variety of inescapable pressures play out their conflicts. If originally science—which in our day has become the surrogate religion of scientism—was a liberating force, freeing the human mind from the chains of religious dogma, it is now responsible for transforming our picture of ourselves from the crown of creation to a society of mindless robots, pushed and pulled by overwhelming influences. If our values turn out to be nothing more than the effects of physical forces—more sophisticated, yes, but no different than our feeling of hunger—then they are no values at all, as it is precisely their radical *difference* from physical necessity that makes them valuable. And a measure of our spiritual life is the degree to which our hunger for such values overrides our hunger for more material satisfactions.

It was this that Steiner recognized, and even if he never wrote a word about Atlantis or etheric bodies, his recognition of the absolute importance of establishing the I as an irreducible spiritual reality would make him one of the most important thinkers of the last century.

Alas, like many today who see this importance, Steiner found few among his peers who shared his concern. Later, when he was studying in Vienna, a school friend with whom he carried on a philosophical debate refused to accept any of Steiner's arguments that human beings were spiritual creatures, and maintained that they were really little more than highly sophisticated machines. All Steiner's talk about the I was, for him, just chemistry. When Steiner said "I think," what was really the case, his friend argued, was that it was Steiner's brain and the chemical processes going on in it that were doing the talking. Steiner couldn't accept this. At the train station—his friend still lived in Wiener-Neustadt and had to return each day after class—Steiner made an effort to make his argument concrete. As his friend's train was pulling out, Steiner hurriedly informed him that, although he believed that his I was nothing more than the effect of brain chemistry, his behavior argued otherwise. "You maintain that to say 'I think' is merely a necessary result of processes in your brain and nerve-system. You consider these processes alone to be real. . . . But do please notice that you never say 'my brain thinks,' 'my brain sees this or that,' 'my brain walks.' . . . You are in fact lying when you say 'I.' But you cannot do otherwise than follow your healthy instinct against the insinuation of your theory."[12]

Steiner himself felt that although this was true, it was a somewhat crude way to refute an idea, and he walked away dissatisfied. But it was a start. Yet what was important to him wasn't to arrive at philosophically convincing arguments, but to present the reality of the I in a way that recognizing it would be unavoidable. Nothing could refute the reality of the I. Of this he was certain. But how to show this to others, especially in a time when the exact opposite belief was taken for granted? Clearly, the task he had taken upon himself wasn't easy.

Steiner spent the summer before entering the Institute of Technology grappling with such questions. But again, practical demands were looming. He had to decide on what course of study he would take—in other words, he had to decide on what he would do for a living. Steiner opted to study to be a teacher in a Realschule. His course work included mathematics, natural history, and chemistry. Yet the true course of his life was to be decided by a subject that until then had been something of an extra.

Along with his studies at the institute, Steiner was able to attend lectures at the University of Vienna; here he heard, among others, the philosopher Franz Brentano, who would have an enormous influence on Western philosophy through the work of his follower Edmund Husserl, the father of phenomenology. Like Steiner, Brentano was concerned about the threat of materialism, specifically an aspect of it known as psychologism. This argued that our thoughts (and, in fact, all mental activity) are really the results of brain chemistry. If I listen to a Beethoven string quartet and am moved by the experience, this is simply because certain chemicals in my brain have produced that result; it has nothing to do with my being aware of any higher value inherent in the music. Likewise my contemplating a triangle or figuring out a mathematical equation (2 + 2 = 4 because our brains are made to see it that way, *not* because it really does). Brentano argued that psychologism fails to recognize an essential difference between a physical act, like a chemical exchange, and a mental one, like listening to music. When two chemicals combine, there is no *intention* involved in the act; the chemicals don't choose to do so. This, in fact, is the definition of a mechanical process: pure physical necessity is the sole force at work. But when I listen to music, I intend to do so. In order to complete the act, I have to pay attention. I *decide* to do it. Brentano saw that *all* mental acts are intentional; they don't happen by accident. Like Fichte, Brentano discovered the necessarily active character of our inner world.

The lectures that would have the most profound impact on Steiner at this time, however, weren't from a philosopher or a scientist, but from a professor of literature. Karl Julius Schröer's lectures on German literature held Steiner "spellbound." They introduced Steiner to the work of two German poets who would have an enormous influence on his future task. One was Friedrich Schiller, whose *Letters on the Aesthetic Education of Man* argued that human development depends on achieving a creative balance between the world of thought and that of the senses, between spirit and nature. Steiner took this lesson to heart, and in his later philosophy, which places the human being in a creative tension between the spiritual forces of Lucifer and Ahriman, arriving at such a balance is a key theme. The other poet was for Steiner an even greater revelation.

Steiner had of course become acquainted with the name Goethe from his talks with the doctor from Wiener-Neustadt. But through Schröer he now became a reality. Schröer was a rarity in the German academic world, or, for that matter, in the academic world in any country: a scholar who loved his subject and, more to the point, wasn't afraid to express that love in his work, and to cultivate it in others. For Schröer, literature wasn't a subject; it was life itself. And at the center of that life was Goethe. Schröer was flattered at the attentiveness and enthusiasm Steiner showed at his lectures, and the two became friends. Steiner read Goethe's *Faust* for the first time then—Schröer had edited Part I—and was bowled over by it, his professor's lectures on the work opening up dozens of new avenues of thought. Schröer then was editing Part II, and he discussed his commentary on this drama of magic, knowledge, and human evolution with his eager student. If Steiner had any lingering doubts about the reality of the spirit world, his meeting with Schröer and, through him, Goethe, blew them away.

Although he is one of the greats of world literature, up there with Plato, Dante, and Shakespeare, Johann Wolfgang von Goethe may be only a name to most English-speaking readers, and an obscure one at that. In Europe, however, he was a historical event on a par with Napoleon or the French Revolution. For one thing, he more or less started the Romantic movement, when his short novel *The Sorrows of Young Werther* had young men all over the continent committing suicide, like its hero, over unrequited love—or only in emulation of it. Yet Goethe grew out of his youthful "storm and stress" period to become, like Steiner, an embarrassingly creative individual, able to turn his hand profitably to just about anything. Master of every literary form, Goethe was also a statesman and, most significant in our context, a scientist. He was an evolutionist before Darwin, as well as a mineralogist and a botanist. He rejected Newton's ideas about color and developed his own theory to account for it. In his own day and for many years after, Goethe's scientific ideas were considered literary and intellectual oddities, the interesting but scientifically valueless extravagances of an irrepressibly creative mind. Today, mostly through the efforts of Steiner and his followers, more serious thought is given to Goethe's scientific ideas than ever before. Steiner himself would first come to public awareness as the editor of Goethe's scientific writings, a fact that had enormous significance for the development of anthroposophy.

Steiner's days as a Goethe scholar are slightly ahead of us, but it may be worthwhile at this point to give some idea why his discovery of the great poet-scientist was such a landmark in his life. For one thing, Goethe totally rejected the dominant mechanistic view of the world. Like his contemporary William Blake, Goethe believed that Newton and his followers falsified the picture of the world.[13] For Goethe, nature was "God's living garment," and it could be understood only as a living being, perpetually involved in metamorphosis and transformation. The mechanical view regarded nature as a dead machine, made up of bits and pieces randomly thrown together. For Goethe, this was sacrilege: nature worked from the center growing *out*, bringing to completion its inner form.

Goethe and Schiller once met at a scientific conference and had a famous conversation, one that Steiner was later fond of repeating. Schiller wished scientists would learn to speak of nature in a different way, one not so fragmentary and disconnected. Goethe explained that there is "another way of apprehending nature, active and living, struggling from the whole into parts." What Goethe was referring to were the results of a series of experiments he had undertaken into understanding plant growth, which he wrote about in his book *The Metamorphosis of Plants.* Goethe explained that through a long process of disciplined "imaginative observation," he had brought himself to the point where he could *perceive*—that is, actually *see*—the archetype of all plants, the original plant from which all others developed, what he called the *Urpflanze.* When Schiller replied that this was interesting but still only an "idea," Goethe answered that, in that case, he had "ideas without knowing it, and can even *see them with my eyes.*"[14] Earlier, as a young man, Goethe had had a similar experience of imaginative vision at the cathedral at Strasbourg, when, after spending many days observing and sketching it from many sides and angles, and even curing himself of vertigo by repeatedly climbing its tower, he remarked to some friends that the building was incomplete. His friends were astonished and asked how he knew; after looking at the original plans, they saw he was correct. Who, they asked, had told him? Goethe replied that the cathedral itself had. "I observed it so long and so attentively and I bestowed on it so much affection that it decided at the end to reveal to me its manifest secret."[15]

For Goethe then, as for Steiner, there were no "limits to knowledge," as knowledge wasn't some hidden information outside of the thought or the thinker engaged in discovering it. Truth, for Goethe, is "a revelation emerging at the point where the inner world of man meets external reality. . . . It is a synthesis of world and mind, yielding the happiest assurance of the eternal harmony of existence." For him "there resides, in the objective world, an unknown law which corresponds to the unknown law within subjective experience."[16] This means that for Goethe—and later for Steiner—the best instrument for examining nature, or the man-made world, is the human mind itself, when, through a discipline of the imagination, the inner and the outer worlds are unified. As a later Goethean would phrase it, "The essential qualities of the world become manifest only through our own participatory inner experience."[17]

Truth, then, for Goethe, isn't out there—*The X-Files* notwithstanding—but in here, and is revealed when the mind and the outer world are brought together in harmony. When we observe the world *not* with the cool detachment of the scientist, excluding any subjective element from our observation—which is still the standard procedure—but, like Goethe, with the warmth and ardor of an artist, then it will reveal its secrets gladly. For someone like Steiner, who believed that through "active thinking" the mind can grasp the inner reality of the world as firmly as we can take hold of its physical reality, Goethe's science must have seemed heaven-sent.

That few scientists in Goethe's time, as well as our own, conducted their experiments in the state of consciousness that Goethe advises is regrettable, and it's not surprising that the vision of the world they arrived at lacks any warmth or vitality: the absence of imaginative participation practically guarantees that they will encounter a dead world. But in some ways this hardly matters. In discovering Goethe, Steiner had found a science that would make the living world available to all who truly sought it, and this was all the encouragement he needed. It's unclear how much he realized it, but Karl Schröer's lectures had introduced the rustic scholar to his destiny.

3. AT THE MEGALOMANIA CAFÉ

S teiner may have found it difficult to share his philosophical ideas with any of his friends, but his attempts to talk with them—or with anyone else, for that matter—about his experiences in the spirit world met with even greater resistance. Until his early forties, the central experience of Steiner's life, his ability to see into a supersensible reality, was something he had to keep to himself. Anyone he tried to discuss this with either had no idea what he was talking about or, more often, didn't believe him. The few who felt some understanding of the young seer's experience related it to ideas of spiritualism, the fascination with séances, materializations, and messages from the dead that had been fashionable in Europe and North America since the early 1850s. Yet Steiner was as repulsed by spiritualism as he was by materialism, even more so. He considered spiritualists "more materialist than the materialists," because they wanted to prove the existence of the spiritual world by grabbing hold of some *physical* evidence for it. This, for Steiner, was worse than absurd. It was something like black magic, a kind of sin. The spiritual world had nothing to do with floating tambourines, ghostly hands, Ouija boards, or rapping tables, and the respect he had for it made him nauseated at the idea that it did. Yet those who felt that through these and other ethereal expedients they were closing in on the unseen world, couldn't understand the young man's hostility. Their literal minds, combined with the scientific pretensions of the day, prevented them from having a true insight into the spirit.

It must have been a tremendous relief for Steiner when, on his daily journey from Inzersdorf to Vienna, the young man made the acquaintance of an individual who felt as at home in the realm of the supersensible as he did himself. Traveling on the same train as Steiner was an herb-gatherer, a "simple man of the people,"[1] as Steiner called him. Steiner was eighteen; Felix Koguzki—the herb-gatherer—forty-six. Felix gathered herbs to sell to pharmacists in Vienna, and on his journey there one day, he met the young student. Steiner doesn't tell us how they fell into conversation, but the meeting must have been tremendously important to him. In the Barr Document, Steiner speaks of this encounter as "the meeting with the representative of the M. [Master]."[2] Who the Master might be we will return to shortly, but it's clear that Steiner didn't regard his meeting with Koguzki as a chance occurrence; given Steiner's belief in karma, it's unlikely that he considered much as the work of chance. Years later, Steiner would pay tribute to the importance this meeting had for him, when he modeled the figure of Felix Balde, one of the central characters in his Mystery Dramas, on Koguzki.

Felix wasn't a learned man; although he had read many books on mysticism, when he spoke with Steiner about his visions, it was from his life, not his knowledge, that his conviction came. Felix "was completely initiated into the mysteries of the effects of all plants and their connection with the universe and with man's nature." "Converse with the spirits of nature was," Steiner said, "a matter of course" for him. Steiner tells us that Felix spoke of these things without enthusiasm, and that this had the effect of kindling Steiner's own enthusiasm even more.[3] Steiner admits that at first he found it difficult to understand what the herb-gatherer told him. But gradually, he grew to appreciate the insights his conversation gave him. Felix told him of the hidden world of nature. "With him," Steiner wrote, "it was possible to speak about the spiritual world as with someone of experience." Steiner felt he was the "mouthpiece for a spiritual content seeking utterance from hidden worlds."[4] Steiner admits that the two of them must have looked odd to passersby as they walked the city's streets: the older man with a bundle of herbs tied to his back and a somewhat distracted expression on his face, and the young student, eagerly listening to his friend's often unintelligible remarks. Koguzki invited Steiner to his humble home in Trumau, a small village to the south of Vienna. Although some in Vienna laughed at the herb-gatherer's odd (to them) remarks, here he was a respected figure, head of a large family and appreciated for his wisdom. Steiner speaks with warmth of his visits and of the generosity that this modest family bestowed on him.

It's generally assumed that shortly after his meeting with Felix, Steiner had an encounter with another individual, this one somewhat more mysterious, as the name of the man involved has not come down to us. Steiner referred to him as the Master, and all we know of him is that he indicated to Steiner certain passages in Fichte that were of crucial importance to him when he came to develop his spiritual science. Schuré speaks of this person in somewhat cryptic terms: "The master whom Rudolf Steiner met was one of those potent personalities who are on earth to fulfil a mission under the mask of some homely occupation . . . Anonymity is the essential condition for their power, but only serves to make their influence more lasting, for they arouse, teach, and guide those who can do their work in full view of the world."[5]

The idea of hidden masters may strike us as somewhat unbelievable, but in the late nineteenth and early twentieth centuries it wasn't uncommon, at least in spiritual and esoteric circles. Madame Blavatsky had popularized the idea, speaking of the Mahatmas residing in the Himalayas, from whom she received direction; later, speaking of the "inner circle" of mankind, P. D. Ouspensky remarked that "men belonging to the esoteric circle, when they appear among ordinary humanity, always wear a mask through which very few succeed in penetrating."[6] The idea appears in earlier writers as well, such as the late-eighteenth-century Christian mystic Karl von Eckartshausen's classic *The Cloud upon the Sanctuary*. It is, however, unusual for Steiner, as he generally speaks of his occult guidance in terms of communication from purely spiritual sources. It is also unclear in what way Felix Koguzki was the "representative" of the Master. Does Steiner mean by this that the Master arranged for him to meet Koguzki, in some literal sense? Was Koguzki aware that he was the Master's representative, or is Steiner here speaking figuratively? Again, these questions will more than likely remain unanswered. Steiner did tell Schuré that the Master gave him some advice on what he now clearly saw as his life's mission, to overcome the materialist spirit of the nineteenth century. "To overcome the enemy," the Master said, "you must begin by understanding him. You can only become the conqueror of the dragon by slipping into his skin."[7] Steiner understood this to mean that if he was to show the errors of materialism and bring a new vision of reality in harmony with the facts of the spirit world to mankind, he would first have to grasp thoroughly the very ideas he wished to transcend. Steiner took this advice to heart, but his diligent observance of it would once again cause him many problems. The Master's wisdom often led Steiner to being associated with the very philosophy he wished to overcome.

It would be a mistake, however, to see the eighteen-year-old Steiner as solely a reclusive introvert, grimly preparing himself to do battle with the spirit of the age. Steiner was, after all, in Vienna, and the Vienna of that time was a city of artists, poets, writers, musicians, and, perhaps most important, cafés. Steiner reminds us throughout his autobiography that he was a very sociable character, and the *Gemütlichkeit* of his Austrian roots came to bloom in this city of strudel, waltzes, and bohemians. One thing Steiner discovered in his new city was music, and he threw himself into the ongoing dispute over the merits of Richard Wagner's operas. Yet even here, he found a way back to his basic obsession. One of the arguments raging in the cultural world then was whether music needed a dramatic element, whether it should express or represent something, in the way that painting and literature did (at least at that time), or whether it could stand on its own as absolute music. Steiner, who saw in music a similarity with the spirit world, argued that it had a content of its own, and didn't need program notes or to tell a story. The followers of Wagner disagreed and saw music as only one element in his gargantuan *Gesamtkunstwerken,* total artworks. Typically, Steiner made friends with a young man who was a fanatical Wagnerian. They went to many concerts together, but where Steiner's friend was carried away by the ecstatic expressiveness of Wagner's music, Steiner himself was bored. They argued endlessly over cups of coffee or while walking the streets for hours. Steiner tells us he was witness to a touching but unrequited love affair between his friend and a girl who would listen to their arguments from her window. The affair never got beyond distant glances, and Steiner's broken-hearted friend soon had to leave Vienna and take a job as a journalist in another city. Years later Steiner found out that his friend had never recovered from his doomed romance and, after years of poverty, had died of tuberculosis. Another young man whom Steiner befriended at this time met a similar tragic fate. A poet of melancholy disposition, he could find no place in the world for himself; all he cared about was poetry, and even this gave him little satisfaction. After leaving Vienna, Steiner stayed in touch with his friend through correspondence; his letters revealed a ominous development: he became obsessed with the idea that he was suffering from some incurable disease. Soon after, Steiner discovered that his friend had committed suicide.

The pessimism that afflicted Steiner's friends was part of the cultural atmosphere in Vienna and the rest of Europe at the time; it has, unfortunately, remained more or less dominant ever since. In a course on public speaking that Schröer gave along with his classes on Goethe, another friend gave a speech on the philosopher Schopenhauer, whose book *The World as Will and Representation* argued, in essence, that all existence was an illusion and that it was better for human beings not to have been born at all.[8] Steiner's idealism couldn't stomach this, and in reply to his friend's speech he thundered, "If the previous speaker is right in his presentation of pessimism, I would rather be the floor on which I stand than a human being."[9] Steiner's friend teased him about this remark for weeks afterward, but it's understandable that a nature so optimistic as Steiner's would find a philosophy that argues that human effort is useless, and that all reality is an illusion, repellent. It was, however, in the air, and once again

Steiner would find himself having to accommodate views absolutely opposed to his own. This was certainly the case in the circle around the young poetess Marie Eugenie delle Grazie. Marie delle Grazie had achieved a degree of fame by publishing her first book of poems at the age of seventeen. Schröer had read them and was impressed; he showed them to Steiner, who went on to read everything the young woman had written. Steiner was so taken with her work, which ironically, but typically, expressed the very pessimism he opposed in his friend's speech, that he wrote an article about her for a small newspaper. They met soon after, and she told him about her new work, an epic poem about the life of Robespierre, the leader of the French Revolution during the years of the Terror. It would, she told Steiner, depict the tragedy of all idealism. Delle Grazie's vision of the world was as diametrically opposed to Steiner's as was possible. She saw all human ideals as powerless against a senseless, cruel, inexorable nature. She also told Steiner about a further work she planned, in which she aimed to portray a vision of an evil Primal Being, the spiritual force behind nature's mindless destruction; Steiner's own vision of the dark spirit Ahriman may have its roots in delle Grazie's poem. Steiner admits that he was shaken by her words, but that he also saw power and a kind of greatness in them. "I was never inclined to withhold my admiration," he writes, "from what I considered great, even when I absolutely opposed it."[10]

When he was invited to delle Grazie's home for one of her literary soirees, he had even more opportunities to admire what he opposed. Schröer came along on Steiner's first visit, but never returned. The atmosphere in delle Grazie's home was so utterly anti-Goethean that Schröer refused to set foot there again. One of the regulars was a Cistercian priest, Laurenz Müllner, who argued that everything Steiner attributed to Goethe really had nothing to do with the stuffy minister of Grand Duke Karl August—a dig at what Müllner and the others saw as Goethe's conservatism and smug complacency as a member of the establishment. (As a Catholic, Müllner also had reason to reject Goethe, who had less than kind words for the Church.) The literary figure whom delle Grazie and her circle admired most was Dostoyevsky, whose sensitivity to human weakness and suffering, and whose often morbid obsession with sin and guilt, was light-years away from Goethe's healthy optimism. Another whom they found stimulating was Leopold von Sacher-Masoch, whose novel *Venus in Furs* depicts a man in the thrall of erotic fetishism; it also provided the world with the term *masochism*. Less kinky was Shakespeare, who was nevertheless a master at depicting human failure and pettiness.

One would think that Steiner wouldn't feel at home in this milieu, but again we have to recall his vow to understand all points of view, even ones as opposed to his as those he was encountering in delle Grazie's circle. But we also have to understand that Steiner was a young man, barely making his way in the world. Like all men of genius, he had a deep belief in his own destiny, but he also had no idea how he would fulfill it. Earlier Steiner had joined the German Reading Room of the Technical Institute. He became its librarian and soon after was elected chairman. One of his first acts as chairman was to write letters to as many well-known writers as he could, asking for copies of their books. He also took every opportunity he had to meet any writers, thinkers, or scholars. In his autobiography Steiner is inclined to speak of these events in a rather solemn, serious way, but as Colin Wilson points out, "it does not take much imagination to place oneself in the shoes of this eighteen-year-old stationmaster's son, with no money and no prospects, and to recognize that what really preoccupied him was the question of getting a 'start in life.'"[11] Steiner was looking for his destiny, and at this point the best way to meet it, he thought, was to meet as many people who seemed to be fulfilling theirs as possible. "So," Wilson writes, "he seized every opportunity to meet writers, artists, philosophers, or any professor who happened to have written a book. The instinct for self-expression is as powerful as the instinct for self-preservation."[12]

With this in mind it's easier to understand why Steiner, after rejecting pessimism in fairly vehement terms, came to write an essay more or less defending it. Discussing delle Grazie's work, Steiner argued that although he didn't agree with her philosophy, he felt that a vision of the world like hers, that didn't shy from facing the "abysses of existence," was more profound than a shallow facile optimism that refused to recognize the drama and poignancy of life. There *was* an enmity between brute nature and human ideals, and it needed to be acknowledged. But, Steiner continued, man's independent inner world creates *out of itself* meaning, value, and purpose, and these, he argued, are stronger than the vicissitudes of life. He also added that our inner being cannot grow if everything it needed were simply given it by nature. Our freedom wouldn't exist if nature or any other external power nursed and protected us as if we were children. "External nature must deny us everything so that the happiness we achieve is wholly our own independent creation."[13]

Steiner needed to be in the company of people like delle Grazie and Müllner, in order to more finely hone his own ideas, but also to surround himself with others who were active in the world and who were taking part, if only in a small way, in the great spiritual struggles of the time. Although he owed much to Schröer, if he had, like his teacher, turned his nose up at the delle Grazie crowd and avoided their company, he would have remained at the same stage of his development and not grown.

Schröer, perhaps understandably, failed to grasp the meaning of Steiner's essay; he also couldn't understand his decision to continue his visits to delle Grazie's home. He felt the essay on pessimism a betrayal of their love for Goethe. It must have seemed like a complete turnaround, especially as Schröer was responsible for Steiner's first step into the wider world of culture. In 1883, when Steiner was only twenty-two, Schröer had urged the editor Joseph Kürschner to hire Steiner to edit Goethe's scientific writings for a series of books titled *German National Literature,* an immense compilation of some 221 volumes, aimed at a popular audience. Kürschner respected Schröer's opinion of his student's ability and agreed. It may seem unbelievable that someone responsible for producing an edition of Germany's greatest poet would hand over the task of editing his work to an unknown and inexperienced young man, but we have to remember that Goethe's scientific writings were considered worthless by most scientists and boring by most literary men. It's a safe bet that no one else really wanted the job. Steiner of course jumped at it. He had already come to believe that in Goethe he had found a thinker of genius who opposed the materialism of the age, and who had also sought to overcome it through its own means, science, a tactic that Steiner himself was then looking for ways to employ. So like his meeting with the Master and Felix Koguzki, Steiner could feel that this offer—which many others may have rejected as a bad career move—was part of the slow revelation of his path.

Schröer threw Steiner a life preserver in another way as well, another reason why he may have felt betrayed by Steiner's insightful but perhaps injudicious essay on pessimism. Since his arrival in Vienna, Steiner had shifted from various cheap lodgings to extended visits to his parents' house (where, in fact, he wrote most of his early books). He also had a less than steady income, and often spent most of his time in cafés, especially the famous Café Griensteidl, known to its artist, poet, and writer habitués, for obvious reasons, as the Megalomania Café. Here he could nurse a cup of coffee for hours, enjoying the warm fire his student's room lacked, discussing the serious questions of the day with fellow aspiring geniuses. For a time, he even gave the Megalomania Café as his address, as it was the one place he was sure to be found. One might think that in this atmosphere of students, artists, poets, and other would-be geniuses, Steiner might have found a girlfriend, but the only affair, if we can call it that, that he mentions in the whole of his autobiography was short-lived and strictly platonic, although the tone of his reminiscences do suggest a certain nostalgia and regret for lost opportunity; one feels that it was the one time in his life when he was truly in love. Whether it was sheer shyness on both their parts, or Steiner's realization that a romantic relationship would turn him away from his chosen path, the outcome was the same: a brief, happy companionship that turned into an even briefer correspondence, followed by bittersweet memories.

Schröer solved Steiner's living problems by introducing him to the Specht family, who were in need of a tutor, especially one for their young son Otto, who suffered from a mental and physical disability, hydrocephalus, water on the brain. Until then, Steiner kept body and soul together by tutoring a variety of different disciplines to several students. The practice forced him to learn an array of subjects, but it was tiring and time-consuming and, more to the point, paid little. Now he entered into the well-to-do Specht household and, for the rest of his time in Vienna, lived in comfort and financial security. Steiner became part of their home; he went on holidays in the Alps with them and, as he says, "shared fully in the joys and sorrows of the family."[14] As the father, Ladislaus Specht, was wealthy and well connected socially, Steiner often found himself in the company of people he would not ordinarily have met; one was the psychiatrist Josef Breuer, who would later become famous as the colleague of Sigmund Freud. Ladislaus was a cotton merchant, and along with teaching the Specht sons, the indefatigable Steiner learned something himself, picking up the essentials of the trade from his employer. With Pauline Specht, the mother, he developed a deep and, one suspects, platonic relationship. Steiner, in fact, developed many deep, "soul" relationships with different women in his life, a tendency that would carry on during his years as a spiritual teacher. With Pauline Specht he could speak about his spiritual experiences, although he admits she was a bit reserved about them; she also took an interest in his philosophical and scientific pursuits. They talked about the problems of life, and for a time Steiner felt it essential that he discuss all his own important decisions with her. Steiner admired her fine personality, her talent and enthusiasm for music, her devotion to her sons, and her own spiritual striving. As Pauline Specht would have been in her late thirties when Steiner met her, it's a reasonable assumption that she would still have been attractive; the ambience of a well-off household, excellent social connections, and warm familiarity would add to her appeal. Steiner was still an impressionable young man, and this formidable older woman no doubt became a kind of mother figure for him. Steiner admits that when it came time for him to leave Vienna, separating from Frau Specht was one of the things that made this difficult.

The most important part of his time with the Specht family was, however, Steiner's relationship with Otto, the disabled son. The boy had been given up as hopeless. At the age of ten, he had not yet mastered the basics of reading, writing, and arithmetic—perhaps Steiner, who could not write grammatically or spell correctly at ten, felt some empathy with the boy. Even the slightest mental effort exhausted Otto. His vitality was low; he suffered headaches, his skin was pallid, and he was subject to emotional fits. Steiner recognized that the problem was essentially physical: Otto's soul had great potential, it was his body that was causing the problems. Steiner saw that he would first have to gain the boy's love and trust, a slow, but rewarding task. The lessons themselves had to be minimal, as even a quarter hour's effort was demanding. Steiner tells us that through his work with Otto, he acquired his basic insights into the relation between the human body and the soul. He had to awaken Otto's sleeping intellect, and gradually guide it as it encountered his resistant body. Through the attention and warmth Steiner showed him, Otto's confidence grew. The work was difficult; Steiner had to spend two hours each day preparing a carefully scheduled lesson that would itself last no more than half an hour. But his efforts paid off remarkably. Otto quickly caught up with his peers; he then passed the entrance examination for the Gymnasium. Even his physical health improved: the hydrocephalic condition diminished considerably, proving Steiner's fundamental insight that our physical health is determined by our inner, mental state. Steiner felt it was important for Otto to grow up with other children, and he advised Pauline to send the boy to the local public school, where he did well. Otto went on to study medicine and become a doctor; he died as a medical officer in World War I. (Pauline, who felt a deep attachment to her son, died soon after him.) Steiner's success with his young student has to be recognized as one of the most remarkable cases of curative education on record. The insights Steiner gained through his work with Otto Specht later informed his work in Waldorf and special-needs education, which became the basis of the many Camphill schools that deal with students "in need of special care of the soul,"[15] as he would later refer to children like Otto. Here is another example of Steiner's astounding versatility: if he had done nothing else besides develop his curative educational philosophy, he would still be recognized today as one of the geniuses of the twentieth century.

One would think that Steiner would have his hands full teaching a handicapped boy, as well as his older brothers, one of whom, Richard Specht, went on to become an important music critic, and who in later years spoke fondly of his tutor. But Steiner was also working on Goethe's scientific writings and had started work on a book of his own, the somewhat dauntingly titled *Theory of Knowledge in Light of Goethe's Worldview,* published in 1886. Steiner was nothing if not busy. And although he had found a comfortable, if temporary niche with the Spechts, he was no doubt still searching for his place in the world. One brief episode was his time as editor of a political newspaper, the *Deutsche Wochenschrift* (German News Weekly). Taking on the job, Steiner was obliged to write about politics and current affairs, a business for which he admitted he was completely unprepared. But again he turned the experience to good use, learning about editing, about how to produce a readable article each week, and about politics and social issues in Austria. He again received some flak from Schröer over an article on educational reform, in which he praised the pedagogical principles of a Catholic minister in the 1850s; Schröer accused him of wanting to return to Church-controlled education. Steiner, in fact, seemed to have a flair for offending friends in his early writings; another article, in which he believed he had expressed himself "quite objectively" on the sensitive issue of the Jews in Austria, opened a rift between himself and Ladislaus Specht, who was Jewish; Steiner seemed unable to recognize that writing critically about the Jews, however "objectively" and fairly, while living under a Jewish roof and being part of a Jewish family, might not be the most judicious of actions. Steiner's tenure as a political editor was mercifully brief, and although he learned much from the experience, he was glad when his editorship was canceled because of a dispute between the owner of the paper and its founder.

In the middle of all this, Steiner's social life grew. His time at the Megalomania Café increased. He became the stereotypical café intellectual, writing his introductions to Goethe's scientific papers in the midst of the noise and hustle about him. The Megalomania Café was just the place for Steiner at this time. Along with poets, artists, and writers, the clientele included Wagnerians, Pythagoreans, astrologers, vegetarians: as was the case in other European capitals, like Paris and St. Petersburg, the late nineteenth century saw a revival of occult and mystical ideas in Vienna.[16] When Steiner wasn't working, his hours at the Megalomania were filled with new friends, new ideas, and, inevitably, new arguments. One ongoing debate was between himself and the writer Hermann Bahr, who was the Viennese equivalent of London's Oscar Wilde or Paris' Stéphane Mallarmé, doyens of the rising tide of decadence and symbolism. Steiner rejected Bahr's aesthetics vehemently, and in many ways, accounts of their exchanges are reminiscent of the political arguments Steiner listened to between his father and his fellow railway employee, when one said yes to the other's no. The regularity and frequency of Steiner's and Bahr's disagreements became something of a running joke, although Steiner himself felt that he was still unable to formulate his own beliefs effectively. Steiner met many other characters as well: the socialist leader Victor Adler, the pastor Alfred Formey (who, like Marie delle Grazie, held literary gatherings at his home), an actress, Ilma Wilborn (who also ran at-homes), and the widow of the dramatist Christian Friedrich Hebbel—names not very recognizable now, but at the time to Steiner they meant that he was gradually making his way into the world. Through his work on Goethe, his brief editorship of the *Deutsche Wochenschrift,* and the articles he was publishing, Steiner was gaining, if not celebrity, at least a certain visibility in Vienna. Yet, even with this, he still felt his attempts to communicate his ideas about the nature of thinking and the reality of the I were feeble and unimpressive.

All this socializing, however, didn't impede Steiner's progress in the other world, the one of things not seen. His work with Otto Specht had depended on Steiner's ability to look beyond Otto's physical form and into his soul. It was through this that he was able to cure Otto and, in fact, do more than cure him, guide him on the path to his own development. Steiner himself says that during this time, his exploration of the spirit world continued, but in a way more disorganized and less disciplined than it would become later on.[17] But there was at least one occasion in which Steiner's strange ability to look into the other world had remarkable results.

The young girl mentioned earlier on whom Steiner had an unvoiced crush was involved in an important experience in his life. Steiner had met the girl through a friend, who had invited him to his home; she was his sister. There Steiner became aware of an unusual situation. Although at first Steiner's friend and his sisters (there were two) never spoke of their father, and although Steiner never met him, his presence in the household was unmistakable. Gradually, the son and daughters began to tell Steiner about their father, who, Steiner discovered, was a recluse who hardly ever left his room. Steiner got to look at many books from the father's library, and through these he seemed to develop an insight into the character of the man he never met, but who sat, alone, in the very next room. Steiner's curiosity got the better of his tact, and he began to ask many questions concerning the strange man. The son and daughters answered reservedly, but slowly Steiner's picture of this odd individual grew, and he began to share the respect that his friend and his sisters obviously felt toward their father. Then one day it became known that their father was ill; soon after this, he died. Although he had not known the man—had not even *met* him—the family asked Steiner to give the funeral address. Steiner's remarkable ability to gain insight into a person's character proved flawless. The tears the family shed after Steiner's speech showed that he had known and loved their father as truly as they had themselves.

What Steiner didn't tell the family, and what he only revealed later on in his autobiography, is that he was able to follow the father into the spirit world *after* his death. Steiner tells us that he became intimate with the family because there was something of great importance that he had to learn from the father in this way—and not, as one might expect, because of his sadly aborted love for one of the daughters. From the father's books, Steiner already knew that he was intellectually a materialist; yet in his supersensible perception of the man after death, Steiner discovered that all his intellectual beliefs meant nothing, and that in spirit, the man's efforts to discover the true nature of reality, although misguided, stood him in good stead in the afterlife. His denial of the spirit worlds in life had no effect on his experience of their reality after his death. This meant for Steiner that honest pursuit of truth, even if it is mistaken, is of greater value than an unquestioned belief in one's spirituality, if by spirituality is meant a smug acceptance of a higher calling that leads to laziness, complacency, and a disregard for the rigors of thought—an insight from which many new age devotees, who eschew the difficult work of thinking in favor of an easy, "go with the flow," attitude, might benefit.

Steiner's experience in following the soul of his friend's father after death, which, strangely, would be repeated some years later within another, even more intimate family setting, convinced him yet again of the reality of the ego, the I. The personality, the you and me that are uniquely ourselves, did not dissolve with the death of the body and the cessation of the brain's activity. It may seem a long way from the philosophy of Fichte to life after death, but if one accepts—as Fichte, Steiner, and many others have—that the I is an irreducible spiritual reality, then moving on from this to survival of bodily death isn't such an incredible leap. It was that irreducible soul that Steiner perceived in Otto Specht and which he helped bring into fruitful activity. With this in mind, it's understandable that Steiner would feel nothing but rejection for the work of the philosopher Eduard von Hartmann, another thinker little read today, but of enormous importance and popularity in Steiner's time. Hartmann had made a name for himself in 1869, at the age of twenty-seven, when he published *The Philosophy of the Unconscious;* knowing this, we can assume at least a smidgen of envy in Steiner. The unconscious here, however, had nothing to do with Freud's ideas, which wouldn't become associated with the term until the early twentieth century. Although today we speak of the unconscious almost as a matter of course (but at the same time having little real understanding of what the term means), in the nineteenth century, it was still a radical and disturbing notion. As Schopenhauer had before him, Hartmann believed that the force behind life was an unconscious will; in this he differed from Darwin, who had posited a mechanical evolution, driven by random mutation and the struggle for survival. Yet Hartmann's will leads to conclusions about human life that are just as pessimistic as those following from Darwin's idea. In animals, the will appears as instinct, yet in human beings, the will seems to have made a blunder. In producing consciousness, it allowed human beings to develop reason, and through reason, human beings have come to recognize the *pointlessness* of the will's striving. While animals are content to follow the impulses of instinct quite unconsciously, we are beset with a nagging need to know the *purpose* of our existence. And this craving has, since the time of philosophers like Socrates, always made us unhappy. In Hartmann's vision, consciousness separates us from our instinctive life, which we can never enjoy as immediately as do animals, yet it also fails to provide us with a reason for living. Hence, it seems, life is meaningless and consciousness a big mistake, since it points this out to us.

Hartmann's philosophy was, in effect, a well-argued version of Marie delle Grazie's view. But while Steiner could good-naturedly assimilate this tragic view of life when presented in the poems of a young woman, it was another thing to see it spelled out in logical sequence by a great philosopher, who had the findings of modern science at his fingertips. Hartmann's worldview infuriated Steiner. Once again, he couldn't accept the dominant view that consciousness was simply a kind of mirror or flashlight, illuminating and reflecting a world that it *could do nothing about.* Consciousness, for Steiner, was an active force in the world, not merely an observer, and certainly not, as in Hartmann's view, a pathetic one at that, surveying the pointlessness of its existence. Yet it would still be some time before Steiner could articulate his arguments against this view with any precision.

In the meantime, fate, karma, or simply good luck was moving Steiner along. Amid his café friends, Steiner could appear bumptious and inept; he was, after all, a rustic scholar in the big city.[18] His physical appearance then was not impressive, and portraits of Steiner at that time contrast with later accounts of him as a charismatic lecturer. He was of small stature, thin, with long unkempt hair, a clean-shaven boyish face (he later sported a professorial beard and mustache), not particularly fashionable or well-fitting clothes (a frock coat and top hat), and metal-rimmed glasses. One friend remarked that he looked like an ill-fed seminarian. Although eager for debate, Steiner was prone to get caught up in his words and, even when he *knew* he was right, would come away from arguments feeling dissatisfied and frustrated. Yet his essential warmth won people over. One of Steiner's closest friends was the wealthy dilettante and occultist Friedrich Eckstein, who was at the center of Vienna's growing interest in theosophy, the spiritual teaching of Madame Blavatsky, which would, some years later, provide Steiner with his first appearance as an esoteric teacher. Eckstein is a fascinating character; a devoted Wagnerian, among his other achievements, Eckstein is noted for making a barefoot pilgrimage to Bayreuth in order to attend the first performance of *Parsifal.* Roughly the same age as Steiner—he was born in 1860—Eckstein was the son of a paper manufacturer. He became interested in the occult in his early twenties through a Dr. Oscar Simony, a specialist in number theory who had a fascination with the fourth dimension, interest in which back then was as widespread as the recent fascination with chaos theory. Professor Nepomuk Zollner, who became famous for employing a celebrated psychic to explore the possibility of a fourth dimension of space, was Simony's friend. Eckstein joined the Theosophical Society after meeting the British scientist Lord Rayleigh, who told him he had seen spirits. Eckstein's motive in joining the Theosophical Society—which had been founded only a decade earlier in New York by Madame Blavatsky and Colonel Henry Steel Olcott—was apparently scientific, as he proposed to investigate Lord Rayleigh's claims. His investigations must have proved fruitful, as he became the most important theosophist in Austria.

In 1884 he traveled to London, where he met Madame Blavatsky; he later met Colonel Olcott, Annie Besant (who would take over leadership of the Theosophical Society), and A. P. Sinnett, the author of an influential book, *Esoteric Buddhism,* a copy of which Eckstein brought back with him to Vienna. *Esoteric Buddhism* provided a kind of digest of Blavatsky's own voluminous tomes, and among its many readers was the poet W. B. Yeats, who converted to the new teaching. Yeats was later an important member of the celebrated Hermetic Order of the Golden Dawn, which included the notorious Aleister Crowley among its participants. More than likely, Steiner met Eckstein at the Megalomania Café, where he was often found with his retinue of vegetarians, Wagnerians, occultists, and other eccentrics. Although Steiner was at first opposed to Wagner, Eckstein's passion for the composer, combined with his personal charisma, no doubt swayed the young scholar; Steiner's later ideas on art have a distinct Wagnerian tone, and it is curious to speculate whether Steiner attended the artists' colony that Eckstein set up in a castle, Schloss Bellevue, and which he tenanted with musicians, poets, and practitioners of ritual magic. Music was always of central importance to Eckstein; for a time he was the secretary and companion of the composer Anton Bruckner.

Steiner, however, was not impressed by the German version of *Esoteric Buddhism,* which he found repellent. Talk of hidden masters and the like no doubt had the same effect on him as had reports of materializations of spirits, although, as we know, Steiner had had contact with a master of his own. Yet he did find himself becoming interested in theosophy. Through Eckstein he became acquainted with Marie and Edmund Lang, who, with Eckstein, were leading Viennese theosophists, although, as Steiner tells us, they were introduced to the teaching through the work of a less than reputable occultist, Franz Hartmann. Steiner started attending the meetings they held at their home and joining in the discussions; he later asked Eckstein to explain to him the basic theosophical beliefs. It is clear that many of theosophy's ideas would appeal to him. Reincarnation, for one; during this time Steiner was more and more coming to the conclusion while speaking with people that they displayed character traits that could be explained only by the idea of what he would later call "repeated earth-lives." Theosophy saw no fundamental division between science and religion; it recognized that one's salvation really depended on one's efforts to achieve self-knowledge; it also acknowledged that the individual soul evolves through many incarnations. All this Steiner could agree with, and, indeed, the degree to which theosophy influenced Steiner's own outlook remains a matter of debate. He states in the autobiography that he was glad that he had arrived at his own understanding of spiritual truth *before* reading Sinnett's book. Yet it is impossible not to wonder how much the ideas and beliefs he was encountering at Marie Lang's soirees informed his later occult teachings. Steiner consistently maintains that he gained *nothing* from theosophy except an audience open to ideas about spiritual reality. But even a cursory glance at Steiner's later occult doctrines reveals a distinct similarity between Madame Blavatsky's picture of things and his own. It is possible to say, as many Steiner apologists do, that they were both looking at the same territory, but that Steiner's vision was less clouded, more accurate than his celebrated predecessor's. Yet it is equally possible to say the opposite: that when Steiner tells us he had already achieved his own unique spiritual vision *before* he encountered theosophy, he is simply obscuring the debt he owes to Blavatsky and company.

The truth is probably somewhere between the two. Steiner clearly was a visionary in his own right, yet the only "ally," as Colin Wilson writes, that he had so far found in his battle against the materialism of the age was Goethe. And although Steiner tried to correct this view with a lecture he gave in 1888, "Goethe as the Father of a New Aesthetic," for all his prestige, Goethe was seen as a kind of monument, an undoubtedly important figure, but still someone of the past. Theosophy, which today seems like a rather loose collection of vague spiritual beliefs, was in Steiner's time an exciting new development. Yeats, Thomas Edison, Abner

Doubleday (the inventor of baseball), the composers Scriabin and Debussy, the artist Kandinsky, and thousands of other intelligent and responsible people found in it an alternative to a fading church and a science that told them that they were meaningless chance events in a pointless universe. So while Steiner no doubt had important spiritual and philosophical insights of his own, he could also recognize the value of this new religious teaching. Later, when he finally developed the self-confidence and ability to articulate his own teaching (or, as he himself would put it, the occult masters declared him ready to do so), he would abandon much of what he now absorbed so eagerly.

But this was in the future. A decade still lay ahead before Steiner the scholar and philosopher would reinvent himself as Steiner the spiritual scientist. What Steiner felt compelled to do now was to once and for all bring his thoughts and intuitions about the I, freedom, spiritual activity, and the true nature of thinking together in a concise, articulate way. The ideas and concepts he had wrestled with for years would later become the basis for what remains perhaps his most important book, *The Philosophy of Freedom* (1894), more recently translated as *Intuitive Thinking as Spiritual Path* (a title, I have to say, that for me obscures the true intent of the book). Helpful in this task was a friendship he developed with another woman, the feminist and poet Rosa Mayreder, who he met through Marie Lang; she is remembered today as the librettist for Hugo Wolf's opera *Der Corregidor*. In his autobiography, Steiner speaks of Rosa Mayreder in warm and respectful tones. She appeared to him to possess "all the intellectual gifts that are humanly attainable," and their "harmonious working made of her the epitome of everything that is human."[19] He discussed with her his ideas about freedom, the self, and everything else that would later go on to form his first major work. Yet although Steiner speaks of Rosa in glowing terms, she too couldn't really enter into his true life. Theirs was a friendship "which was in a certain sense independent of the views" they held. Neither the way he thought nor the way he felt was congenial to Rosa. His attempts to gain a conscious experience of the spirit held no appeal for her, and what was for him an "absolute necessity" had no meaning for her. His ideas about art she found worthless, as well.[20]

Yet none of this altered anything in Steiner's feeling for her. Again, he had befriended someone who really didn't understand him, and one begins to wonder if Steiner's irrepressible sociability didn't somehow obscure his own emotional needs. Steiner, at least at this point in his career, seemed unable to drop an acquaintance over the simple matter that he had nothing in common with the person. This isn't a criticism, merely an observation, yet I can't help but feel that Steiner's determination to appreciate others, regardless of their appreciation of himself, smacks of something more than the "selfless surrender" that he tells us is essential to spiritual development. Was he simply incredibly lonely, accepting whatever companionship he could find, even if it was with someone incompatible? Is it possible that along with his profound belief in the truth of his insights, and in his own destiny as an agent of spiritual progress, Rudolf Steiner in his mid-twenties had difficulty assessing his own needs and felt a less than invincible self-esteem? That Rosa Mayreder was an older, accomplished, and fiercely independent woman may account for his attraction—again, we have little to go on regarding Steiner's relationship with his own mother. Was he seeking acceptance?

In any case, Steiner's friendship with Rosa marked the end of his Vienna days. In 1889, Schröer once again gave his destiny a push. He had recommended to the Goethe-Schiller Archive in Weimar that they employ Steiner as editor of Goethe's scientific papers for their complete edition of the poet's work. On a visit to the Athens of the North, Steiner had little difficulty in presenting himself as the man for the job, and a year later he headed for Germany.

4. IN THE GOETHE ARCHIVES

teiner paid his first visit to Weimar in August 1889. Upon Schröer's suggestion, he was invited to join the team of scholars then working on a definitive edition of Goethe's works, under the auspices of Grand Duchess Sophie of Saxony. Although he appreciated Vienna and the café life, Steiner thoroughly enjoyed his first experience as a traveling scholar. Aside from the satisfaction he must have felt knowing that he had convinced Bernard Suphan, the Goethe Archive's director, that he was the best candidate for the job of editing Goethe's scientific writings, and that securing the position meant steady work for the next few years—at, admittedly, a less than princely wage—he was a dedicated lover of German culture and this was his first visit to its homeland. It was arranged that he would return a year later, to begin work in earnest, but for the moment, Steiner allowed himself to enjoy his time as a tourist. Steiner's capacity to sink into his thoughts and to let the spirit of a place enter into him served him in good stead. He visited Martin Luther's room in the Wartburg and found the experience profoundly moving. In a letter to Richard Specht—Otto's brother—Steiner wrote that "there is quite a special feeling about knowing that one has beneath one's feet the ground that the German masters trod . . . I have known few days in my life comparable to yesterday, when I entered Luther's room."[1] Weimar had an impressive list of previous inhabitants. There were Goethe and Schiller, of course. But also Johann Sebastian Bach, when he was the court organist. Franz Liszt had been the city's director of music, and the first performance of Wagner's *Lohengrin* had taken place there. A few years after Steiner's arrival, the composer and conductor Richard Strauss would be making a name for himself in the city.

The central spirit of Weimar, however, was Goethe, and Steiner could feel his presence everywhere. He had occupied himself with Goethe's ideas for years; now he had an opportunity to visit the scene of their inspiration. He enjoyed studying Goethe's original manuscripts at the archive and meeting some of his soon-to-be fellow workers, like Hermann Grimm, Gustav von Loeper, and Wilhelm Scherer. Steiner would soon discover that his own approach to Goethe was very different from that of these men, but right now, this didn't matter. What he learned from looking over the material at hand made him feel that his initial insights into Goethe's scientific work were accurate. If anything, this first perusal of Goethe's unpublished scientific writings only strengthened Steiner's conviction that in the act of knowing—in Goethe's sense—Goethe believed a new form of consciousness was produced. Steiner's question now became how he could build upon what he already gained from Goethe, so that from Goethe's insights he could forge a link leading to a direct perception of the spirit world, something that he himself already experienced.

His stay in Weimar lasted a few weeks, and on the return trip to Vienna, Steiner decided to visit Berlin and Munich. In Munich he took in the artistic sights, but his trip to Berlin had a more personal agenda. There he intended to look up the philosopher

Eduard von Hartmann, whose work he disagreed with so thoroughly. It's not exactly clear what Steiner thought he would get from visiting Hartmann, aside from perhaps an opportunity to argue his views in person with someone whose ideas he rejected completely. He and Hartmann had corresponded for a long time, but one gets the impression that letters from the young Steiner were like many the famous philosopher received, and that he didn't take particular notice of them. But again, it isn't difficult to understand Steiner's reasons for seeing the older thinker. Hartmann was at that time an important figure, and even though he disagreed with him, Steiner still respected him and could appreciate his significance. And it would not be a small boost to his own self-confidence if he was able to explain to the established, successful thinker that, with all due respect, his views on some things were open to debate.

The meeting with Hartmann, however, was disappointing. Hartmann had for years suffered from a knee ailment that forced him to spend most of his life sitting upright on a couch; even granting Steiner's powers of tact, it must have seemed an awkward way to meet a brilliant thinker. Steiner says that the two spoke for a long time, but from the description Steiner gives of their conversation, most of it must have been disagreeable to him. Hartmann voiced his convictions with the confidence of age and achievement; this, however, according to Steiner, prevented him from appreciating his guest's point of view. And when Steiner argued that we had no right to assume that our "mental pictures" of reality are in fact *only* that, only pictures, and affirmed conversely that through an effort of will our consciousness can reach into reality directly, Hartmann would have none of it. For him, reality—that is, the world beyond our mental pictures—would forever remain outside consciousness. In fact, the very term "mental pictures" itself suggests that our thoughts have no privileged access to reality; quite the opposite. No, reality, so said the philosopher, whatever it may be, is for us locked in the unconscious, and we must accept this and resign ourselves to living in perpetual uncertainty. . . . Steiner came away chilled, feeling that Hartmann's games with language—"word definition"—were avoiding the real issue. Yet Steiner would later dedicate his doctoral thesis to Hartmann, and when his major work *The Philosophy of Freedom* was published, one of the first copies went to Hartmann—who read it, made many notes in the margins, then sent it back, still having failed to understand what Steiner was talking about. Steiner's patience with uncomprehending acquaintances was phenomenal.

Steiner felt that the move to Weimar constituted a new era in his life. His philosophical and spiritual goals still lay before him; but in respect of his career, he could feel he was making headway. And although he had enjoyed his time as a bohemian, arguing between coffees at the Megalomania Café, what he really needed was the peace and quiet to work out his ideas. Weimar may have been the cultural capital of Germany, but it was a less lively place than Vienna, and its stuffy atmosphere forced Steiner back on himself. One product of this was Steiner's dissertation, mentioned above. Because he had graduated from the Technical Institute, Steiner had been unable to receive a doctorate. Although he had given himself a Gymnasium education, and had even tutored other students in it, because of the nature of Austrian education he was denied official recognition of his scholastic status. He had already been accepted as a colleague on the Goethe project, but it was suggested that having an academic qualification certainly wouldn't hurt. Toward the end of his time in Vienna, Steiner had come upon an enormous tome, *The Seven Books of Platonism,* by a Professor Heinrich von Stein, who taught philosophy at Rostock University. Steiner enjoyed the book immensely and was especially taken with Stein's view that true Platonism received its culmination in the rise of Christianity. Steiner himself would later place Christ at the absolute center of human experience. Now he appreciated Stein's conviction that philosophy was a kind of preamble to the revelation of spiritual reality to be found in Christ's teachings. Steiner sent Stein a copy of his dissertation, which he accepted, and later, as part of the procedure in the German educational system, Steiner traveled to Rostock for an oral exam. Steiner speaks warmly of Stein, remarking that the professor's tone of voice revealed him to be a true philosopher. Stein himself proved agreeable, although he informed Steiner that his dissertation "was not written in the style one usually expects." "It is clear that you have not been under the guidance of a professor." The dissertation, however, was accepted, and Steiner passed his oral examination easily.

Steiner arrived in Weimar for the second time soon after his meeting with Stein, and the ideas he had absorbed from the older man's book were fresh in his mind. How did Plato experience ideas, he asked himself, and how did this differ from what they meant to Goethe? This was an early surfacing of an idea that would become central to Steiner's later work, the notion that consciousness *evolves.* The ancient Greeks saw the world differently than Goethe did, and even more differently than we do. As Owen Barfield would later point out, this isn't the same as a history of ideas, which recognizes that the *contents* of the mind change, but a more radical insight into the fact that the *mind itself* changes.[2]

Steiner's initial excitement over being in the city of Goethe soon cooled when he got down to the daily business of work. Although Steiner met many people, and found the work congenial enough, the differences between Weimar and Vienna, and between his colleagues and himself, soon became apparent. Some people, like Hermann Grimm and Gustav von Loeper, were closer to his feelings toward Goethe than others. Grimm and Loeper, although scholars, didn't approach the poet in an academic way; both had an appreciation of him as a living influence, as a personality and artist. This wasn't true of Wilhelm Scherer. Although Grimm and Loeper had distinguished themselves in their research on Goethe, Scherer, because of his academic standing, was recognized in the archive as the official Goethe expert, and he more or less made the major decisions. He brought to the project a deadening philological approach, a meticulous, painstaking, piecemeal textual analysis that, more than likely, Goethe himself would have snorted at. Steiner himself soon found it unbearable, and the usually tolerant and accommodating philosopher quickly complained that the experts had just as little understanding of what Goethe was about as did the scientists who rejected his work. The philologists, for their part, were often critical of Steiner's approach, pointing out errors in his interpretation of the texts. Steiner himself admits that he was not concerned with getting it right in their sense, but in bringing to life Goethe's *ideas*. Steiner tried to inject a bit of his own sense of Goethe through a lecture he gave titled "Imagination as the Creator of Culture," but one gets the feeling that not many in his audience appreciated his efforts.

Steiner began to speak of Weimar as a home for "classical mummies," where he stood "coldly aside from the life and activity."[3] He confided in Friedrich Eckstein—whom he called Eck: "You can have no idea how alone I feel here, and how little understood."[4] To Rosa Mayreder he wrote, "Here I am all alone. There is no one here who has the remotest understanding of what motivates me and what goes on in my mind,"[5] although, as we've seen, he also believed that Rosa herself didn't really know him. But perhaps Weimar had this effect on people. Another who also felt alone, but whose reaction to his feelings was more radical, was Bernard Suphan, the man who had hired Steiner. Suphan had been married twice, and both his wives, who were sisters, had died young. He lived in Weimar with his sons and seemed lost in mourning the past. Steiner noted that something in Suphan's character prevented him from coming to terms with life, and he watched as he slowly descended into a deep depression. Eventually Suphan committed suicide, immune, apparently, to Goethe's robust philosophy of life.

The free time Steiner had he put to good use, gathering material for his first major work. Along the way he came into contact with the work of another thinker with whom he had little in common, but which, following the advice of the Master, he felt compelled to understand and even to defend. This would lead to much misunderstanding about Steiner in later years. Indeed, Steiner's defense of the now little read Ernst Haeckel, who was immensely popular at the end of the nineteenth century, was precisely one of the reasons why he felt obliged to write his autobiography and set the record straight.

Haeckel was a biologist who had taken up Darwin's ideas and more or less ran with them. He developed a philosophy that he called monism, the idea that there was a single reality and that everything in the universe is a result of matter going through the process of evolution. Unlike Darwin, Haeckel was an out-and-out atheist and materialist, and through his gift of writing very readable prose, his books, like *The Riddle of the Universe,* became bestsellers and his name became something like a household word. Steiner, who also considered himself a monist, but for the exactly opposite reason—spirit, not matter, was the fundamental reality—had given a lecture to the Vienna Scientific Club on his version of monism during his first year in Weimar. Haeckel had heard of Steiner's lecture, and he sent Steiner a copy of a lecture he had given a few months earlier. Steiner reciprocated by sending him a copy of his lecture. Steiner points out that anyone who bothers to read his lecture will see that his version of monism is radically different from Haeckel's. Nevertheless, Steiner, the antimaterialist, soon found himself defending Haeckel the materialist in print, and understandably getting tarred with the older philosopher's brush.

Steiner bends over backward to explain that, given the choice between an account of the creation of life given by Darwin and Haeckel and that by religious fundamentalists (today we call them creationists), he would unreservedly choose the former. Yet he is as fundamentally opposed to their view, which has no place for the spirit, as he is to the other, which ignores the reality of scientific observation. Steiner remarked that Haeckel was a child when it came to philosophy and that his reserves of intellectual energy were consumed in his appreciation of sensory phenomena, something, we know, that Steiner himself had much difficulty with. Haeckel was in essence an artist, Steiner says, and anyone who has seen the beautiful illustrations in his book *Art Forms of Nature* will agree. Yet the conclusions he came to were naive. Nevertheless, as in the case of Marie delle Grazie and Hartmann, Steiner found himself drawn to defend Haeckel's views. Steiner met Haeckel in 1894, on the occasion of the biologist's sixtieth birthday; although he tells us that he had no particular wish to meet him, the idea that he was invited to the birthday celebration in Jena— which had something of a festival about it—must have gratified him considerably. Although established, Steiner was still unknown, and it must have been some boost to his confidence to be considered important enough to be invited to what was almost a national event. As in the case of Hartmann, although he rejected Haeckel's ideas, he recognized his significance, and Steiner's own ambitions must have been piqued when he saw the kind of success the older man enjoyed, and which might be possible for him. Haeckel must have occupied Steiner's mind considerably, as he even saw into the spiritual life of the great scientist. Steiner tells us that in a former life, Haeckel had in some way been a fanatic involved in the Church—the Inquisition?—and that this, combined with his essentially gentle nature, had made him a dogmatic opponent of religion. Steiner would later say something along the same lines about Eduard von Hartmann.

Something similar happened with Steiner and the philosopher Nietzsche. Steiner first came upon Nietzsche's work in Vienna, when the philosopher's ideas were part of the heady brew served up in the Megalomania Café. He read *Beyond Good and Evil,* one of Nietzsche's most provocative books, and entered into a love-hate affair with the brilliant but dangerous thinker. Steiner loved Nietzsche's style and his boldness, but given Steiner's belief in the spirit world, he couldn't love his ideas. In essence, these were materialist, but not materialist in the way that Haeckel's was. Nietzsche was no "positivist," one of those who argued that only what has been arrived at through a methodical scientific analysis could be considered true. Nietzsche's materialism consisted of his rejection of any higher world to which we can appeal to give life meaning. Man, he said, must learn to abandon comforting notions of an afterlife; he must be able to draw a meaning and purpose to his present life out of *himself,* an idea that Steiner had expressed in his essay on pessimism. Nietzsche believed that human beings are far stronger and much more creative than they know, and that all ideas about our present life being a prelude to a real life after death merely provide an excuse to avoid realizing our possibilities. Unfortunately, Nietzsche, who was a gentle, shy, and profoundly lonely man, too often expressed himself in questionable ways and went to extremes that led him to being mistaken for an advocate of cruelty and domination. Steiner had the intelligence to not make this mistake and to appreciate Nietzsche's battle against the spiritual timidity and mediocrity of the time, something in which he himself, in a less explosive way, was engaged.

Steiner later expressed his appreciation of Nietzsche in his book, *Friedrich Nietzsche: A Fighter Against His Time,* published in 1895; again, this led to his being called a follower of Nietzsche, although Steiner does make the differences between himself and the philosopher clear. At the time, Nietzsche was something like the cultural flavor of the month; after years of obscurity and neglect (culminating in his madness), he ironically became the most talked and written about figure at the turn of the century. Steiner was trying to make a name for himself as a cultural writer, so for him to write a book about Nietzsche isn't surprising. Indeed, he almost found himself doing for Nietzsche what he was doing for Goethe. Elisabeth Förster-Nietzsche, the philosopher's sister, approached him about the possibility of helping her set up a Nietzsche archive. Elisabeth Nietzsche had married Bernard Förster, a

German nationalist and anti-Semite, and together they had tried to set up a pure Aryan colony in South America. The plan failed, and on the death of her husband and her return to Germany, she took over care of her now famous but insane brother. Before this, she had absolutely no interest in her brother's—or anyone else's—philosophy, which was just as well, as she lacked the capacity to understand it. Elisabeth took some considerable liberties with Nietzsche's work. Along with adding passages expressing her own anti-Semitic views, she falsified some of Nietzsche's letters to his mother, so that his expressions of affection seemed to be addressed to Elisabeth. In actuality, Nietzsche detested her and her husband for their anti-Semitism, as well as for what he called their "cultural philistinism." But Elisabeth had gotten control of Nietzsche's unpublished manuscripts and was seeking someone to help her arrange them for publication. Nietzsche's own choice as literary executor, the composer Peter Gast, was, sadly, pushed out of the picture when he objected to Elisabeth's less than respectful approach. She later went on to endorse Hitler and the Nazis, who made scurrilous use of her brother's work, and had the pleasure of hosting the Führer on his visit to the Nietzsche archives during a trip to Bayreuth. Nietzsche himself would have had nothing but disgust for Nazism, and it is one of the grave ironies of history that his work still remains associated in the popular mind with the ruthless hacks who appropriated it.[6]

Steiner is being either extremely gracious or naive when he describes Elisabeth as "a versatile and charming personality." Accounts of her at this time relate that she became quite fond of Steiner, describing him in letters as "attractive," "unusually interesting," and a "genuine admirer of Nietzsche," and she confided in friends that she felt he was better equipped to edit the archive than the man currently in charge, Fritz Koegel.[7] One can assume Elisabeth paid considerable attention to Steiner, and it's difficult to believe he wouldn't have known about her Aryan experiment in Paraguay, not to mention that her ideas about race and Germany were distinctly at odds with her brother's. (Nietzsche once described himself as an anti-anti-Semite, and he had nothing but scorn for German nationalism, which really meant militarism.) Elisabeth's ignorance about her brother's work was so great that Steiner, the irrepressible teacher, even offered to tutor her in it. Here one can either accept Steiner's delicacy or find fault in him for not remarking on these dubious characteristics.

But his acquaintance with Elisabeth, and his brief period spent arranging the philosopher's library, led to an opportunity to visit Nietzsche himself. One can't say that Steiner actually *met* the philosopher, for at the time Nietzsche was insane, as a result almost certainly of an untreated syphilis infection. Elisabeth had taken to dressing Nietzsche in a toga and positioning him near the window, where he would appear to be gazing out onto the horizon. In actuality he was oblivious of the world around him, his brain and nervous system rotting away with the disease.

For dedicated readers of Nietzsche (like me), Steiner's account of his visit to the philosopher requires some patience, and it's safe to say that Nietzsche himself would have found it nauseating. Steiner speaks of Nietzsche's "beautiful forehead" and "ensouled" eyes. Steiner says he saw Nietzsche's soul "hovering over his head, infinitely beautiful." It had "surrendered to the spiritual worlds" it had longed for, but was unable to find until illness set it free. In Nietzsche, Steiner recognized a soul "who had brought from former lives . . . golden riches of great spirituality," but who had been unable to let this come to light during his present life.[8]

Previously, Steiner had admired Nietzsche's writings; now he saw the spirit behind the work.

Steiner was disappointed that his time at the Nietzsche archive was cut short, but circumstances made it impossible for him to carry on. Steiner discreetly sidesteps the incident that caused him to withdraw from Elisabeth's offer of working on the archive, and sadly, space doesn't allow me to do more than mention the story of how Fritz Koegel, believing that Steiner had conspired with Elisabeth to unseat him as editor, had challenged him to a duel. Steiner had become friendly with Koegel; when Elisabeth lost interest in Fritz she offered the job to Steiner; he was tempted, but his ethics wouldn't allow it and he declined. Given Steiner's predilection for older women, and Elisabeth's attraction to him, it's a good thing he did.

Along with his work on Goethe, Steiner was given the task of editing complete editions of Schopenhauer (whose pessimistic philosophy he disagreed with so violently) and a writer who is little known in the English-speaking world, but who deserves more recognition, the Romantic novelist Jean Paul. Although Steiner felt closer in spirit to Jean Paul, whose novels often touch on magical or occult themes, his feeling for Schopenhauer was unchanged. He appreciated Schopenhauer's literary skill—with Nietzsche, he is one of the few philosophers who can write—but his ideas still struck Steiner as misguided. Steiner once again had an opportunity to grapple with points of view that strongly contrasted with his own. The work brought him into the social circle of Hans and Grete Olden, a group that considered itself modern, in contrast to those who saw Weimar as a citadel of the past. Hans Olden was the author of light comedies, but at his home, the talk focused on weightier matters. Here the subjects for discussion were Ibsen, Nietzsche, or Strindberg. Although Steiner believed that modern culture was in decline and that the past of Goethe, Schiller, and Hegel represented a high-water mark, he again entered a milieu very much in opposition to his own feelings. One result was his meeting with yet another intelligent, independent, and creative woman, the Egyptian-born writer Gabrielle Reuter. Like Rosa Mayreder, Gabrielle Reuter was a feminist, and one wonders if the high incidence of feminist writers in Steiner's life was simply a product of the time, or if he was somehow attracted to women of strong character and well-defined personalities, who rejected the traditional role of women. Steiner may simply have admired their independent spirits. But it's possible that such women allowed a certain intimacy without danger that the relationship would become something more than platonic.

It's clear, however, that another relationship Steiner formed with a woman at this time was of a different character. As in Vienna, Steiner had been forced to live in cheap rented rooms in Weimar. Although not given to luxury or ostentation—later accounts of his living conditions emphasize their simplicity— Steiner did find such accommodation unsatisfactory; a few years later, he would speak of the "utter misery of living alone." So when through a friend he was introduced to a recently widowed woman who was looking for a lodger, he was delighted. Steiner's biographer Stewart C. Easton remarks that the widow was, like Pauline Specht, in search of a tutor to oversee the education of her children, four daughters and one son. Yet Steiner himself doesn't mention this in his own account. He goes on at length about a remarkable coincidence, however. As before in Vienna, when Steiner met the family of the reclusive father, whom he got to know so well spiritually—without ever meeting him—that he was asked to give the funeral address, here too in Weimar was another family, with a very similar situation. Her husband had died only recently, and the widow in whose home he had now found himself mourned her loss. In his new lodgings, Steiner found himself exploring the library of the deceased, just as he had in Vienna and, more recently, during his visits to Elisabeth Förster-Nietzsche, when he helped arrange her brother's books. During these visits, Steiner found that looking through Nietzsche's collection gave him deep impressions of the philosopher's soul. Now, once again, Steiner was receiving a powerful sense of a dead man through his library, this time one in whose home he had taken up residency.

Like the man in Vienna, the widow's husband had been something of a recluse. He had, Steiner tells us, lived in a world of his own and had been thought of by others as a bit eccentric— something that could easily be said of Steiner himself. And like the man in Vienna, Steiner found that he was able to follow this individual in his path through the afterlife. Like the man in Vienna, here too, the deceased had been a materialist thinker during his life, which means that he accepted the prevailing scientific doctrines. But, Steiner tells us, he wasn't materialistic in his life, meaning that he acted decently and with compassion. This, Steiner explains, is altogether more important in our life after death than any of our purely intellectual ideas. In their thoughts they were materialists. But in their *wills* they were not.

Steiner admits that what he has to say about these two individuals will appear fantastic to many, and we will save a discussion of Steiner's uncanny ability to peer into the spiritual worlds for a later chapter. What is important here is that the man in Weimar into whose spiritual path Steiner gazed, was the husband of the woman who would in a few years become Steiner's first wife. Yet

Steiner's remarks about Anna Eunicke, the widow, are few and less than enlightening; he's certainly at pains not to tell his readers much about their relationship. It's only after a lengthy account of his spiritual perception of the deceased, and the importance this had for his book, *The Philosophy of Freedom,* that he mentions that the name of the family he had entered was Eunicke. A few pages later, he tells us that he lived with the family in Weimar, and that Anna, with whom he became close friends, did everything for him, which, we can assume, meant kept house. He was given a part of the house for his own use, and he tells us that although Anna appreciated that he would help in the upbringing of the children, he only saw the children when the opportunity arose, which seems to be at odds with the idea that he was tutoring them. Steiner goes on to say that his friends enjoyed visiting him there, then we hear nothing more about Anna until several chapters later, when he tells us that she had followed him to Berlin, where he lived with the family again. Only then, as if in passing, does he mention that they were at that time married.

Steiner devotes considerable space in his autobiography to Marie delle Grazie, Rosa Mayreder, and Gabrielle Reuter; later, his second wife, Marie von Sivers, is a central character in his life story. Yet we can assume that his relationship with Anna Eunicke must have been of equal, if different, importance. Yet he barely talks about her and seems reluctant to announce that they were married. Earlier I remarked on Steiner's reticence regarding his personal life. Again, we can respect his wish not to provide details and it is understandable that his followers would want to avoid the kind of biography that aims at pandering to prurient interests. Yet respecting Steiner's privacy doesn't stop us from wondering.

In fact, his reluctance to speak about his private affairs only piques our interest.

We can assume that Steiner's relationship with Anna wasn't romantic. One writer characterizes their relationship as "too familiar for a boarder and a landlady, too distant for man and wife."[9] Yet Steiner must have found the arrangement satisfactory; as mentioned, when he left Weimar for Berlin, Anna and her children followed him, and he again set up house with them. As Anna's daughters by this time would have been too old to need a tutor, and as Steiner himself would only be in his late thirties, and still relatively young, it may have seemed advisable to avoid any talk about a single man living with a family of young women by marrying their mother. Yet, from all accounts, the marriage didn't affect the relationship. Again, Anna was almost a decade older than Steiner, and as the "utter misery" of living alone in cheap rooms proved intolerable, moving in with the Eunickes provided Steiner—as it did with the Spechts—with a kind of surrogate family. This one, however, was not as well-off, or socially connected, and lacked the cultural and intellectual background that Steiner enjoyed in Vienna. A later account, of their life in Berlin, includes the comment that Anna and her daughters shouldn't be considered "ladies"—not because of any personal misbehavior on their part, but because they weren't upper class. One gets the impression, in fact, they were quite the contrary, and their devotion to Steiner indicates that he must have appeared something of an anomaly in their midst. From this I think it's safe to assume that Steiner may have felt some misgivings about his relationship with Anna Eunicke and her family, and so played this down when telling his life story.

Some of this may have been a kind of snobbery: Steiner was a figure in Weimar's cultural life, and Anna's background was working class at best. But given Steiner's own humble beginnings and basic peasant sensibilities, I think this unlikely. It's more likely that he later felt he had perhaps taken advantage of Anna when his position as boarder and possible tutor slipped into that of husband and stepfather. Understandably, Steiner wanted someone to take care of the boring necessities of life for him, a task, at least in those days, most often allotted to a wife. Yet he either had no romantic needs, or felt obligated to deny them, and so couldn't approach a woman in the usual way. When he met Anna, she was still piously mourning the loss of her husband, who had already given her five children; she was also in her early forties and may no longer have felt any romantic inclinations. But she probably appreciated having a man around the house, especially one as learned and respected as Dr. Steiner. So the arrangement made sense, at least for a time.

One thing Steiner certainly did owe the Eunicke family was the influence his experience with the soul of the departed Herr Eunicke had on the writing of what remains his most important book, *The Philosophy of Freedom*. Steiner tells us that the book was the outcome of all the philosophical questioning of his Vienna days, as well as the insights he gained through his spiritual perception. His experience following the souls of the two dead men— the one in Vienna and more recently Herr Eunicke—helped him to understand the advance in evolution that human beings owe to the development of science, an odd remark to make about a revelation of the afterlife. Yet by this Steiner means that a scientific approach to life need not result in a loss of spiritual experience; both of the deceased pursued scientific ideas, yet they were still able to participate fully in the spiritual world after death. (Steiner in fact speaks of seeing their spirits filled with the images of the spiritual beings who are engaged in the work of creating the world.) Their scientific pursuits helped these men develop a power of discrimination they would otherwise have lacked. Steiner insists that this power—basically the ability to think clearly and purposefully—is absolutely necessary in order to make any headway in the spirit world. Steiner says that the two men in question shied from turning their discriminating minds toward the spirit world, because in their life they had no opportunity to do so. Only after death was this possible for them. Yet it's Steiner's central belief that it *is* possible to approach the spirit world scientifically, that means in clear consciousness and with a discriminating mind, in *this* life. For years he had tried to communicate this insight to his friends, sadly unsuccessfully. It was this obsession that led his friends to consider him either a bit eccentric, or, ironically, a kind of abstract hyperrationalist, who had to approach everything through ideas.

When we realize how intently Steiner focused on this insight, and for how long, it's surprising that he didn't suffer some kind of breakdown—and in fact later, it seems that Steiner did go through what the historian of psychology Henri Ellenberger calls a "creative illness." Steiner admits that during his Weimar years, whenever he withdrew from social life—which, during the Goethe festivals, could be demanding, especially for Steiner, who was a part of both the official and the unofficial cultural worlds—he felt the only world he really knew was the spiritual one. The other world, that of "things seen," still remained unreal for him. The outer world, he wrote, "appeared to me somewhat shadow-like or picture-like," while the inner world for him always had a "concrete reality." It must have been a trying time for Steiner. He talks of visiting friends and, as usual, entering into their world and their way of seeing life. But no one ever entered his world. He was at home in the world of others, but no one was ever at home in *his* world. "My innermost being had always to remain within itself," he writes. And perhaps most telling: "My inner world was really separated from the outer world as if by a thin wall."[10] Again, this is a feeling shared by many creative individuals, yet it is also a characteristic of Anthony Storr's schizotypical personality.

It's clear that the need to bring his thoughts together and to finally make the reality of this inner world absolutely unequivo-cal, had something more than intellectual ambition behind it. Although written with all the apparatus of philosophy and logic, and couched in a dry, academic style, *The Philosophy of Freedom* is more than a book of ideas. It's Steiner's assertion of his own real-ity. It's also a work of genius, and one suspects that Steiner's later occult reputation has prevented the book from receiving the kind of attention it deserves.

Although practically all commentators on Steiner's work agree that *The Philosophy of Freedom* (or, as it has also been translated, *The Philosophy of Spiritual Activity*) contains within it all of the essentials of anthroposophy, the book itself makes no mention of a spiritual world, in the sense of an actual other world accessible to human consciousness, nor does any other standard anthropo-sophical theme, like karma, the afterlife, or reincarnation make an appearance. It's rigorously and exhilaratingly a book about think-ing. Steiner believed that he had succeeded in carrying Nietzsche's own thought to a higher level, and said so in a letter to Rosa Mayreder. Steiner may have thought twice about linking the fate of his book to Nietzsche; although at the time of writing, the mad philosopher was the focus of almost worldwide attention, during his career, he was even more obscure and lonely than Steiner. Steiner's book was marginally better received than Nietzsche's, although not by much, and the fact that his publisher issued a first edition of only 1,000 copies argues that he didn't expect it to sell (in fact another edition wasn't published until 1918). It's curious that the book Steiner expected the most from, and into which he poured years of thought and reflection, is one that many people who develop an interest in anthroposophy have the most difficulty with—at least according to an informal survey carried out by the present writer. Steiner's later books dealing with outright anthroposophical ideas, like *Theosophy, Knowledge of the Higher Worlds and Its Attainment,* and *An Outline of Occult Science,* although filled with rather provocative material about astral bodies, chakras, and planetary evolution, seem to provoke less resistance than this admirably clear, albeit abstract, account of the nature of human thought. Steiner himself insists there's no essential difference between his occult teachings and this early essay in epistemology, and he accounts for the fact that he kept his spiritual insights to himself until he was forty by referring to an "occult law" that allowed him to speak openly about them only then. (In the Barr Document, Steiner states that his occult master required "everything in the clothing of Idealist philosophy."[11]) Many followers of Steiner agree, and insist that his early philosophical activity was in preparation for the spiritual teaching to come. Yet to an unbiased reader, it's clear that there's nothing occult about the early writings, and anyone who follows Steiner from *Theory of Knowledge in Light of Goethe's Worldview* (1886) to *Friedrich Nietzsche: A Fighter Against His Time* (1895), will see in him a passionate Idealist, trying to throw a monkey wrench into the machinery of materialism. In *The Philosophy of Freedom,* he succeeds.

Steiner's fundamental idea is that, when we open our eyes, what we take to be a simple, immediate perception of the external world, is already infused with the content of our inner, spiritual world, our consciousness. So when materialists insist that our consciousness is a product of the material world (as many of them still do today), this is really a case of putting the cart before the horse: the material world they refer to is already shot through with their own consciousness. Steiner speaks of "percepts" and "concepts" and the reader lacking a philosophical background can get sidetracked by his vocabulary, but his basic insight is easily enough grasped. Once we see that the materialist, in speaking of matter—or whatever form of it he or she says is at bottom the source of consciousness—is really speaking about his or her *ideas* about matter, we are halfway to intuiting what Steiner is on to. Steiner said as much in his early work on Goethe, when he wrote that "When one who has a rich mental life sees a thousand things which are nothing to the mentally poor, this shows as clearly as sunlight that the content of reality is only the reflection of the content of our minds."

Anyone trying to come to terms with the current fascination with explaining consciousness should repeat this last sentence as a kind of mantra. It's a version of the basic Idealist position and has been voiced by people like William Blake, Samuel Taylor Coleridge, Emanuel Swedenborg, Edmund Husserl, and dozens of others in different ways. The dominant view of consciousness, going back at least to Descartes and carried on by philosophers like John Locke, is that consciousness is essentially passive. Locke argued that there was nothing in the mind that was not first in the senses and that at birth our interior world is a tabula rasa, a blank slate, waiting to be written upon by the outside world, a proposition that any parent will find preposterous. (Cognitive scientists may pooh-pooh the idea, but most parents recognize that their children arrive with the kernel of personality already present.) What Steiner and his fellow Idealists are saying is that you would not even have an outside world unless you first had something inside. This is a variation on Goethe's notion of objective imagination, the idea that truth is not something out there, waiting to make a mark on our virgin minds: it's a product of the harmonious meeting *between* out there and in here. Far from a passive recipient of impressions from an inaccessible outside world, consciousness is a kind of hand, reaching out and giving shape and form to what would remain mere empty chaos. We find it difficult to grasp what an world perceived *without* thought would be like, because since around our second year, we have only seen a world already informed by consciousness. It takes the equivalent of an epistemological crowbar to wrench our contribution to our perceptions apart from their recipients. When we look at a garden and see a tree, we see *a tree,* and not the alleged molecules and atoms it is made of, nor the blotches of light and color that make up its surface. One of the most difficult of philosophical methodologies, phenomenology, is precisely the discipline of separating what we *know* from what we *see;* it requires us to describe *not* what something is—for example, a book—but how it *appears,* a rectangular surface of a certain color, and so on.

Along with undermining the materialists, Steiner also wants to refute his old nemesis Kant, by showing that there are no limits to knowledge, in the sense that there is a realm or area of life or the world which is off limits to cognition. Kant (and Schopenhauer and Hartmann after him) had argued that *behind* the sensory world lay (metaphorically) an inaccessible real world, of which our senses produce impressions which we translate into mental pictures, which are merely subjective, with no relation to reality. Our consciousness of the world is, in this view, like a video monitor relaying the images sent to it by a camera; for Kant and his followers, all we can ever *know* is what we see on the monitor; we can *never see for ourselves* what the camera is showing us. Steiner argues that this is untrue and that we are already directly aware of what the camera is showing us. There is no world behind the sensory one, but within it, as Goethe had argued, lies the *complete* reality, which is made accessible (or rather manifest) through our own spiritual activity, that is, the act of knowing. As thinking beings we are already inhabitants of the spiritual world—the world, in metaphysical terms, of the *noumena,* or causes, of which the sensory world, or world of phenomena, constitutes the effects. And it is through our recognition of thinking as a free, spiritual act—as Steiner calls it, a *supersensible* one—that we can come to an experience of ourselves as free spiritual beings and of our own inner worlds as portals into the world of spirit itself.

The problem, Steiner recognized, is that we are unaware of ourselves as free, spiritual beings. We are also unaware of the immense creative power of our own consciousness, and so our "normal" perception of the world is far removed from the kind of world we would see if into our daily encounters with it we put the kind of energy and attention Goethe did when he went in search of his *Urpflanze.* Most of the time, we stare blankly at the world, accepting the poker face it returns, unconsciously confirming the misconception that our consciousness is passive and undermining any possibility of motivating ourselves into pouring more energy into our awareness. Steiner's extraordinary insights into the spirit world, and the vividness with which he experienced his own inner world, combined with Goethe's ideas on imagination and produced in him the conviction that our everyday consciousness is a kind of lie. Or, if not a lie, than a dangerous half-truth, as in it we perceive only half of reality, yet accept it as the complete picture. This incomplete picture gives rise to a host of debilitating consequences. The philosophy of materialism is one; our picture of ourselves as passive, near automatons is another. Our abuse of nature and the environment, which we falsely perceive to be dead and merely material for use, is another. Our general belief that at death the personality disappears is yet another. In fact, Steiner hit on the paramount intuition that our unconscious beliefs about ourselves and the world dictate the kind of world we live in and the kind of people we are. If anyone reading this book—or any book by or on Steiner—were to *really* grasp the importance of Steiner's insight, grasp it, that is, deep down in his most fundamental convictions, his or her world would be transformed. And that is precisely what Steiner had in mind in writing it.

After finally producing *The Philosophy of Freedom*, Steiner could rightly feel that he had answered the materialists and Kantians and that he had provided a firm foundation for the work that lay ahead. It mattered little that the book received minimal attention; after all, most books on philosophy do. What was important was that he had managed to turn his nagging intuitions into expressible ideas, and when the mind achieves this kind of clarity, half the battle is won. Now Steiner felt it was time to get the message across, and he set out to find ways to do this.

5. BERLIN AND THE TURNING POINT

lthough Steiner was generally well liked and could count many people as warm acquaintances, if not close friends, it has to be admitted that to many of them he must have appeared a bit odd at times. Throughout his autobiography, Steiner makes no apology for stating several times that he had difficulty dealing with the external world, the world of "things seen." His inner world, whether of ideas, mathematical figures, or perceptions of the spirit, was, for him, absolutely concrete—vivid and unmistakable in a way many of us may find difficult to appreciate. The outer world, the world that most of us bump up against everyday with numbing regularity, he found dreamlike and shadowy. And again, I think it's significant that we remember that Steiner spoke of an earlier form of human consciousness, what he called Old Moon consciousness, in just this way. Steiner's firm anchor in the world of the spirit, and his unsure footing in the mundane world, suggests that he was frequently, as the saying goes, not all there. Not, of course, in any sense that suggests simple-mindedness. But Steiner wasn't as deeply rooted in the physical world as the rest of us, and from his earliest years, he had access to inner worlds and an ease and familiarity within them that perhaps only a few of us could approach after years of spiritual and mental training.

Yet we know that Steiner, although privy to the spirit, bore no malice toward the physical world, and that in fact, as a scientist, he recognized his responsibility to go against his inclinations and come to some understanding of it. Toward the end of his time in Weimar, a change came over Steiner that helped facilitate this. He writes that, at around the age of thirty-five, a "profound transformation" began to take place in his life. Halfway through life's journey—as Dante has it—Steiner became able to perceive the outer world with a new clarity and acuteness. While he had been able to grasp clearly the wider systemic connections among things, as these were mainly conceptual, to firmly grasp the isolated thing before his eyes was always a challenge. Yet now, with little apparent reason, all this changed. Within him, a "new awareness of sense-perceptible things" had awakened. Although his abstract prose softens the impact, the development must have affected Steiner profoundly. Details stood out, and he felt that the world of the senses had something to tell him that only it could reveal, an insight that his mentor Goethe could have shared with him. "One ought to learn to know the physical world, purely through itself, without adding thoughts of one's own,"[1] Steiner told himself. Years later, the German poet and essayist Gottfried Benn would write about such perception in an essay called "Primal Vision," in which he speaks of seeing things with "matchless clarity." Steiner, it seemed, was experiencing a kind of primal vision of his own and, Zen-like, the very is-ness of things hit him with an exhilarating freshness.

It's curious that Steiner recognized that what he was experiencing then, at thirty-five, was a change that most people go through in childhood. As was the case when learning how to play only as a tutor in his twenties, Steiner was now experiencing the kind of shift that takes place at a much earlier age, when the young child first recognizes that there is an independent, objective world *outside* himself. Autistic and profoundly introverted children fail to make this shift and remain bound within their own subjectivity. Yet many, perhaps most of us, also tend to live within our own worlds, recognizing the *objective* reality outside sufficiently enough to deal with it, yet not in any real or deep sense. Hence the effect of some psychotropic drugs, which seem to increase the degree of reality we are aware of, rather like turning the volume up on a stereo. Less hazardous and perhaps more beneficial are meditative disciplines like Zen, the aim of which is precisely to bring their practitioners to the kind of immediate awareness of the here and now that Steiner was experiencing. The result of both is often that the person involved says of a flower or a tree or a stone that it was as if they were seeing these things for the first time.

Steiner in a way was discovering what would later become the core insight of phenomenology, the branch of philosophy I briefly mentioned earlier: its motto was "back to the things themselves," which, in essence, was Goethe's approach as well. Steiner is talking like a phenomenologist when he says that if "the sense world is approached objectively, independent of all subjectivity, it reveals aspects about which spiritual insight can say nothing."[2] This, he discovered, was most true in his encounters with people. Steiner found himself able to observe people as they are, without making any judgments or criticisms or bestowing any approval. He found this also helped in his spiritual perceptions which, he tells us, were not in any way lessened by his new appreciation of things seen. When the physical could be perceived for what it is in itself, then the spiritual, too, could be recognized with greater clarity. Steiner recognized that one advantage of coming to this new relation to the outer world late in life was that, in contrast to most people, who experience it in childhood, for him the two worlds did not mix. They remained distinct, which allowed him to grasp their separate realities with exactness. A too early introduction to the reality of the outer world—which is what, he says, most of us experience—causes it and the inner one to flow together, making a kind of undifferentiated blend. This is why most of us have difficulty in separating the two and confuse one with the other.

Steiner's new relation to the outer world gave him a greater grasp of the spiritual one and allowed him to recognize more sharply the *differences* between the two. And this he felt was the essential clue to achieving a greater understanding of the world as a whole. Again, Steiner's abstract way of expressing himself lessens the impact of his insight, but here he echoes previous spiritual explorers like Nietzsche; even more, Steiner's insight is reminiscent of William Blake, that visionary poet we've had occasion to refer to earlier. Blake's vision, like Nietzsche's, is of a dynamic world of complementary forces and energies, engaged in a perpetual dance of antagonism and reconciliation. Nietzsche expressed this in his first book, *The Birth of Tragedy*, when he speaks of the contrast between Apollo, the god of contemplation, and Dionysus, the god of ecstasy; through their union the masterpieces of Greek tragedy were born. Blake's poetry is shot through with images of spiritual forces struggling with each other; he writes that "opposition is true friendship" and "without contraries there is no progression."[3] (The title of one of his most well-known works, *The Marriage of Heaven and Hell,* seems to say it all.) Steiner is less succinct, but the insight is the same. Unlike some philosophers and mystics who strive to do away with the contrast between the spiritual and physical worlds—curiously, Steiner singles out monism—Steiner celebrates it and makes it the key to life itself. "Where there is life," he writes, "the disharmony of contrasting factors is also *active*. Life itself is but a continuous overcoming and re-creation of opposites."[4] In years to come, Steiner would arrive at his own characterization of this fundamental clash of opposites, in his teachings on the influence of the two spiritual beings Lucifer and Ahriman.

Steiner tells us that this insight made him want to enter into life's riddles actively, to participate in them, rather than to understand them only theoretically. Steiner saw that when life presents a problem, we usually try to solve it by *thinking* about it, but that actually, it is *life itself* which solves it, by throwing up a situation or an event or another person, which is itself the answer to the mystery.[5] Steiner at thirty-five was recognizing that to think about the world was one thing, but to actively overcome its difficulties was something else. The whole world, in fact, is just such a riddle, and the solution to it, Steiner was sure, was the human being. This brought home with greater force and clarity the insight that Steiner had experienced years earlier: that cognition, the act of knowing, is a real process, an essential element in the evolution of the world.

Human beings, Steiner saw, were not simply observers, dispassionately gazing at the cosmic processes going on around them. Knowledge was not our private, subjective possession. It was part of the cosmic process itself. The world might exist if there was no consciousness to be aware of it, but its existence would be limited; the world, Steiner saw, only reaches completion through the act of knowing. Hence my, your, and everyone else's cognition of the

world is not something extra, tacked on to it through the chance
event of intelligent life arising in an accidental universe. Our
knowledge of the world is a part of the world; through our knowing the cosmos becomes complete. Without it, it would be only
half a world. For Steiner, this meant again that our knowledge is
not simply a collection of mental pictures located in our individual heads, an assortment of images produced by our senses and
brains, having nothing to do with a reality which we can never
experience directly and having no effect on it whatsoever. We,
Steiner clearly saw, were not "copyists" but "co-creators," equal
partners in the business of the evolution of the world. "Man," he
said, "is not only there in order to form for himself a picture of the
finished world; nay, he himself cooperates in bringing the world
into existence."[6] Although his way of expressing this is less explosive than Nietzsche's, Steiner's insight is every bit as revolutionary.
Steiner tells us that at this point, he once again understood the
absolute necessity of arriving at a perception of the spirit in full
clarity, and not in the kind of indefinite, vague, and emotional
way that mystics before him—or so he believed—had achieved it.

Yet, of the many riddles that lay before him, a particularly
pressing one stood out. His work at Weimar was coming to an
end and Steiner had to decide what to do next. Very likely he
could have found a way to stay on, but he was beginning to feel
that the atmosphere in Weimar was becoming cloying. He felt the
need to move on and, perhaps more powerfully, to communicate
his insights more directly than through his books. Perhaps it was
his friendship with the von Crompton circle, a group of writers
and musicians who felt that the cultural climate in Weimar was
stifling, and who embraced Steiner as a devotee of Nietzsche, that
prompted him. In fact, Steiner became the resident Nietzsche

expert among them, which must have meant he was respected, as the entire group considered themselves true Nietzscheans. This group felt that for all its past glory, Weimar was now more of an obstacle in the way of Germany's cultural life than an asset. Steiner must have agreed. It was from his experiences in this circle that he drew inspiration when writing *Goethe's Conception of the World,* a book which, like his earlier ones, expressed his understanding of how Goethe saw the world, yet in which he spoke in a much more personal voice, at least according to his own account. Steiner was still speaking through Goethe, yet his passion for Goethe's vision of the world is unmistakable. In this book he was taking a chance and saying, "This is what I believe." Any of Steiner's colleagues at the archive who read it must have felt that a promising scholar had sadly manifested a serious breach in academic etiquette.

But if any of them voiced this opinion, we can be sure that Steiner ignored it. He had already decided against following an academic career. He knew that, more than likely, Hermann Grimm, who occupied a chair at the University of Berlin, could have found a comfortable niche for him somewhere. But Steiner wanted a more direct means of spreading his ideas. He had already written several books, none of which reached many readers, and his attempt to attract established thinkers like Eduard von Hartmann, was, as we've seen, unsuccessful. He liked and admired Grimm, but he also knew that at bottom there were profound differences in their outlooks. For example, after the publication of *The Philosophy of Freedom,* Steiner became troubled by the popularity of a "Society for Ethical Culture," whose beliefs he felt trivialized the issue of how a free human being should conduct himself in the world. The society argued that it was necessary to adopt moral principles regardless of how they related to the different worldviews then in vogue. It was possible to lead a good life, they said, whether you were a materialist or a spiritualist; your worldview didn't matter. Steiner took vehement exception to this. For him, it was impossible to believe in any ethical or moral order if one was a materialist. This would mean that a purely mechanical, mindless process had somehow given rise to a purely spiritual code of conduct. For Steiner, it was clear that the two are mutually exclusive: either we recognize a spiritual reality in which we can anchor our moral ideas, or we admit that they have no foundation outside their social utility. Steiner knew that a rigorous investigation of thought leads to the recognition of a spiritual world, but the followers of the ethical culture society had no interest in Steiner's arguments. Steiner published an article about this in a small magazine, *The Future*, but he wanted a wider readership. He went to Berlin to ask Grimm for help, but Grimm couldn't understand why he was making such a fuss. The members of the ethical culture society were, he said, "nice people," and he told Steiner to meet with them and have a chat. At that moment, a chasm opened between himself and Grimm, and once again Steiner found that his path led through a deep and rarely relieved loneliness.

Steiner decided to kill two birds with one stone. He answered the questions of what he would do in his career and how he could get his ideas across to more people by once again becoming a magazine editor. He was offered the editorship of a failing weekly periodical in Berlin, the *Magazine for Literature*. Although Steiner's only experience of such work was his ill-fated and fortunately brief tenure at the *German News Weekly*, he jumped at the chance. Throughout his autobiography Steiner remarks that he never questioned the twists and turns fate put before him, and he regarded this development as another step in the unfolding of his destiny. But Steiner was determined to get out of Weimar and to Berlin, and editing a magazine, although not necessarily his forte, at least offered the chance to do this. Berlin was earning a reputation as the center for Germany's avant-garde, and it was better suited as an arena for Steiner's plans than Weimar was.

The *Magazine for Literature* had an impressive history. Established in 1832, the year of Goethe's death, it had gone through many changes, and when Steiner came on the scene, it had become something of an organ for new trends and ideas, without, Steiner tells us, being too opposed to more traditional approaches. The magazine, however, was less than steady—its subscribers had dwindled perilously in recent times—and to help keep it afloat, it had become associated with the Independent Literary Society, a kind of reading group that put on lectures focusing on the new literature. As part of the agreement for his becoming editor, Steiner was obliged to lecture to the literary society and also to more or less use the magazine as a means of furthering their aims—something, we know, that Steiner intended to do for his own ideas.

As the tastes of the Independent Literary Society were much more modern than Steiner's, the task fate had set him was less than enjoyable. Another thorn in his side was the requirement that he accept as coeditor a likable but useless dilettante named Otto Erich Hartleben, whom Steiner had already met during the Goethe Festivals in Weimar. Hartleben was a character. Steiner relates how during the festivals, which Hartleben always traveled from Berlin to Weimar to attend, he would spend his time in bed in his hotel room, avoiding all the meetings and lectures. In the evenings he would gather with some like-minded individuals and stay up until the morning hours drinking and talking. On one such occasion, Steiner endeared himself to Hartleben by calling Schopenhauer an "obtuse genius." That a genius could also be obtuse struck Hartleben as profound. Steiner says he liked Hartleben—Steiner seemed constitutionally incapable of *not* liking someone—yet we can assume the relationship had its difficulties.

Being saddled with Hartleben, who spent most of his time in Italy or sitting in cafés, and who did practically no work on the magazine, would seem a sufficient burden for Steiner to bear. But Steiner also had to contend with producing a magazine for readers he was not particularly in tune with, and whose shaky financial base expressed ideas and opinions he found repellent. At the same time, he was eager to use the publication to express his own ideas. Steiner admits that he had some doubts about the enterprise. The people who had been involved with the magazine before him were not, he tells us, "particularly serious-minded," and he soon found himself asking whether he could justify his participation in this arrangement at all. Once again, the old theme of finding himself in the middle of a group with whom he had nothing in common had cropped up. Steiner says that, in looking back on this episode, he wished for nothing different. Yet it doesn't take much imagination to see in it a recipe for disaster. It was, he said, a constant source of anxiety for him.

In his autobiography, Steiner laments that the necessity of having to spend time in Hartleben's circle prevented him from maintaining contact with people in Weimar. It also made it almost impossible for him to see the few people in Berlin he knew, like Eduard von Hartmann. Both Stewart C. Easton and Johannes Hemleben, another of Steiner's biographers, are almost apologetic in describing the milieu Steiner had entered. Steiner himself must have felt some misgivings, not only about the magazine and his do-nothing coeditor; it must have seemed like a strange rerun of his life in Vienna a decade earlier, with endless coffees, late night chat, miserable lodgings, and bad meals. Yet, having to once again plunge into café life had its own rewards. He did at least meet other individuals of genius, like the playwright Frank Wedekind, who had gained notoriety in 1891 through his scandalous play *Spring Awakening,* which dealt with the then taboo themes of teenage sexuality and suicide, and whose later plays *Earth Spirit* and *Pandora's Box* would be the basis of an opera by Alban Berg and a film by G. W. Pabst. We can assume that Steiner thought little of Wedekind's work, yet he found himself spellbound by his "truly extraordinary" form. Wedekind's hands in particular fascinated Steiner. He believed that such hands in previous lives must have done remarkable things. Wedekind's head must have offered Steiner some solace, too, as it gave him the impression of "a spirit alien to the present age."[7]

Another who interested Steiner was the fantasist and poet Paul Scheerbarth, who Steiner felt had a true calling for the spiritual worlds, but whose taste for the strange and bizarre prevented him from achieving any clarity in these realms. He too, along with Wedekind, provided Steiner with more insights into the facts of repeated earth-lives. Among other things, Steiner realized that meeting them, as well as the other characters he now encountered, was a necessary part of his own karma.

Yet Steiner found it impossible to enter into any kind of warm, simply human relationship with these, and other, writers. All of them were dominated by what Steiner called the "literary mind," which we can assume meant that, like all writers, they invariably talked shop. Steiner remarks that although *he* knew why he was there, no one else did. For him, being in this uncongenial circle was part of his destiny, and he was convinced that at that time no one else could have taken his place. But for the writers and poets trying to make a name for themselves, he must have seemed one editor among many, and from his own account, not a particularly good one at that, at least from their point of view.

But Steiner's uncomfortable milieu at least gave him an opportunity to learn. The *Magazine for Literature* was associated with an Independent Drama Society, and as editor, Steiner was elected to its board. The society put on plays that were considered too experimental for regular theaters—meaning they couldn't expect to draw large audiences—so the productions usually went on during afternoon matinees. One such production was Maurice Maeterlinck's *The Intruder.* Steiner took part in the rehearsals, and adapted the play for the performance. Although Steiner didn't think much of Maeterlinck's work, feeling his "symbolism" was simply a dilettantish way of dabbling in spiritual matters, he threw himself into the task and, from his account, appears to have enjoyed himself. He also gave an introductory talk before the performance, in which he tried to "convey a mood of true spirituality."[8] Given that the audience for this and other performances was drawn from the subscribers to the *Magazine for Literature,* and, one suspects, had an interest in Maeterlinck, one wonders how Steiner's talk went over.

Steiner's other link to Berlin's theatrical world was his position as drama critic. Steiner tells us that his approach to writing reviews was unusual, in that he felt it was necessary for him to give not an opinion about the work—which is what most of us expect from a reviewer—but an "artistic picture" of the ideas behind it. Not surprisingly, Steiner's ideas about theater reviews led to his own not being very well understood. Yet in years to come, Steiner would put what he learned in Berlin's theater world to good use, first when he wrote and staged his own series of mystery plays, and then later, when he gave a course on dramatic art in the last year of his life.[9]

Yet not all of Steiner's experiences among Berlin's avant-garde were unsympathetic. One person he became close to was the Jewish poet and social thinker Ludwig Jacobowski, who had started an artistic-political group called Die Kommenden, "the coming generation" or "the coming age." Jacobowski, who, sadly, died of meningitis in 1900 at the age of thirty-two, only a few years after Steiner met him, combined poetry with a study of folklore, and, until his death, combated the anti-Semitism it was his fate to endure. He also started a magazine called *The Society,* which he used as a vehicle for his social philosophy, rather as Steiner wanted to do with the *Magazine for Literature.* (Steiner published an article in *The Society* passionately defending Haeckel's *The Riddle of the Universe,* a book he would later ridicule, thus adding to the confusion about his position on this important thinker.) Steiner remarks that Jacobowski was a tragic figure and that he suffered deeply his destiny as a Jew in a time of rising anti-Semitism. His association, Die Kommenden, carried on after his death, and soon Steiner became a regular speaker at its meetings.

Another important friendship was with the Scottish anarchist John H. Mackay. Steiner had already met Mackay in Weimar through Gabrielle Reuter; he had been drawn to him because he had expressed interest in the second part of *The Philosophy of Freedom,* in which Steiner advocated a moral philosophy he called "ethical individualism." Mackay was attracted to Steiner's ethical ideas because he had edited the works of the German philosopher

Max Stirner, whose book *The Ego and Its Own* had advocated a peculiar form of individual anarchism.[10] To Steiner, Mackay seemed a man of the world. He had lived in England and America, but had moved to Berlin in 1898. Steiner was impressed by Mackay's travels and accomplishments, but also by his strong convictions against the use of force to achieve social or political aims. Mackay was very critical of communism because, even though its ends were laudable—a just and equitable society—the means it was ready to employ to achieve those ends—force and violence—undermined its own goals. Yet Steiner remarks that his association with Mackay—and through him, Stirner's philosophy—became for him a kind of a test. The ethical individualism that he had expressed in *The Philosophy of Freedom* was, for Steiner, an account of the individual's inner experience of the reality of the moral life. Yet his contact with Mackay—and, no doubt, the atmosphere of the time—began to draw Steiner into turning his ideas toward an outer, political end. As Steiner expressed it, he felt himself being drawn into an abyss. What for him had been an *esoteric* insight, was now taking shape as an *exoteric* theory. And although Steiner would later actively pursue social and political aims, he was at this time still concentrating on the spiritual experience of the individual.

Steiner must have passed through this trial successfully, and his friendship with Mackay must have remained strong, as Mackay was the witness at his wedding to Anna Eunicke on October 31, 1899. It's a bit unclear whether Anna followed Steiner to Berlin or, as Johannes Hemleben states, she had moved there before Steiner did.[11] What isn't in doubt is that Steiner welcomed the chance to move in with her and her family again, this time in a house in the suburb of Friedenau. Although he was, as we've seen, saved from the "utter misery" of living alone, Steiner has little to say about their renewed relationship. He briefly remarks that his "friendship with Frau Eunicke was consolidated in civil marriage,"[12] and then, as mentioned earlier, states flatly that he will say nothing more about it. We do, however, get a more detailed picture of what their life may have been like from an account by someone who was about to provide Steiner with the platform that would launch him on his true destiny.

It was soon clear to Steiner that the *Magazine for Literature* wasn't going to become the organ for his ideas that he had hoped for. When he took on the job, the magazine was already doing poorly, and since he had become editor, sales had plummeted. Steiner seemed unable to reach any sympathetic readers with his articles and reviews; on the contrary, he invariably alienated them, and even went out of his way to do so. Whatever reputation the magazine had in the past, under Steiner's leadership, it was "undermined completely."[13] One of his earliest editorials criticized the "philistinism" of his fellow Berliners and singled out the people associated with the magazine and the avant-garde in general as particularly reprehensible. His defense of Émile Zola in the Dreyfus Affair turned many subscribers away. His theater reviews were considered incomprehensible, and an article he wrote criticizing his critics was met with contempt. His association with Mackay also caused understandable confusion. Although Mackay clearly rejected violence as a political tool, in naming his own philosophy he had unfortunately retained the word "anarchism," and most readers were neither subtle nor discerning enough to recognize the difference between "individual anarchism" and the kind that had suspicious-looking characters lobbing bombs at kings and presidents. One ironic upshot of this was that the *Magazine for*

Literature was banned in Russia, because of its editor's relationship with a well-known and dangerous anarchist—doubly ironic, as Russia would fall to the communism to which Mackay was adamantly opposed. And Russian aristocrats weren't the only ones troubled by Steiner's friendship with Mackay. When Steiner published extracts of their correspondence, many academics, outraged that a Goethe scholar was rubbing elbows with such ruffians, canceled their subscriptions.

A young writer who belonged to Hartleben's circle wrote an article in which he referred to Steiner as an "unpaid peripatetic theologian" who didn't really belong in the group, as, aside from Steiner, it was composed of "young idealists."[14] And Steiner's article on Goethe's hermetic fairy tale "The Green Snake and the Beautiful Lily" was, we can assume, for the readers he was trying to reach, impenetrable. Steiner remarks on all this that he had "the knack of offending readers—but not the Spirit of the Age," and that while it was in his hands, the *Magazine for Literature* did not cater to "modern bourgeois philistines." Depending on how you look at it, this can be taken as a wry comment on the spiritual poverty of the time or an expression of sour grapes. Steiner's optimism and self-belief are remarkable and admirable, but if professors and philosophers couldn't make head or tail of *The Philosophy of Freedom*—whose ideas Steiner was hoping to promote—it was probably too much to expect the readers of the *Magazine for Literature* to succeed where they failed.

So, only a short time after taking on the job, Steiner must have felt that it had been a useful learning experience, but that once again, he needed to move on. His finances alone demanded some action. The magazine paid its contributors practically nothing, and Steiner himself could barely keep body and soul together with what he got from it. On top of this, he had contracted to pay its former owner in installments, so each month was something of a crisis, with Steiner desperately trying to come up with the money. With Hartleben thrown in, it must have been little more than a constant headache. We can forgive Steiner if he occasionally wondered what karmic debt he was paying when fate placed this white elephant in his path, and appreciate the eagerness with which he accepted an opportunity for a change.

That opportunity came when Dr. Steiner and Frau Eunicke—they were not yet married—were visited by Alwin Alfred Rudolph, a delegate from the Working Men's College in Berlin, with a request that Steiner give a lecture course on history at the school. The Working Men's College had been started in the mid-1890s by Wilhelm Liebknecht, a Social Democrat member of the German Reichstag, and its faculty taught according to the Marxist principles of dialectical materialism, a philosophy, like Haeckel's, diametrically opposed to Steiner's. At the time, many leading socialist thinkers had the idea to bring higher education to the proletariat, and similar schools were formed elsewhere, like New York's Cooper Union and the Workingmen's College in London, one of whose teachers was the art and social critic John Ruskin. Although the tone of the school was socialist, when Steiner agreed to lecture, the main concern was to open up higher education to the masses, and so some leeway in what was taught was possible. Nevertheless, to be associated with the school suggested one was at least a fellow traveler, and once again Steiner found himself wearing a hat that didn't really suit him. It was inevitable that people wondered what had made Dr. Steiner change his mind again, and this time become a Marxist materialist? He was, after all, speaking at the same podium as "Red" Rosa Luxemburg, who would become famous as one of the leaders of the Spartakus communist rebellion in 1919.[15]

Herr Rudolph and his colleagues had never met Steiner before; in fact they had decided to ask him to lecture only after others had turned down the job. Finally, a poet they asked had suggested Steiner and had given them his address. Without any warning, they turned up at the house in Friedenau, not knowing what to expect. Any apprehension they may have felt was soon dispelled by the warm reception the young socialists received. They were met at the door by a woman, who showed them into a large, well-lit space, a kind of combination living room and study. An enormous desk littered with books and papers stood by the window, and in the middle of the room was Dr. Steiner. Dressed in black, Steiner was very slim, sported a thin mustache on his upper lip, and was wearing what would later become a kind of trademark: a long, flowing bow tie. Steiner greeted the men so warmly that they soon felt they were all old friends. Rudolph remarks that they were then introduced to an older woman, whose position in the house they were at first unsure of, although it became clear that the young woman who had let them in was her daughter. (This suggests that it wasn't obvious that Anna might have been, or might become, Steiner's wife.) Rudolph and his colleagues were invited to coffee and sat down. The young woman brought in a tray of pastries, which Steiner took and offered to the young men, explaining that they had been baked according to the secret recipe of his friend the poet Ludwig Jacobowski. Then after spending a pleasant hour drinking coffee, eating cakes, and chatting, the group left, having got Steiner's enthusiastic agreement to give the course.

The experience had been so unexpectedly charming that

Rudolph and his friends forgot to mention that they could pay only a paltry sum for the entire series, eight marks, and when they returned to the school they were chastised for this. Rudolph was ordered to go back to Steiner and explain. When he did he was once again treated to a warm reception, as if the family, whom he had known for years, had not seen him for some time. Rudolph remarked that he had never received such hospitality from any of the Social Democrat lecturers, nor were their hand-shakes as firm and hearty as Steiner's. Rudolph says that although Steiner looked like an ascetic, his smile radiated happiness and cheer. Any idea that it might be inconvenient to drop in un-announced, *twice* in one day, on a man he had never met before, especially one as busy as Dr. Steiner, dissolved when Rudolph looked at Steiner's face. The reverence, too, that the women dis-played was evident, and seemed to make the idea that Steiner could have been married to either of them preposterous. Frau Eunicke remained silent and waited for the Doctor to speak, although she did converse a bit with Rudolph. When more coffee and pastries appeared—Steiner seems to have had a sweet tooth—Rudolph made conversation by asking how the water for the coffee was heated, as he couldn't tell from the machine. Steiner replied that it was heated by spirits (methylated), which led to Steiner's making a play on the word, which struck the materialist Rudolph as a bit odd. Frau Eunicke then showed Rudolph a rag doll made in the likeness of Steiner, complete with black coat and bow tie. The doll had come from Ludwig Jacobowski, and under its coat was a bottle of cognac. It was, Anna explained, a joke of Ludwig's, and meant that the body is really spirit. The follower of dialectical materialism must have found this a strange remark as well.

Steiner told Rudolph his plans for the lectures, going into detail and refusing to allow him to mention the fee. He then asked when he would like them to take place, and Rudolph said they had in mind a series of ten lectures, two hours long, on Thursday evenings, starting at eight o'clock. When Anna pointed out that the Doctor was already lecturing to Jacobowski's Die Kommenden group on Thursdays, Steiner replied that he didn't need to be at those lectures until after ten, and so would have enough time to do both. He then asked when they proposed to begin the series, made a mental note of the date, declined the offer of a written reminder, and said he would be there.

At two minutes to eight on January 13, 1899, Steiner arrived at the small hall where the lectures would be held, accompanied by Anna and her daughter. The previous lecturers had been so dull that attendance at the course had shrunk drastically, so it was a complete surprise when the room quickly filled; the space was soon packed, and more chairs had to be brought in to accommodate the people standing. Although Steiner had something of a reputation—and not a particularly good one—in Berlin's literary world, he wasn't yet that well known, and the audience at his first night is a testament to the hunger Berlin's workers had for an education. Steiner greeted the hall with a smile, then launched into his talk—as he would for the rest of his lecturing career—without notes. According to Rudolph, those present soon grasped that they had been incredibly lucky to find such a lecturer. Here was a man overflowing with knowledge, and whose evident passion was nothing less than to pass it on to others.

Steiner, however, was not lecturing in the manner these students were used to. When the "slender, dark man mounted the platform,"[16] he was not about to confirm the theories of Marx,

nor extol the idea that material forces and the means of production were the paramount engines behind history. In his powerful
Austrian voice, Steiner informed them that, although it was true
that in relatively recent times, materialism was the dominant force
behind history, this had only been true since the sixteenth century. Prior to this, spiritual forces were at work. Therefore, Marx's
belief that economic factors were the central means of moving history along was only partially true . . . a statement that any Marxist worth his salt would have snorted at. Steiner's audience,
however, didn't, and sat there in awe, spellbound by his massive
erudition and the ease with which he distributed it among them.
We can see Steiner's pedagogical sleight-of-hand as either a gentle
way of leading his audience toward his own vision of the world, or
as an opportunistic ploy, although the idea that he would camou-
flage his worldview with lip service to Marx, in order to collect a
meager fee, seems highly unlikely. Just as he did with the readers
of the *Magazine for Literature*, Steiner felt it his mission to introduce the reality of the spirit into the minds of his listeners. The
fact that they were all indoctrinated with a philosophy that denied
everything he stood for was negligible. The fact that they were listening was enough. It would, he realized, have been useless to try
to deny Marxism directly. What he needed to do was to let their
own idealism, which had brought them to Marxism in the first
place, carry them beyond it, to a recognition of the spirit. At his
first attempt, Steiner displayed the innate charm, charisma, and
sincerity that would in a few years make him one of the most
successful speakers in Europe. As one member of his audience,
described as a "specially active comrade," remarked when Steiner
had finished: "That was not by any means the materialistic view
of history, *but it was interesting.*"[17]

This "specially active comrade" was not the only one who found Steiner's lectures interesting. Steiner's audience grew each week, and after only a few months, a group of about two hundred came to every lecture. This meant of course that they had to be moved to a larger hall. One reason for Steiner's popularity was that he invited his listeners to comment and ask questions and to participate in a way unusual in Germany, where most students respectfully listened to the speaker, took notes, and went home. Soon it wasn't uncommon for the lectures to go on till after midnight, and some of the most engaging material emerged from the students' questions and comments. Steiner also lectured on other subjects besides history: German literature; Indian, Persian, and Arabic culture; philosophy; science; and social history. He even gave a class in public speaking, and when students presented him with papers for his comments, corrected them all with a delicacy and encouragement many had never known before. As one student remarked, "Many of his students really accomplished things which previously could never have been expected of them."[18] If there's any doubt that Steiner was a born teacher, this account of this period in his life is enough to dispel it.

When Steiner accepted the job, he made clear to the school's council that he demanded a free hand in what he taught. At first this presented no problem, as most of the council paid little attention to him, happy that the lectures were well attended and that the lecturer was content with a mere eight marks. Steiner was soon approached by other workers, who had heard of his talents. One group asked him to lecture on Haeckel's *The Riddle of the Universe*. Steiner of course accepted and solved the problem of how to handle Haeckel's atheism by praising the biological chapters of the book, and instructing his audience to throw the rest away. Steiner's success was so impressive and his reputation as a speaker so great that on the five-hundredth anniversary of Gutenberg's invention of printing, he was asked to address an audience of seven thousand members of the Typesetters and Printers Union at the Busch Circus, the only auditorium in Berlin able to accommodate such a crowd. Eventually, though, Steiner was recognized as a spiritual wolf in materialist sheep's clothing. His very popularity proved his unmasking. After hearing so much about the inspiring Dr. Steiner, some of the council members thought it would be a good idea to hear him themselves. Although in his account in his autobiography he states that he was given carte blanche to teach what he liked, in a lecture given in October 1918, he painted a somewhat different picture.[19] There he remarks that he was allowed to lecture as he liked on every topic except one: freedom. To his Marxist employers, to speak of freedom was a dangerous business, and one wonders if they knew that their star lecturer had as his life's mission to spread the message of his book, *The Philosophy of Freedom*. At one meeting when Steiner was arguing the reality of spiritual values, a committee from the council attended and interrupted him throughout. When he asserted that socialism could have a future only if teachers like himself were allowed the liberty and freedom to express their deepest convictions, one of the true believers shouted back, "In our party there can be no question of freedom, only of reasonable constraint."[20] And even though Steiner had hundreds of students on his side, he was inevitably forced to resign. It was made impossible for him to lecture to other working men's associations as well, so virulent was the antagonism to this spiritualist counterrevolutionary. It took

some time for the materialists to oust him, though, and he continued to lecture at the school until 1904, by which time he had
found a new, perhaps even more receptive audience.

Steiner must have found his work as a lecturer stimulating.
Alwin Rudolph remained in touch with Steiner throughout this
time, and provides a glimpse of his life after his marriage to Anna.
The change in their legal status provoked no change in their personal relations. Anna continued to look after Steiner with "moth-
erly attachment and modesty," and remained as reserved as
before. On fine days, Steiner would take some of his students on a
walk in the countryside. There, Rudolph recalls, they would lie on
the grass and listen to Steiner as he spoke on a variety of subjects:
literature, the theater, the Greek poets and philosophers, Confu-
cius, Zola and Dreyfus, the altar of Pergamum. Then, after some
fascinating comment about the latest scientific developments (or
ancient history or Goethe), Steiner would turn to speaking about
the flowers before them or about the insects flying around them.
On one occasion some students discovered a rare type of cater-
pillar; Steiner was able to tell them the family it belonged to and
gave them an exact description of it. There seemed to be nothing
that this "silo brimful of knowledge"[21] didn't know.

Another student outing lead to Steiner being asked why so few
people are happy, although that is precisely what they want out of
life. Steiner replied: "But perhaps life is not given us in order that
we may be happy." "But what else can it be for?" his students
replied. "Well, suppose we had life *in order to fulfill a task*?" the
Doctor answered. The students didn't know what to make of this,
but for Steiner it was a self-evident truth.

Along with the Working Men's College, as mentioned, Steiner
also gave lectures to Ludwig Jacobowski's Die Kommenden

group. Among others they heard his memorial address on the occasion of Nietzsche's death in 1900. Like the Working Men's College, Die Kommenden was at first open-minded and allowed Steiner the freedom to speak on whatever he chose, even Christianity, about which, after a long inner struggle, Steiner was at this time arriving at many new insights. Another group, with a more rigorous agenda, was the Giordano Bruno Bund, named after the Renaissance mage burned at the stake by the Church for his advocacy of the Copernican model of the solar system. The Bund espoused a monistic philosophy of the spiritual kind, and Steiner attended their opening lecture. It was given by a friend, the philosopher Bruno Wille. Even here, Steiner was still unintentionally stepping on toes. Wille lectured on Goethe's belief that there is no matter without spirit, and after the lecture, Steiner, in all innocence, spoke up and commented that Goethe had later added to this view, informing the audience of his ideas on "polarity" and "intensification." The upshot was that Steiner more or less corrected Wille in public and was later baffled when his friend was less than appreciative of this. Steiner, however, was asked to give another history course, this time at the new Independent College started by Wille and the Bund. Yet Steiner again put his foot in it when he lectured on monism for the group. That their hero had been burned at the stake by the Church understandably made the members of the Bund less than receptive to the views of Christian thinkers. They also had a low opinion of Haeckel, who Steiner had both praised and criticized. Steiner may have had the best intentions when he decided to lecture to the group on how Church thinkers like Duns Scotus and Thomas Aquinas were monists too, but it infuriated his audience, who believed he was trying to "smuggle in Catholicism" while they were trying to deal it its death blow. It was doubly confusing as Steiner seemed to be making a U-turn on his ideas about Christianity, a topic we will return to in the next chapter. Although Steiner's membership in the Bund survived this talk, a later one proved too much for the group and after it he was never again asked to speak. A similar fate was in store for his relationship with Die Kommenden, and even his long friendship with Anna Eunicke would not survive the remarkable change that was about to come over Dr. Steiner. After an absence of more than a decade, theosophy, which Steiner had not thought about much since his encounter with it in Vienna in 1888, was about to come back into his life.

6. THEOSOPHY AND COSMIC MEMORIES

Most readers of the *Magazine for Literature* made little sense of Steiner's article on Goethe's alchemical fairy tale "The Green Snake and the Beautiful Lily," but for at least one it was a revelation. A young member of the Berlin lodge of the Theosophical Society, Fritz Seiler,[1] read the article and was impressed; it was clear to him that its author had insight into esoteric knowledge and that he would be perfect to speak to the lodge about the philosopher Nietzsche, a timely topic that theosophical groups in other countries found themselves tackling as well.[2] Count and Countess Brockdorf, leading members of the lodge and hosts to its weekly lecture series, agreed, and on September 22, 1900,[3] at the Theosophical Library at 54a Kaiser-Friedrich-Strasse, Steiner gave his first lecture to a theosophical audience. He must have been a success, because he was asked to return a week later, this time to lecture on Goethe's fairy tale itself.[4] This second lecture was something of an historical event: for the first time, Steiner allowed himself to speak publicly about his spiritual experiences. In recent times he had despaired over finding a means of communicating his vision to the world, and he had already decided to throw in the editorial towel at the *Magazine for Literature*, having failed to increase (or even maintain) its readership through his efforts to spread the message of *The Philosophy of Freedom*. In the same month he gave the lectures, he passed the magazine on to other hands. And although his associations with the Working Men's College, Die Kommenden, and the Free Academy of the Giordano Bruno Bund would continue for a few more years, they, too, were shaky, and it was really just a matter of time before he would have to cut his ties here as well. The question "Must I remain silent?" had troubled him—so much so, that of the thirty-eight chapters in his autobiography, only one, chapter 24, dealing with his decision to take on the editorship of the magazine, has a title, that being the question itself. Steiner had followed the commandments of his Master rigorously, and had, at least to his own satisfaction, laid the philosophical foundations of his spiritual research. He was convinced that the esoteric message he had to give to the world was rooted in firm ground, but aside from some disgruntled readers and some slightly mystified Marxists, he was still pretty much without an audience. Until now.

Count and Countess Brockdorf, like Fritz Seiler, were impressed with Dr. Steiner, and Steiner himself was taken with his new surroundings. It seemed that in his audience he could detect individuals who had a deep interest in things of the spirit. This shouldn't be surprising, as they were all members of the Theosophical Society, which in the last decades of the nineteenth century had risen from an obscure group of occultists to something like a worldwide religion. Steiner felt a great relief in finally speaking openly about his insights, laying down his protective coverings, and communicating the knowledge he had acquired from experience directly. The count and countess were in no doubt that they had come into contact with a man who knew and who could communicate his knowledge brilliantly. It was soon decided that Steiner would return again, this time to give a series of regular lectures to the society's members. The topic was mysticism. Ten years earlier, Steiner confesses, he "would not have dared to agree to such a request."[5] Now he was ready.

As usual, Steiner insisted on complete liberty in what he would talk about; he would only lecture on what he himself had experienced through his own spiritual research. And in any case, Steiner confessed that he had little knowledge of theosophy, and what he did know of it didn't impress him. Although he had spoken with Friedrich Eckstein about it in Vienna, what he had read didn't attract him. He had even published some very critical remarks about it, particularly about the brand of theosophical wisdom offered by a disreputable occultist, Franz Hartmann. More recent encounters hadn't changed his opinion. He found most theosophical literature distasteful, and, as far as his own work went, useless.

Nevertheless the count and countess wanted him back and Steiner must have suspected that he had found his audience after all. In October he began the series of lectures that would later be published as *Mysticism at the Dawn of the Modern Age*.[6] Here Steiner set a precedent that would last for the rest of this association with the Theosophical Society. Although in its very early days its cofounder Helena Petrovna Blavatsky had looked to Egypt for esoteric guidance, she soon turned her sights further east, toward India and the Himalayas, and for the Theosophical Society, that's where they've remained ever since. More than anyone else, Blavatsky is responsible for the love affair millions of Westerners have had with the mystic East for more than a century now. The East has always had an attraction for the West (just as the West has had for the East), and important thinkers like Leibniz and

Schopenhauer had explored aspects of Eastern religions and philosophies earlier. But Blavatsky brought the East to a wider audience than ever before, and made hitherto obscure practices like meditation and strange ideas like reincarnation acceptable to the average person.

In doing this Blavatsky wasn't entirely impartial, and, like Nietzsche and other modern thinkers, she too had little good to say about Christianity. Many of her criticisms were valid; Steiner himself had strong words about some aspects of Christianity. Unfortunately, the recognition that Eastern thought has much to offer the modern West has too often been translated into the belief that the West itself has little of spiritual value. Steiner was adamant that his own approach would follow a Western tradition that in his time was either completely rejected by materialist philosophies or eclipsed by exotic imports. In doing this, Steiner was tackling a problem that is still an important issue in spirituality today.

Steiner spoke to his audience about people with whom most rank-and-file theosophists weren't familiar: Meister Eckhart and Jakob Boehme, for example, both Christian mystics; the alchemist Paracelsus and Giordano Bruno himself, too. These and other medieval and early Renaissance mystics were important because they showed that mysticism was a vital way of knowing, an alternative to the materialist tradition that characterizes the modern period. What was needed was to complement the one-sided materialist view with the insights of the West's own spiritual tradition.

Most of his audience accepted what Steiner had to say, although some were critical. When one theosophist informed Steiner that his ideas were at variance with the received message of the society's head, Annie Besant, he replied with the equivalent of "Oh, really?"

and simply carried on. One listener, however, found nothing to criticize at all. Marie von Sivers was an attractive thirty-three-year-old Baltic Russian who had studied drama in Paris, but who had recently given up the stage because she could find no place for herself in modern theater.[7] Marie's ideas about acting were focused on declamation and the use of a poetic voice; she had no use for naturalism and felt out of touch with the likes of Ibsen, Strindberg, Wedekind, and Shaw (although Yeats's "Celtic Twilight" would have appealed to her). This in itself gave her something in common with Steiner. She was an excellent linguist and in Paris had become the friend and translator of Edouard Schuré, intimate of Richard Wagner and Nietzsche, and author of *The Grand Initiates* (1889). Schuré had in fact spoken to her about theosophy, but at the time Marie could find no way into it. Marie had left Paris for St. Petersburg, called home by her mother, who objected to her interest in acting, and on a trip to Berlin she had seen an advertisement for Steiner's lectures and decided to go. The decision changed her life. At one lecture, Marie approached Steiner and started up a conversation. He asked what she intended to do with her life, and she told him of her profound feeling for the "living nature of speech." This would later translate into the new art form of "living speech" that she and Steiner developed, eurythmy, in which the participants develop physical movements and gestures which themselves communicate in a kind of moving language. Today eurythmy is a staple of anthroposophy. She would also be essential in staging Steiner's mystery dramas. It was during another conversation that Marie asked Steiner whether it wasn't time for a new spiritual movement, built on the foundation of modern science, to be introduced to the modern world—the implication being that he himself would be the man to do it. Steiner agreed, but insisted that he could only "ally myself with a movement that is connected exclusively with Western occultism and cultivates its development . . . such a movement must link on to Plato, to Goethe."[8]

At that moment, Steiner tells us, he mapped out the whole program needed for the undertaking. If it's true that behind every great man is a woman, it seems this includes founders of modern spiritual movements too. Although he was married to Anna Eunicke and would remain so until her death in 1911—they separated, but never divorced—from that moment on, Marie von Sivers became the most important person in Steiner's life. They would marry in 1914. And unlike some great men, Steiner never obscured the influence Marie had on his work. In his autobiography he speaks at length of her devotion to him and the spiritual movement she sparked.

Marie's enthusiasm for theosophy must have been apparent to Count and Countess Brockdorf, for she was soon asked to go to Bologna to help in setting up a Theosophical Section there; she in fact became one of the society's most energetic members, displaying remarkable organizing skills. While she was away, Steiner gave his second lecture series, this one on "Christianity as Mystical Fact," later published in book form. In the same year, 1901, Steiner gave a series of lectures to Die Kommenden on a theme that would soon cause much friction between himself and his new associates, "From Buddha to Christ," also later published as a book. Steiner argued that, in essence, although the Buddha was a remarkable individual who achieved a high level of spirituality and was rightly considered one of the world's great teachers, Christ was *unique*. While the Buddha and other spiritual teachers could guide individuals toward the truth, Christ's birth, death, and resurrection was an event of cosmic proportions, one that made it possible for humanity as a whole to achieve a new participation in the spiritual worlds. In effect, mankind had enjoyed a significant advance in its progression from the "Buddha event" to the "Christ event." For Steiner it was clear that humankind itself reaches its culmination in what he called "the mystery of Golgotha," the significance of which came to him, as he says, during his first years in Berlin.

The idea that Christ was unique was antithetical to the religious tolerance adopted by theosophy. Although many of her remarks about Christianity suggest otherwise, in principle Madame Blavatsky held to the idea—at the time very radical—that all religions are equally valid, as all are different paths to the truth, a belief in keeping with our own multifaith sensibility. For a West that had for centuries focused exclusively on Christianity, this liberal view was fresh and inspiring. But for Steiner, for all its good intentions, it was wrong. Christ's descent and incarnation, he declared, was the single most significant event in human history. This aspect of Steiner's work is, to put it bluntly, a turn off for many people. It smacks of narrow-mindedness and fundamentalism, although Steiner's approach has nothing to do with either. Yet while many, probably most, anthroposophists would disagree, I think it's possible to put aside Steiner's Christocentric beliefs, without losing what remains of importance in his work.

Steiner came to his new understanding of Christ through direct spiritual experience. In his early days in Berlin, and during his difficult time as editor of the *Magazine for Literature,* Steiner went through what the historian of psychology Henri Ellenberger calls a "creative illness."[9] Steiner's own account is regrettably abstract, but it seems that his conversion, if we can call it that, occurred during the trials he endured through his friendship with John H. Mackay, when Steiner felt he was being tempted to apply his inner "ethical individualism" to the outer world of politics. In chapter 26 of his autobiography, Steiner remarks that some of the comments he made about Christianity then could be taken as contradictions of his later view. Steiner is less than specific, but it's clear the aspect of Christianity that triggered his earlier remarks was its belief in a world beyond, a spiritual world unattainable through the intellect and from which were revealed the moral and ethical precepts that were to guide one's life. Steiner rejected this view and had dedicated his life to the opposite belief, that through rigorous and active thinking we can gain access to the spirit world ourselves. And although he disagreed with Nietzsche on many points, on one important issue the two thinkers were in accord. Steiner had no patience for individuals unwilling to make the effort to actualize their freedom and who relied on the state or the church to tell them what to do. A Christianity that expected passive obedience would find little commendation from an advocate of *The Philosophy of Freedom*.

Yet during the years preceding his appearance on the theosophical stage, Steiner went through "inner battles" and "inner struggles," in which he was forced to rescue his entire world conception. He felt the presence of demonic spiritual beings, whom he later called Ahrimanic, whose aim was to impede humankind's evolution and to turn the scientific method into a complete acceptance of materialism. Steiner emerged from his battles victorious, he tells us, through contemplating the evolution of Christianity with "spiritual perception." And shortly before the turn of the century, he found himself "standing in the spiritual presence of the Mystery of Golgotha in a . . . profound and solemn festival of knowledge."[10] We can assume from this that Steiner in some way *saw* that the "Christ event" was unlike any other in history and, regardless of the consequences, was obliged to stick to this empirical fact.

Some of this knowledge Steiner passed on to his audience. In "Christianity as Mystical Fact," Steiner posits the Christ event as the culmination of the ancient "mystery tradition," into which he places Plato and pre-Socratic thinkers like Heracleitus, Empedocles, and Pythagoras, a theme he may have absorbed from Schuré's *The Great Initiates.*[11] Whether his view jibed with theosophy proper or not, Steiner was impressive enough to be asked to join the society. He was, in fact, asked to become the general secretary of the Theosophical Society's German section, which the members intended to found if Dr. Steiner would accept their offer. Steiner accepted in principle and made only two conditions: that he be allowed to speak as he wished, and that Marie von Sivers be called back from Italy to become his assistant. The Brockdorfs, who were planning to leave Berlin but didn't want to interrupt the work of the society, were so anxious that Steiner accept their proposal that they offered Marie the apartment that had housed the Theosophical Library. At this, Steiner formally accepted their offer and, almost immediately, he and Marie were invited to attend the Theosophical Congress to be held in London in July 1902.

As the charter for the new section hadn't yet been received, Steiner and Marie attended the London congress as guests. There Steiner met some theosophical notables: Annie Besant herself; A. P. Sinnett, whose *Esoteric Buddhism* he had disliked; the author and scholar G. R. S. Mead (whose home became something of a pit stop for traveling theosophists, playing host a few years later to

P. D. Ouspensky); and Bertram Keightley, at whose house Steiner stayed. Steiner didn't meet the Reverend Charles Leadbeater, one of the society's more colorful figures, but he did hear him speak, although he wasn't impressed. Steiner gave a brief speech, in which he informed his new associates that in Germany there was a great deal of interest in theosophy, but little understanding of its concepts. Yet he believed that in German philosophy, the work of thinkers like Hegel, Fichte, Schelling, and Leibniz was in the true theosophical tradition, and that their thought should now be brought within the mainstream of the society—a clear enough indication of Steiner's own intentions. And once again he declared that he was against dogmatism of any kind and that his own work would be informed by his own spiritual research. In his free time, Steiner and Marie visited London's museums; her background enabled her to introduce Steiner to many works of art, while he supplemented her remarks with his own spiritual perceptions, a practice that would continue whenever the two traveled together.

Steiner returned from London a changed man. Even his appearance was different. He had shaved his mustache and had brought back a souvenir: a bowler hat. It seems he took the occasion of a lecture at the Giordano Bruno Bund on "Monism and Theosophy" to announce that from now on things would be different. Those close to him couldn't mistake it. Alwin Rudolph felt that Steiner had placed some distance between himself and his old friends, and that the intimacy they once enjoyed was lost. Steiner even treated his audience differently: instead of looking at the faces before him, he now kept his eyes above the crowd, fixed on the back of the room. The lecture began with a powerful denunciation of spiritualism, a clear sign that although he had adopted theosophy, he was dissociating himself from its founder, and any others who had followed her practice of trance communication, what today we would call channeling. Spiritual knowledge must come through clear, waking consciousness—mediums were a thing of the past. Steiner then informed his listeners that all serious philosophies of life must be in accord with the findings of genuine science and that theosophy was indeed a serious philosophy of life. Modern science, however, was in danger of succumbing to a one-sided belief in materialism. Finally, he went on to exasperate and alienate the members of the Bund by insisting that if it did not let into itself the revivifying truth of the religious impulse, the science of the modern world would be nothing but an empty shell. If it were to fail to do this, the men of the present were in danger of appearing little more than pygmies to generations to come.

According to one account, when Steiner finished no one clapped, in fact no one made a sound at all. The hall quickly emptied, and Steiner was left, one suspects, with the distinct feeling that he had burned several boats. (Another account relates that some of the audience remained outside until the morning hours, discussing Steiner's talk.)[12] Alwin Rudolph broke with him almost immediately after the lecture. Anna Eunicke, who we can imagine was not entirely thrilled by her husband's new friends, was "strangely withdrawn and closed up, speaking very little."[13] She had no interest in theosophy and couldn't understand her husband's decision to give up his career as a liberal academic to associate himself with a society founded by a well-known charlatan, which was the general view of Madame Blavatsky at the time. Most of Steiner's friends and colleagues shared Anna's bafflement. Anna would become, as one writer put it, a "casualty"[14] of Steiner's new task. A year later, Steiner would move out of their house and into what would become the Theosophical headquarters in Berlin, at 17 Motzstrasse.

The question of Steiner's relationship with Marie von Sivers during his marriage to Anna Eunicke has raised some eyebrows among occult historians and warrants a few words here. In his brilliant if critical study, *The Occult Establishment*, James Webb remarks apropos of Steiner's marriage to Anna that "the possibility of his having married a rich widow for her money cannot be ruled out."[15] Webb also records a story told by one of Steiner's stepdaughters of how Anna once found Steiner in bed with one of his disciples—if true, this was most likely Marie von Sivers. Webb, it has to be admitted, is less than sympathetic to Steiner, although he does remark that the story of Steiner's infidelity must be taken with a grain of salt as its source may not be entirely reliable. Steiner's stepdaughter could very possibly have held a grudge against a man whom her mother had taken in and cared for, and who then abandoned her for another woman, and simply made up the incident. And the fact that throughout his autobiography Steiner comes across as sexless casts doubt on his being caught in bed with anyone.

Anna Eunicke wasn't the only casualty of Steiner's new career. Steiner never again lectured for the Giordano Bruno Bund, and his reputation as a theosophist ended his tenure with Die Kommenden. But Steiner's long apprenticeship was over. Ten days after his lecture, the charter for the German Section was ready, and Annie Besant herself came to Berlin to present it to him. Not everyone in the Berlin lodge was happy about the idea of Steiner becoming the leader of the Theosophical Society in Germany, Switzerland, and Austria-Hungary, but the opposition accepted the decision. Steiner, it seems, had finally found his audience.

Almost immediately he plunged into the torrent of activity that characterized his life for the next twenty-three years, writing, publishing, and lecturing practically nonstop. In July 1903, during a second visit to London, Steiner was gratified when one leading theosophist told him that his book *Mysticism at the Dawn of the Modern Age* "contained the truth about theosophy." Steiner surely agreed. Although until the break in 1913 and the founding of the Anthroposophical Society he would call himself a theosophist, Steiner's own reading of the Akashic Record differed considerably from that of his predecessors, and it wouldn't be long before that difference became clear. One of the first things Steiner did in his new capacity was to start a journal. *Lucifer*, later *Lucifer-Gnosis*, became the organ for his ideas that Steiner had been searching for. Steiner wrote practically the whole magazine, which he and Marie published from their new headquarters. In the beginning they would address all the issues themselves, then carry them down to the post office in a laundry basket. Soon they needed several baskets. Steiner must have felt that he had vindicated himself as an editor; within a few years, subscriptions had increased so much that he had to turn the journal over to a professional distributor. By 1909, the increase in lecture tours and other demands led to Steiner's taking a less active role in the magazine's production, and it had to be abandoned. Steiner had by this time found a more effective means of disseminating his message, through the publishing house founded by Marie von Sivers, which issued his books and transcriptions of his lectures.

Steiner serialized two of his earliest and most important occult works through the book *Knowledge of the Higher Worlds and Its Attainment* (1909) and the essays later published as *Cosmic Memory* (1937), a kind of first draft of the longer *Outline of*

Occult Science (1910). Along with *Theosophy* (1903), these form the three basic books of anthroposophy, and at this point it would be good to give some idea of their contents. As the title suggests, *Knowledge of the Higher Worlds and Its Attainment* is a handbook on developing spiritual perception. Steiner believed that his supersensible perception wasn't an anomaly, but a potential of everyday consciousness, so it followed that it could be taught. As there were no limits to knowledge other than those set by laziness and ignorance, anyone willing to spend the time and effort should be able to learn how to do it. If the ground has been prepared by an experience of consciousness as a free, spiritual activity—as set out in *The Philosophy of Freedom*—the exercises Steiner provides should lead to the development of distinct stages of supersensory consciousness, which Steiner called Imagination, Inspiration, and Intuition.

Steiner's exercises involve both detailed meditations and general maxims. Patience, reverence, open-mindedness, respect, detachment, tranquillity, and other basic virtues are emphasized, along with specific disciplines, such as meditating on the growth and decay of plant forms. This, Steiner says, will convey a sense of the timeless *idea* of the plant—the *Urpflanze* of Goethe's metamorphic studies—which transcends its transitory life. In the process one's own eternal spirit would be revealed. One result of practicing Steiner's exercises is a change in one's dreams; from being vague and distorted, they take on a more orderly pattern. A further change is a kind of continuity of consciousness; one's ego awareness is strengthened in sleep and is retained during dreams, much like the phenomena of "lucid dreaming." Another result is a perception of the aura, the astral form that envelops our physical body; likewise the refinement of the chakras, those centers of esoteric force which theosophy claimed existed within the physical body and which many readers today may be familiar with through Tantric yoga and other methods of awakening Kundalini, the spiritual serpent. The ultimate aim of the exercises, however, was initiation, which culminated in a confrontation with the Guardian of the Threshold, a projection of one's unredeemed karma.

Subtitled *An Introduction to the Supersensible Knowledge of the World and the Destination of Man, Theosophy* relates the sevenfold nature of the human being and the mechanics of karma and reincarnation. Steiner argues that, contrary to church teaching, human beings are not creatures of body and soul alone, but are really threefold; spirit, the third element, was abandoned by Christianity in the ninth century, when the belief in a human spirit was branded a heresy, much to the detriment of Western civilization.[16] To these three Steiner adds the etheric and astral bodies, familiar to theosophy.

The physical body is the only one recognized by modern science, and although many of us believe in a soul, we generally see this as a metaphor for our inner life, our feelings and emotions. The notion that we have two additional bodies, then, may strike us as strange. We can think of the etheric body as a kind of life force, giving shape to and animating the minerals that constitute the physical body, which it leaves at death.[17] The astral body we can see as our feelings and emotions, our likes and dislikes, much as I characterized the soul above. The notion of spirit (rather than a spirit, which suggests a ghost) some readers may have difficulty with.

Unlike the soul, which is personal and which, according to Steiner, we receive anew with each incarnation, the spirit transcends our personality; it's that part of ourselves which looks on in the midst of disappointment or joy with bemused detachment. Although Steiner associates it with our I, which would seem to make it very personal, it's really that part of us which goes beyond our self, that's driven by impersonal aims and purposes and works toward *objective* knowledge of reality, and not merely for our likes and dislikes. If the senses tell us *that* something is, and our feelings tell us whether we like it or not, spirit is drawn to discovering what the thing is *in itself.* I can look at the sky and notice dark clouds moving in—that's sensory knowledge. I can decide it's going to rain and be disappointed that I'll have to cut short my walk—here I use knowledge for *personal* reasons, how the coming rain will affect *me.* But I can also become fascinated with the whole phenomenon of weather. How do clouds build up, what's involved in precipitation, how do these clouds differ from others? I may even become so interested in this that I won't get out of the rain when it comes. This is the "disinterested curiosity" of the scientific or philosophical mind, the kind of mind that Steiner argued is the prerequisite for any success on the path of spiritual development. Spirit is that in us which will endure discomfort, even hardship, because it's certain of the value of the things it pursues, a value not utilitarian, or merely personal, but *objective,* that exists *outside* us. Again, Steiner's way of communicating this is at times abstract, but he nevertheless hits on a fundamental truth about human nature, much as he did in *The Philosophy of Freedom,* and it's a truth that's valid whether or not etheric or astral bodies really exist. Put in its simplest form, we can say that, unlike animals, human beings can become deeply interested in things that do not concern them personally, and that, in fact, it's precisely those things—like science, art, philosophy, or religion—that, for many, are the most important of all.

In life, by ennobling our passions and desires, we work on our different bodies, transmuting them into finer substances. The result is a sevenfold hierarchy. The first four—the physical body, the life or etheric body, the astral body, and the I—are given in each incarnation. Through our efforts, three additional bodies can be created: the spirit-self, which is the transmuted astral body; the life-spirit, which is the transmuted etheric body; and the spirit-man, which is the transmuted physical body. (Steiner altered his terminology in later years, but early on he continued to use Sanskrit words like *buddhi, manas,* and *atman* in speaking about these transmuted higher bodies.)[18] From the physical body we receive only sensory knowledge. But from the etheric body we can gain *imaginative* knowledge, from the astral body we can gain *inspirational* knowledge, and from the conscious experience of the I or the spirit, *intuitive* knowledge is granted us. These forms of knowledge relate to previous forms of consciousness that existed prior to the development of the conscious I, and Steiner's aim in attaining knowledge of higher worlds is the reawakening of these earlier forms of consciousness, while retaining full possession of the I. Imaginative knowledge is conveyed in the form of pictures; it's a kind of spiritual seeing, and through it we can observe etheric forms and the aura. Here the images that come to us from objects—stones, plants, animals, people—are anchored to their source, but with inspirational knowledge, which is a kind of spiritual hearing, these images are set free and can be observed independently of physical reality. Intuitive knowledge is a direct, unmediated awareness. At present, the only thing of which we can have intuitive knowledge is our own I, and Steiner rightly points out that it is only of ourselves that we can say I, and that no other being, in referring to us, can use that term. With intuitive knowledge, this kind of intimacy will, presumably, be made available to us in "all things." As Steiner said in a later lecture series (which serves as a good introduction to his ideas on the evolution of consciousness), with intuition "man has a universal consciousness . . . he will see not only what proceeds on his own planet, but in the whole cosmos."[19]

Steiner's account of what takes place after death is perhaps the most fascinating and most difficult part of *Theosophy*. It takes three days for the etheric body to dissolve after death, and during this time the individual experiences his entire past life in a kind of simultaneous panoramic vision, the source, perhaps, of the many accounts of people near death seeing their whole life flash before their eyes. The astral body, which has assimilated this instantaneous replay of one's life, then continues to exist for a period equal to one third of the individual's life—so if you die at seventy-five, your astral body carries on for another twenty-five years, a time during which the soul experiences in full awareness the content of its sleep life. This period of time Steiner calls *kamaloca*, using the Sanskrit term. Here the ego undergoes a process of purging (the Christian notion of Purgatory expresses the same idea). As the astral body is the seat of our desires and passions, in this part of *kamaloca*, it experiences profound frustration, as it still seeks to gratify its hungers, but cannot—this may account for the many ghost stories that suggest the departed don't know they're dead and continue to seek out what they enjoyed in life.

Eventually the ego endures the pain of ungratified desires and is purified of these. Following this, the ego then experiences its entire life again, only backward, from death to birth, and from an unusual perspective. Here we are made aware of the consequences of our actions, unknown to us in life. Viewing these karmic connections can be profoundly painful, as one becomes aware of all the suffering one's actions caused. This is necessary, however, in preparation for one's next incarnation. Having been cleansed of our desires and made aware of our karma, the I, with the assistance of higher spiritual beings, then decides on what conditions in the next incarnation will be best suited to its further development. The I decides who its next parents will be, where it will grow up, what kind of physical body it will have, what disposition, and so on, in order to provide itself with the best material for its spiritual growth (so it's no use complaining about your life, as you chose it before you were born). During the time prior to rebirth, the soul travels out into space and comes under the influence of spiritual beings, the planets, and the stars, which assist in the creation of our next physical body. Traveling past the sun and stars, the astral body is formed; from the influence of the moon we receive a new etheric body. These two are then linked to the seed in the womb which we have already chosen. Our new threefold body then joins its soul and spirit, ready to take advantage of the opportunities for spiritual growth provided by its new incarnation.

This process of birth, death, and rebirth, Steiner tells us, is part of a vast cosmic evolution, the most elaborate description of which can be found in *An Outline of Occult Science* (here I can provide only a brief summary, taken from several sources). According to Steiner, the earth (like ourselves) has gone through three previous incarnations, which he calls Old Saturn, Old Sun, and Old Moon, and is destined to pass through three further stages, Jupiter, Venus, and Vulcan. We shouldn't confuse these names with those of the heavenly bodies (or with the home planet of *Star Trek*'s Mr. Spock), and why Steiner chose them is unclear; many commentators agree they are not the most inspiring. During the Old Saturn incarnation, matter didn't exist, although the first rudiment of our physical bodies developed here and was worked on by several spiritual beings during seven "cycles." A kind of heat-permeated space. On Old Saturn the entities that would eventually evolve into human beings experienced what Steiner calls "a very dull deep condition of consciousness." Only a few present-day humans experience this kind of consciousness, those capable of trance states, or mediums—in our language, channelers. This consciousness was aware of "cosmic conditions," but in a very vague, dull way. Steiner says that minerals still share in this kind of consciousness, and if they could speak, they would tell us what life was like on Old Saturn.

After a period of rest, what Steiner, using the Sanskrit term, calls a *pralaya*, we enter the Old Sun incarnation. Here the warmth of Old Saturn has hardened slightly into a kind of air. On Old Sun we first received our etheric bodies, which, like our rudimentary physical bodies, are worked upon by several spiritual beings, through a series of seven cycles. Our physical bodies at this point are plantlike. On Old Sun, consciousness existed in a kind of deep, dreamless sleep, a slightly less dull awareness than on Old Saturn. On present-day earth, plants have this kind of consciousness, and if we could speak with them, they would, Steiner tells us, share their memories of Old Sun.

After another *pralaya,* Old Sun mutates into Old Moon. The hardening that began on Old Sun continues, and Old Moon is characterized by water. A repetition of the previous two incarnations takes place, resulting in the first appearance of the astral body. Now the Moon, which had been embedded in the Sun, splits off and becomes an independent body, on which develop certain beings involved in human evolution. Again our body, now composed of physical, etheric, and astral parts, is worked on by spiritual beings. As we were mineral on Old Saturn and plantlike on Old Sun, on Old Moon there existed a kind of animal-man. Old Moon consciousness was a kind of dreamy, symbolic state, what Steiner calls "picture consciousness," and which animals today experience. Again, if they could speak, they would tell us what it was like on Old Moon.

Eventually the hardening that had begun on Old Saturn reaches our present earth, where the kind of physical body we know makes its first appearance, along with our present-day waking state consciousness, which eventually gives rise to the I.[20] Here what we might call the descending phase of cosmic evolution, its increasing materialization, reaches its nadir and begins to turn back toward its spiritual origins, the decisive point in this being the incarnation of Christ. Present-day human beings are the bearers of this evolution, and Steiner saw his task as nothing less then turning them in the right direction. We have within us the remnants of the previous incarnations, but also intimations of future states of consciousness that will come with further incarnations of the earth, which, Steiner tells us, is dying.[21] The next incarnation is Jupiter, which will be characterized by a return of the Old Moon picture consciousness, along with our waking, rational consciousness; this is what Steiner calls Imagination. Next comes Venus, which is a return of the Old Sun consciousness, then Vulcan, which is a return of the Old Saturn consciousness, both with our rational I intact, and providing Inspiration and Intuition, respectively.

Before getting to this point, however, human history passes through a series of "epochs." When our earth was in its infancy, human beings were still only slightly material, their bodies little more than a kind of vapor. On Lemuria, the earliest civilization, we had telepathic powers, a deep intuitive awareness of plants and minerals, and could use our willpower to move tremendous weights. Ideas of good and evil first appeared then, and it was also at this time that the moon (the one we know) split off from the earth. This was brought about because the "moon forces" were speeding up the hardening process, which interfered with our proper evolution. Other forces working against lawful evolution appeared then too, the Luciferic and Ahrimanic beings, who rebelled against the spiritual hierarchies, thus bringing about the possibility of free will. Ahriman tempts man into materialism, while Lucifer is the source of hubris and overweening pride.

After the destruction of Lemuria comes Atlantis, where our solidification continues. (Both Madame Blavatsky and another important theosophist, W. Scott-Elliot,[22] had written about Atlantis, and Steiner's account was meant to supplement and correct theirs.) The Atlanteans had terrific powers of memory and could harness the life force in plants. They, however, fell victim to the temptations of Ahriman and were corrupted. Our Atlantean ancestors fell deeper into materialism, egoism, and pride, which, according to a strange occult law, brought on a violent reaction from nature, resulting in the catastrophic sinking of Atlantis, echoes of which we hear in legends around the world and which Plato speaks of in the *Timaeus*. Then follow seven post-Atlantean epochs; we are currently in the first half of the fifth, with two more to come. Each epoch, which lasts roughly 2,160 years,[23] is characterized by an increasing "materialization of consciousness" until the descent of Christ takes place in the fourth, at which point an upswing occurs. Previous epochs had a greater participation in the spirit worlds, and now, with the incarnation of Christ, which ensured the possibility of freedom and the development of the I, we are moving back to spirit. In our current stage, the European-American epoch, which started in 1413 and will continue until the year 3573, our task is the development of what Steiner called the "consciousness soul," whose mission is to combine the clear consciousness of the scientific mind with the vital awareness of the spiritual world present in our earlier incarnations. The previous epochs—Ancient Indian, Ancient Persian, Egypto-Chaldean, and Greco-Roman—had as their task the development of the etheric body, astral body, and what Steiner called "the sentient soul" and "the intellectual soul," respectively.

I apologize for this unavoidably sketchy overview, which does little justice to Steiner's fascinating, challenging, and sometimes bizarre account. Readers who wish to explore Steiner's occult history further, can find an excellent introduction to it in Robert A. McDermott's *Essential Steiner* and a more detailed summary in Stewart C. Easton's exhaustive *Man and World in Light of Anthroposophy.* Elsewhere I have discussed how Steiner's "epochs" parallel the "structures of consciousness" of the philosopher Jean Gebser.[24]

I wouldn't be surprised if the last few pages have taxed some readers' capacity for giving Steiner the benefit of the doubt and left them wondering who could possibly believe this science fiction story. Yet this cosmic history is the backbone of Steiner's work. How, we want to ask, could he possibly know these things? Although Steiner had been privy to the spiritual worlds since childhood, he tells us that around the time that he became involved in the Theosophical Society, he "stood within the spiritual world in full consciousness." In 1902 and for the next few years, Steiner had "imaginings, inspirations and intuitions regarding many things." During this time he received impressions of "the facts and Beings of the spiritual world" and out of this experience he developed "specific details of knowledge." Steiner modified and supplemented his description over the years, remarking in several places that his account was never to be taken on blind faith alone, and that, as in all attempts at gaining knowledge, mistakes were inevitable. "Spiritual perception," he told his readers, "is not infallible." One can perceive in an "inexact, oblique, wrong manner." "No man is free from error in this field."[25] Having said this, Steiner nevertheless insisted on the overall accuracy of his "reading," admitting that while some mistakes in specifics were possible, the general picture was true. He also added the caveat that he was "obliged to remain silent" about the sources of his information. It must also be remembered that this account of human and planetary history is actually a history of consciousness. For Steiner, the world of matter, which seems so obdurately there for us, is actually a product of consciousness, or spirit, which is the ultimate reality. At an earlier time matter did not exist, as it will not in the future.

What exactly the Akashic Record is remains an open question.[26] For Steiner, "everything which comes into being in time has its origin in the eternal." But while the eternal is not perceivable by the senses, it can be perceived through heightened consciousness. "At a certain high level . . . man can penetrate to the eternal origins of things." At this level the past does not appear as "the dead testimony of history," but "in *full* life. . . . In a certain sense, what has happened takes place before him."[27] Colin Wilson has suggested that Steiner was a powerful psychometrist, a person with the ability to perceive the history of an object, simply by touching it, an idea first proposed by Maurice Maeterlinck.[28] Elsewhere I have discussed how Steiner's visions may be linked to the phenomena of hypnagogia, the half-waking, half-dreaming state we all pass through on the way to sleep, and how this can be seen as a form of our Old Moon consciousness, the return of which Steiner posits as the next stage in the evolution of consciousness.[29] The detail Steiner provides in *Cosmic Memory, Outline of Occult Science,* and in the lectures making up *Karmic Relationships,* seems to preclude the idea that he was inventing his account of cosmic history or reincarnation as he went along. Reports by people like Friedrich Rittelmeyer and Guenther Wachsmuth, two early biographers of Steiner who knew him personally, suggest that Steiner did indeed see what he says he did. At his lectures, which he always delivered without notes, oftentimes changing the topic depending on the mood of the audience, he seemed to be relating to his listeners something he was actually *perceiving* right then. Steiner seemed able to shift his awareness from the external world to his own inner landscape at will. We also should recall his own admission that, until his thirty-fifth year, the external world, which most of us find stubbornly real, appeared to Steiner shadowlike and fleeting, very much in the way that he tells us consciousness perceived the world during the Old Moon incarnation, in "picture-form." We also recall Steiner's predilection for his "picture books" as a child. In some cases, hypnagogic imagery can appear with such startling clarity and depth that it seems like a concrete, three-dimensional reality, a characteristic that it shares with "eidetic imagery," which the *Encyclopaedia Britannica* describes as "unusually vivid subjective visual phenomena." An eidetic object appears in minute photographic detail, and the person perceiving it behaves toward it as if it were really there. (One famous eidetic person was the inventor Nikola Tesla, who could visualize an entire device in his head, and use this as a blueprint for the actual object; likewise, Mozart reportedly heard an entire piece of music before setting the notes to paper—a form, apparently, of eidetic hearing. An often quoted account of the neurosurgeon Wilder Penfield is suggestive too: accidentally stimulating an area of his patient's brain, Penfield evoked the total sensory recall of some past event.[30]) And there are, of course, innumerable accounts of precognition, second sight, clairvoyance, and other forms of super- or extrasensory perception, unrelated to Steiner's.

Some combination of these possibilities could account for the vividness of Steiner's visions, but not, clearly, for their accuracy, or lack thereof. Steiner, we've seen, admitted to the possibility of error, and in some cases, his visions seem to have been inaccurate.[31] We also know that his visions differed from Madame Blavatsky's, and also from those of other well-documented seers, like Swedenborg or Edgar Cayce. Yet this doesn't mean that he was fooling himself or that the others were wrong—although confirmed anthroposophists might think so. We know that dreams can present a series of apparently absurd images, yet also be astoundingly accurate; as Steiner said, "picture consciousness" presents knowledge in *symbolic* form. From my own experience I know that dreams can be precognitive, yet this information is invariably delivered in symbols and metaphors, usually jumbled up with a great deal of nonsense.[32] More commonly, many of us have been amazed at a dream's ability to comment accurately on our lives, providing us with profound self-knowledge. Steiner's visions, then, can be seen as astonishingly detailed and vivid lucid dreams, or a form of what the psychologist Carl Jung called "active imagination," a kind of induced waking dream or hypnagogic state. And while most of us will balk at the kind of detail Steiner relates in, say, his account of Atlantis or Lemuria, or even less fantastic reports of the machinery of karma, we can still, I believe, glean much insight from the general drift of his scheme. Again, I think there's good reason to suspect that, while more than likely inaccurate in the details—which, in any case, seem impossible to prove one way or the other, and of which I've presented only a minute fraction—Steiner's account does provide a good working hypothesis of a possible evolution of consciousness. The fact that some other accounts tally significantly with his supports this view.[33]

Ultimately, it's for the individual reader to decide what to make of Steiner's occult history. Depending on your point of view, you can accept it as truth, reject it as absurd, or, as the present writer finds most profitable, enjoy it for its sheer imaginative vitality, gleaning whatever insights from it you can. Whatever we make of it, it was against this backdrop that, almost overnight, Steiner rose to prominence as the most important esoteric teacher of his time.

7. THE RISE
OF DR. STEINER

Although Annie Besant and the others who welcomed Steiner's arrival saw him as a way of injecting new blood into the Theosophical Society, they soon realized with some chagrin that they were getting more than they had bargained for. It's hackneyed to speak of a meteoric rise, but in Steiner's case the phrase is apt. Upon becoming general secretary of the German section, Steiner swiftly rose to prominence and quickly established himself as a powerful and charismatic figure, a brilliant thinker with a mind of his own and no hesitations about using it. This sudden transformation from a respected but obscure scholar to a spiritual leader is reminiscent of some strange plant whose seed, dormant for years, had found its proper soil and immediately burst into rapid growth. It's understandable that some members of the society were suspicious of his motives; they would have no difficulty agreeing with the historian of the occult James Webb, who remarked that "if we allow Steiner a consistency of aim and purpose, he cannot be acquitted of the charge of joining the theosophists with the intention of taking them over."[1] Steiner himself admits something of the sort when he says that he became involved in the Theosophical Society because it was only there that he discovered a suitable audience for his message. By all accounts, that audience grew rapidly, and one reason for the increasing friction between Steiner and his new associates was that, instead of becoming members of lodges in their own countries, which was the usual procedure, many new recruits joined the German section, simply because of Steiner. Although Steiner didn't go out of his way to encourage this, it's understandable that Annie Besant and other leading members would see in his popularity a dangerous rival to their own authority.

In the first few years, however, Annie decided that the best policy would be to try to heal any threatening rifts. In 1907 she wrote to an old-guard German member, Dr. Hübbe-Schleiden, who was unhappy with Steiner's influence, assuring him that although different, Steiner's vision and her own were compatible. "Dr. Steiner's occult training," she said, "is very different from our own. He does not know the eastern way, so cannot . . . teach it. He teaches the Christian and Rosicrucian way, and this is very helpful to some, but is different from ours. . . . I regard him as a very fine teacher on his own lines, a man of real knowledge."[2] And in 1908, in an introduction to Steiner's short book *The Way of Initiation,* Annie could write that "Dr. Steiner's views . . . are of great utility, supplying a side of Theosophical thought which might otherwise miss fitting recognition."[3] It may have been true, then, as some felt, that Steiner "gladly recognized the profound depth of Hindu wisdom and offered it a brotherly hand."[4] But nevertheless clouds were gathering, and it was only a matter of time before the storm broke.

Steiner himself may have been keeping his options open. In 1906, Steiner met the occultist Theodor Reuss in Lugano, Switzerland, and Annie Besant's remark that Steiner taught a "Rosicrucian way," may have originated in Steiner and Reuss's brief and somewhat mysterious association. Reuss, along with two other Germans, Joshua Klein and the disreputable Franz Hartmann, was given a charter by an English Freemason, Jonathan Yarker, allowing them to set up a lodge of a semi-Masonic group, the Order of the Temple of the Orient, otherwise known as the Ordo Templi Orientis, or OTO. Strangely, the OTO—which is still active today—is most known for two things: its use of rituals involving sexual magic, and the fact that at one time the notorious Aleister Crowley was its head. That Steiner was involved in this group is surprising, and he later admitted that it was probably a bad idea.

One reason for Steiner's misgivings is that, along with other abuse, he was at one point accused of using sex magic for diabolic purposes, a charge that, considering Steiner's evident celibacy, seems almost comical. Nevertheless, for a brief time Steiner became the head of the Mysteria Mystica Aeterna lodge of the OTO. Steiner says he was invited to accept this position, much as he had been by the Theosophical Society, and that his sole intention was to exercise the "formal right to establish, in historical succession, my own symbolic ritual activity." It's possible, however, that in the OTO, Steiner saw another means of spreading his message. Steiner wanted to secure the "historical continuity" of the rituals because of a "need that arose among the members." This seems to indicate that Steiner's intellectual approach must have been too dry for some of his followers, and he recognized that something more dramatic was wanted. Steiner himself, we remember, was deeply moved by the church rituals of his youth, and the need to incorporate drama and ritualistic elements into Steiner's work was soon made clear. Steiner insists that the aim of the rituals was not to create a secret society or magical order, nor to confer any degrees of initiation on any of their participants—which is their usual purpose in Masonic or magical societies, like the Hermetic Order of the Golden Dawn—but to illustrate the path of spiritual ascent, and that their content was absolutely determined by his own spiritual research. Steiner remarks that, as far as he was concerned, the fact that he and Marie von Sivers signed the certificates they were given was a mere formality. It was a formality, unfortunately, with unwanted consequences. Steiner's meaning isn't exactly clear, but it seems that some of the people who participated in the rituals didn't get what they were looking for, and later spoke negatively about it—Steiner speaks of "slander," the source, perhaps, of the sex magic accusations. Steiner explains that at the time he still assumed that people would behave honestly and decently, and that the alternative, to be constantly suspicious of people's motives, would make it impossible to do anything. This is true, yet it's difficult to avoid seeing this as another instance of Steiner's tendency to involve himself with groups and activities that inevitably caused misunderstandings about him.[5]

Any need for the OTO, however, was made redundant in the summer of 1906, when Steiner appeared in Paris at the Theosophical Congress. Here he was introduced to Edouard Schuré, who became one of his most important followers. To Schuré, Steiner possessed "that self-mastery . . . which gives mastery over others," and he was certain that in meeting Steiner he had for the first time met an initiate.[6] Steiner's lectures at the Congress itself were a success, but his real triumph was the series of talks he gave to a group of Germans and Russians in the suburb of Passy, which were not part of the official program. Steiner had been scheduled to lecture in Russia in 1905, a tour set up by Marie von Sivers.

Like Paris and London at the turn of the century, St. Petersburg and Moscow were caught up in an occult revival. Marie knew that Steiner's Christianized theosophy would appeal to the members of the Russian intelligentsia who had a strong interest in mysticism and the esoteric but who weren't attracted to the Eastern approach of their countrywoman, Madame Blavatsky. Mother Russia had always had a strong religious yearning, and mystical thinkers like Vladimir Soloviev and novelists like Fyodor Dostoyevsky had sparked an obsession with the absolute and created a generation of God-seekers. The October Revolution of 1905 had made it impossible for Steiner to travel to Russia, but many of the intelligentsia, fearing reprisals by the tsar, had fled the country and headed to the exile capital of Europe, Paris. It was arranged, then, for a series of talks to be given for them at a private house. At first attended by only a few dozen people, after word got around, the house was soon overflowing, and the French theosophists, who resented Steiner's popularity, were eventually forced to offer him a lecture hall. Some of the most important names in Russian literature attended: the novelist Dimitri Merezhkovski, his wife, the poetess Zinaida Hippius, and the poets Konstantin Balmont and N. M. Minski. Their reports helped pave the way for the remarkable spread of Steiner's ideas in Russia, which lasted until World War I and the Bolshevik revolution. One reason for Steiner's success in Russia is that he believed that the Slavic folk soul had an important part to play in humanity's evolution and that Russia was the country best suited to embody a new cultural epoch, an idea that many in the intelligentsia agreed with. For some contemporary readers, however, Steiner's notion of folk souls—the idea that each race has a particular character and destiny—is suspect. This is understandable, but it often means that Steiner's ideas are lumped in with the sort of *völkisch* notions which tragically helped pave the way for Hitler and the Nazis, with whom Steiner had nothing in common—he was, in fact, on an early Nazi hit list. (C. G. Jung's ideas about the German and Jewish "souls" is a similar case.) By 1913, when Steiner gave a series of talks at Helsinki specifically for his Russian followers, there were already several discussion groups and workshops dedicated to his ideas in St. Petersburg and Moscow. Even after the revolution there was an attempt to harness Steiner's ideas to the goals of the new Marxist regime.[7]

But Steiner's popularity wasn't the only reason why some of the older theosophists regarded him as a threat. Steiner's ideas about theosophy's role in the wider world were clearly very different than the orthodox view. When traveling, it was Steiner's habit to visit as many museums and art galleries as he could. Although in 1888 he had given a lecture to the Goethe Society in Vienna on "Goethe as the Father of a New Aesthetics," until he met Marie von Sivers, Steiner had given little thought to art. Now it became a central item on his agenda. No doubt his ideas about the importance of the arts and their meaning for mankind's spiritual development had been stimulated by his stay in Paris, a city Marie knew well. It was through her that Steiner met Schuré, and the older man spoke with Steiner about his ideas on the place of drama in the ancient Greek mystery schools. Schuré himself had written a play based on this idea, *The Sacred Drama of Eleusis,* an imaginative recreation of the Greek mystery drama that was performed every five years at the close of the Eleusinian Mysteries. Schuré, we know, had been a friend of Wagner and had written a study of the master. He had been a frequent visitor to Bayreuth, where he met Nietzsche. Nietzsche's first book, *The Birth of*

Tragedy, is a poetic investigation into the origins of the Greek drama; in it he celebrated Wagner's operas as a return to art's sacred roots. In his early days in Vienna, Steiner hadn't been a fan of Wagner's music. Now he was beginning to understand what the master was getting at.

Wagner had envisioned his operas as "total art works" through which he could transform society. A similar idea was beginning to make sense to Steiner. Theosophists, he believed, were too content to focus exclusively on the spiritual world. The sensory world, for them, is merely transitory. But Steiner, we know, had achieved a new insight into the sense world, and he recognized that the creative imagination was an essential part of spiritual growth. Although artists like Wassily Kandinsky, Piet Mondrian, and others would be influenced by theosophy, the society itself had no living connection to the arts and culture in general.[8] This, Steiner saw, was a mistake, one he decided to rectify as soon as possible. His first opportunity was the Theosophical Congress of 1907, to be held in Munich, a city home to many artists. Steiner decided that for this congress some changes would be made. The six hundred delegates who arrived at the Munich Concert Hall were treated to a sight unseen at any other congress. The floors were covered in red carpet, and Steiner had draped the walls with a deep red material, against which he had positioned seven boards; on each of these he had painted a column, creating the illusion of a temple. Different planetary signs were inscribed on the columns' capitals, and between the columns Steiner had put the seven seals from the Book of Revelation. On the two columns at the head of the hall, painted red and blue, Steiner had put the letters J and B, the initials of Joachim and Boaz, signifying the two pillars of Solomon's Temple, thereby adding a Masonic touch. This is an early example of Steiner's belief in the importance of the experience of color, which would become a core theme in both his artistic and his homeopathic work of later years. In the room Steiner had also strategically placed busts of the German Idealist philosophers Fichte and Schelling, as well as one of Hegel, which had been a prized possession of his for many years.

There wasn't a Hindu deity or Hidden Master in sight, and if the décor of the concert hall wasn't enough to ruffle a few theosophical feathers, Steiner also treated his audience to a performance of Schuré's *Sacred Drama of Eleusis*, with costumes and scenery he had devised himself. Marie von Sivers played the role of Demeter, during which she demonstrated the art of speech formation she was then creating with Steiner. Marie and Steiner believed that in modern times speech had become constrained by the requirements of logic and communication, and they sought to liberate words from these restraints, allowing pure vowels and consonants, phrasing and rhythm to convey a deeper, more soulful meaning. In doing this, Steiner was very much in keeping with the spirit of the times, as the idea of somehow liberating language from the constraints of logical meaning had been a common theme of Symbolist poetry for decades—Rimbaud and Mallarmé were perhaps its most influential advocates—and was taken up by practically every school of poetry that followed.[9] Like Steiner's use of ritual and decoration, the idea was to circumvent the critical mind and reach down into the soul directly. Steiner had already had some success with this approach when, at a Christmas lecture given in Berlin, "Signs and Symbols of the Christmas Festival," he had spoken to the audience while standing in front of a Christmas tree, which he had decorated himself.[10]

As could have been expected, Steiner's initiative didn't go down well with the old guard, who resented the arty atmosphere and the distinct shift to the West. Annie Besant expressed her admiration, commenting on Germany as a land of philosophers and mystics, but it was at this congress that she realized that the best that could be expected now was a peaceful coexistence between her own esoteric group and Steiner's, and she decided on a clear separation. One member of the audience, however, was profoundly moved. Karl Stockmeyer, a young mathematician, wondered what Steiner's planetary columns would look like as part of an actual building. He asked Steiner, who gave the young man some ideas. Stockmeyer then went on to create a model building, based on Steiner's designs. Steiner later also directed the decoration of a lecture hall in Stuttgart, where he was developing a large following. These were early steps toward what Steiner would soon recognize as a growing need, the creation of a center for his work, what he would later call his own Bayreuth.

Another nail in the coffin of Steiner's good name among his non-German theosophists at this time was a lecture series he gave in association with the congress on the "Theosophy of the Rosicrucians." Most authorities on the Rosicrucians, a hermetic and alchemical brotherhood said to have been active in the early seventeenth century, are unsure whether they ever existed or not; the pamphlet announcing their appearance, *The Fame of the Fraternity of the Rosy Cross,* published in 1614, is very possibly a hoax. In any case, Steiner's theosophy bore little resemblance to what most theosophists understood by the term, and it has to be said that his ideas on Rosicrucianism are equally unlike what most historians would recognize.

While the ideological lines were being drawn, more concrete clashes were in the offing. Steiner's lectures in Germany, Czechoslovakia, Austria, Hungary, Norway, Denmark, and the Netherlands—mostly on the theme of esoteric Christianity, and Steiner's highly eccentric ideas about the true nature of Christ[11]—were paying off, and the number of new groups had increased appreciably. Steiner's star was clearly rising, and in 1909 he began to speak to his followers about a change that had occurred in the spiritual worlds. With that year, which had marked the end of the first seven-year cycle of his involvement with theosophy—an important number for Steiner, which would have great significance in his educational ideas—the possibility of a new relationship with Christ had arisen. Steiner, in fact, had begun to speak about a "second coming," but not in the way the idea is usually understood. For Steiner, the second coming of Christ wouldn't be a physical return of the individual known as Jesus. It would be a spiritual event, what Steiner later called the "etheric Christ," who would at first be visible to a few people, through a kind of natural clairvoyance, but who would gradually appear to many—over, it has to be said, the course of the next three millennia.

Some, however, were less patient than Steiner, and less inclined to accept a second coming not housed in flesh and blood. While Steiner spoke to his audience about the "etheric Christ," assuring them that in the near future, many would begin to notice the presence of a mysterious stranger, bringing words of comfort or direction, who would suddenly disappear (rather like a spiritual Lone Ranger), a more visceral incarnation of the Messiah had been spotted in, of all places, India. In 1909, the Reverend Charles Leadbeater had come across a young boy on a beach at Adyar, home to the Theosophical Society's headquarters. Leadbeater was struck by the boy's beauty, and also, he claimed, by his aura; it was, he said, exceptionally spiritual. That Leadbeater was also what we would today call a pedophile may, however, have had something to do with his interest in his discovery. Leadbeater persuaded the boy's father, who was a civil servant and fervent theosophist, to allow him to take twelve-year-old Jiddu and his brother Nitya into his home.[12] Leadbeater was convinced that Jiddu, later to be known as Krishnamurti, was the avatar of the new age, a reincarnation of the master Maitreya, as well as of the Christ. Upon meeting the boy, Annie Besant agreed. Perhaps the fact that Leadbeater, no stranger to the Akashic Record himself, had investigated the boy's previous thirty lives—beginning in 22,662 B.C.—helped persuade her. And although the official announcement of Krishnamurti's mission wasn't made until 1911, one wonders if the young and handsome Jiddu's real purpose was not so much the inauguration of a new age, but to stand as a rival to Steiner's growing celebrity, and to show that old school theosophy, too, could provide fascinating and charismatic figures.

There was still some time, though, before the final break, and on the surface it seemed that the amiable détente that had lasted the last seven years could continue. In 1909, Steiner's *Knowledge of the Higher Worlds and Its Attainment,* which had originally been serialized in *Lucifer-Gnosis,* won an award as best theosophical book of the year. Another congress was held that year as well, this time in Budapest. Here proceedings were back to normal, and nothing like the extravagances of Munich were in sight, much to the disappointment of Steiner's group. It was at this congress that Annie Besant and Steiner met for the last time. It was clear that their conversation, cordial enough, would resolve nothing, although it was good to clear the air and bring matters into the open. Both felt that a confrontation was inevitable, but neither wanted to make the first move. Throughout his autobiography, Steiner repeatedly remarks that he felt subject to an occult law, which prevented him from taking any steps that would further his own designs, relying rather on destiny or events to call forth the appropriate action. It's also likely that neither he nor Annie wanted to be seen as the one responsible for a rupture that would throw the society into turmoil.

Steiner, however, knew the direction he was heading in. After the Congress of 1907, Steiner's interest in art was evident, and he lectured on the theme in various cities, speaking of two "sisters," Knowledge and Art, and their need for each other to achieve wholeness, a theme Steiner had first encountered in Schiller's *Letters on Aesthetic Education*. But Steiner wasn't satisfied with simply talking about art. Schuré's sacred drama had affected him deeply, and in 1910 he decided to try his hand at writing one himself. Steiner had been interested in the theater since his early days as editor of the *Magazine for Literature*, and now he felt it was time to put what he had learned back then into practice. After another intensive series of lectures in Scandinavia, Berlin, Cologne, Stuttgart, Munich, and Vienna, and a trip through Italy to Sicily and then Rome, Steiner returned to Berlin and over a few weeks wrote his first of four Mystery Dramas, *The Portal of Initiation*. The play was premiered at the Theosophical Congress in Munich in August, with a cast made up of amateur actors of different nationalities, all followers of Steiner, trained and supervised by Marie von Sivers. Steiner directed and designed the sets and costumes, all according to Goethe's color theory. Another of Schuré's plays, *The Children of Lucifer*, which had been translated by Marie von Sivers, was also performed.

The audience of two thousand people, all of them followers of Steiner, filled the rented hall, and the expectation was of witnessing a sacred event. The troupe overcame several hurdles, not the least of which was memorizing lines that Steiner provided just days before the performance. It would be difficult to give a précis of the play and those that followed; interested readers may benefit from Stewart C. Easton's detailed commentary.[13] It may be that, as the poet and later Steiner student Albert Steffen claimed, the play embodied a "renewal of an art as it arises from the mysteries," and that the participants at its premiere, coming from all walks of life, found "themselves on the threshold of the awakening to their higher humanity."[14] Yet as theater, Steiner's Mystery Dramas are, I think, an acquired taste. Without doubt they deal with the deep concerns of the spiritual life and, for those committed to Steiner's ideas, can provide a moving and transformative experience. For this reason, performances of the dramas for Steiner's followers continue to be an annual event. But for the uninitiated, they can appear stiff, and redolent somewhat of Sunday school. Even for an audience sympathetic to spiritual ideas, the plays, for my taste at least, suffer from being heavy on message and light on movement. There are many long speeches, and what there is of action seems to consist of the characters' engaging in extended arguments about the need for a new spiritual vision.

The message *is* important, and it's understandable that Steiner's followers insist that the plays should be judged on their intent. But other playwrights have had messages, yet were able to communicate them and entertain their audience too—Bernard Shaw, for example, whose plays form a theater of ideas, remarked that if, like a dentist, he performed a necessary but unpleasant act (pointing out society's inequities), he nevertheless made sure he gave his patients plenty of laughing gas. Steiner, and Marie von Sivers, seemed to think that any thought of mere entertainment would be an unacceptable concession to the materialism of the time, and they were determined to maintain a lofty level throughout. The problem with this is that too extended a stay in the higher realms can lead to boredom. The central character, Benedictus, is a spiritual teacher most likely based on Steiner himself. Around him gravitate a collection of seekers: Johannes, a painter; Maria, who is involved with Johannes; Capesius, a professor; Felix Balde, a herb-gatherer modeled on Felix Koguzki; Felicia, a storyteller; Theodora, a clairvoyant who speaks of the new Christ. All have gathered to hear Benedictus speak of his experiences of the spiritual worlds, and their intertwining lives are meant to express the twists and turns of karma. The poet Christian Morgenstern, who became one of Steiner's followers, managed to highlight the work's good points, while faintly acknowledging that as theater, there was still some work to be done. "It is not a play," he wrote to a friend, but "it mirrors worlds of the spirit and great truths. It introduces—perhaps burdened with the labor of a beginning work—a new era of art. . . . The era itself is still distant; it may well be hundreds of years before there are enough human beings who want this pure, spiritual art."[15] Morgenstern's remark about a "pure, spiritual art" is a good way of describing what attracts many to Steiner's various artistic endeavors—painting, poetry, eurythmy, architecture—but also what turns others away. For many, myself included, there is something too soft and precious, too—for want of a better word—ethereal, about much of it. Pastels abound, and edges are practically nonexistent. The limits of Steiner's and his followers' execution, however, do not detract from the ideas that Steiner had about art, and which became an important influence on some major figures of the twentieth century.[16]

The success, at least in terms of attendance, of *The Portal of Initiation* and the plays that followed—*The Soul's Probation, The Guardian of the Threshold*, and *The Soul's Awakening*, each one performed in successive years (a fifth was proposed but never finished)—convinced Steiner that it was essential for his teaching that a center be found, a space wholly dedicated to creating the kind of total impression he was aiming at. The creation of such a space would mark a new phase in his work, and would allow him to concentrate on developing new ideas, like the work he was doing with Marie von Sivers and the young Lori Smits on eurythmy. The hired halls they were currently using were insufficient, and the headquarters on Motzstrasse seemed pushed to capacity. We can get a picture of Steiner at this time from an account by the Russian novelist Andrei Belyi, who met Steiner in 1912, and spent the next several years following him across Europe on his lecture tours. Belyi is most known to English readers for his remarkable novel *Petersburg*, a masterpiece of modernist literature, and a work deeply influenced by Steiner's ideas.

Steiner's apartment in Berlin, Belyi tells us, "was like a command post":

All the inmates . . . rushed in constant haste from one floor to another with papers and copies, clattered on typewriters and made telephone calls. . . . Every minute is already scheduled, and there are tasks, tasks, tasks. Here somebody is editing; there . . . tickets for a lecture are being distributed; here, books are being handed out. . . . Past these . . . rooms . . . stream . . . all those who have announced themselves for a consultation with

Steiner. . . . Each comes with a question that is more important to him than anything else in the world. . . . They are ushered into a small waiting room where every upholstered place is occupied by waiting people. . . .

One pictures the personal meeting with the "Teacher" within a certain ceremonial framework; but here simplicity rules and an atmosphere of intense everyday work. . . . In one of the back rooms there are probably some open, unpacked suitcases standing about. He returned from Switzerland and tomorrow he leaves for Hanover. . . . Then, suddenly, right in front of your nose, the door . . . is opened, and quick as lightning . . . the Doctor appears. . . . His visiting hours last for hours and hours.

Belyi remarks that Steiner often appeared a "little worn, with a tired pale face," which is no wonder, considering the amount of activity that made up an average day for him. One suspects that even at this early stage, Steiner must have felt that his commitment to help those who came to him, and his refusal to turn anyone away, was draining. In the end, it would be those "hours and hours" of visitors that would lead to his death.

It's worth staying with Belyi's account a bit longer, as it gives us an endearing picture of the Doctor. Steiner, he says, wore "a tight short jacket . . . that is no longer new. On occasion he wears slippers; his pince-nez dangle and dance on a little ribbon and sometimes become entangled in the drapes as he rushes through them." The Doctor was also a bit hard of hearing, Belyi tells us, and turned his good ear to his visitors when they spoke. He had "a therapeutic smile; the countenance blossomed. . . . He had the gift of the smile, the faculty of direct expression from the heart."

Belyi confesses that it's difficult to express how, in the "simple interior of this room there occur such dramas of every kind, dreadful and joyous ones," and settles for just saying that he was, "after all, Rudolf Steiner, and he has the capacity to transform every situation into an unforgettable moment." It was this ability to elicit something very close to love from those who became involved with him that, perhaps more than his actual teaching, accounts for the devotion Steiner received from his followers.

Steiner must have known it was a time for new beginnings. On March 17, 1911, Anna Eunicke died, leaving Steiner free to legitimize his relationship with Marie von Sivers, although they wouldn't marry for another three years. And by this time a gauntlet had been thrown across his path in the form of the Reverend Leadbeater's protégé. Annie Besant had agreed with the reverend that the boy Jiddu was indeed the new avatar, and with all the pomp such a revelation required, she had founded a brace of new occult orders to help usher in his ministry: the Yellow Shawl Group, the Order of the Purple Ribbon, and, the most offensive from Steiner's perspective, the Order of the Star in the East.[17] Aside from the sheer absurdity of promoting a twelve-year-old Indian boy as the new Christ, the fact that Leadbeater was involved in a lawsuit with the avatar's father disgusted Steiner, and he must have suspected that the Reverend's interest in the Messiah more than likely exceeded his spiritual aims. Steiner recalled with revulsion a similar scandal involving Leadbeater in 1906.[18] Steiner had also garnered some flak from Besant's followers when he expelled a certain Hugo Vollrath from the German section. Vollrath was a disciple of the despicable Franz Hartmann, about whom even Madame Blavatsky had once remarked that "the magnetism of that man is sickening." Steiner had no use for Hartmann or his followers, and when Vollrath had formed a literary section without Steiner's permission, the Doctor felt it was time to draw the line. In any case, he always had a low opinion of many of the old-time German theosophists, and they in turn resented him for using the society to further his own aims. Besant came to Vollrath's defense, saying Steiner had exceeded his authority, but this fracas was merely a warm-up to the main attraction.

The Order of the Star in the East was created for the express purpose of preparing the world for the return of the master Maitreya, also known as Christ, in the form of Jiddu Krishnamurti, and Besant made it clear that all good theosophists should consider becoming a part of it. When Steiner caught wind of this, he immediately refused to allow the order to operate in Germany and sent out an edict requiring any German members who had already joined the order to resign from it. He then sent a telegram to Besant in Adyar, demanding her resignation as head of the Theosophical Society. She had no doubt seen this coming, and she responded by revoking the charter she had given Steiner in 1902, thereby canceling the German section and excommunicating Steiner. The peaceful coexistence had ended, and Dr. Rudolf Steiner was no longer a member of the Theosophical Society.

But by this time this was irrelevant. Fourteen of the fifty German lodges followed Besant's decision and abandoned Steiner; these were left under the leadership of Dr. Hübbe-Schleiden. The rest stood by the Doctor. Destiny had made its call, and Steiner was now ready to follow it. When the regular annual meeting of the German section took place as scheduled in January 1913, Steiner informed those who attended that in actual fact no meeting could be held, as there was no longer a German section to hold it. This minor detail was soon dealt with when those present announced the formation of a new, independent body, which was to be known as the Anthroposophical Society. A month later the new society held its first meeting. Anyone who desired to remain a member of the Theosophical Society was free to do so, but they could not be a member of the Anthroposophical Society. Steiner himself did not become a member, but accepted instead the title of honorary president, preferring to remain its spiritual, rather than its legal head. At the time of its conception, the new society could boast of a membership twenty-five hundred strong.

Steiner had used the term "anthroposophy" as early as 1901, when lecturing to Die Kommenden,[19] and gradually, during his years as a theosophist, the worldview behind the ideas and aims he communicated had shifted from that of the older society to that of the new dispensation. Toward the end of his life, in a collection of meditations Steiner wrote for a newsletter for members of the Anthroposophical Society, and later published as *Anthroposophical Leading Thoughts,* Steiner provided what is probably the most quoted definition of this term. "Anthroposophy," Steiner wrote, "is a path of knowledge to guide the spiritual in the human being to the spiritual in the universe." The term, however, did not originate with him, which he always made clear. One of Steiner's teachers in Vienna, Robert Zimmerman, had used it as the title for a work on aesthetics. Steiner had also come across it in the work of the philosopher Immanuel Hermann Fichte, son of the more well-known Johann Gottlieb Fichte. Its earliest use was perhaps that by the alchemist Thomas Vaughn in his *Anthroposophia Theomagica,* published in 1650. In the early nineteenth century, the Swiss Romantic philosopher Ignaz Troxler defined it as "a cognitive method, which, taking as a starting point the spiritual nature of man, investigates the spiritual nature of the world,"[20] which seems a less concise expression of Steiner's own definition. Etymologically the word derives from two Greek terms, *anthropos,* "man," or as it is now more often translated, "human being," and *sophia,* "wisdom." Its link to theosophy is clear, the distinction being that the older term—it had been used by Jakob Boehme in the fifteenth century—designates the wisdom of "God" or "the gods." (Readers will recognize the link with the more widely used *philosophia,* or "love of wisdom.") "Anthroposophy" became the term Steiner used to designate the methodology and body of knowledge that derived from his own spiritual experiences; he also used, as we've seen, the phrase "spiritual science," to emphasize that this knowledge was not revealed, as was that promoted by theosophy and most established religions, but was achieved through one's own efforts. Along with its emphasis on Eastern thought, this last point was something that Steiner also found troubling in the Theosophical Society. Except for vague and general suggestions as to how to lead a spiritual life, theosophy had no pedagogical program, no method of teaching its followers how to experience the spiritual directly, and so was left with the revelations of a few gifted individuals, who passed these on to the rest. While theosophy originally served as a valuable rallying cry and encouragement for the many who felt disenfranchised by the rising dominance of materialist science, it soon deteriorated—at least in Steiner's eyes—into an amiable but ineffective club for eccentrics, or, in the case of Franz Hartmann and the Reverend Leadbeater, downright scoundrels. Steiner the tutor was determined to offer stronger resistance to the growing decay of the spiritual in modern life. Anthroposophy would not be a cosy in-group, where one could chat about things spiritual, in the meantime leaving the wicked world outside to go its way. For Steiner, anthroposophy's business was to *change* the world, a task generally set aside for religions. From the outset, Steiner was adamant that he was interested in actual *objective* knowledge about man and the world—knowledge that could be communicated and assimilated by others in the same way that mathematics or history could be, and was not, by definition, dependent on any one individual. The distinction here is crucial, and although in many ways for some anthroposophy became, as many spiritual or esoteric teachings do, a kind of lifestyle, Steiner wanted to anchor it with the same weight of verifiable fact as that which steadied physics or astronomy. The name, at least initially, was unimportant, and Steiner admitted that he would have gladly called it something different each week, except that doing so would have confused everyone even more than they already were. Later, however, the term took on a deeper, more evocative value, until to many, including Steiner, it designated not merely a body of thought, but a kind of spiritual being in itself.

Having made the break with theosophy, Steiner now saw the need for a new home for his new teaching more urgently. At first the idea was to build a theater suitable for the Mystery Dramas, and the most obvious location seemed to be Munich, which was Germany's artistic capital. Stuttgart, too, which had a strong Steiner following, was a serious contender. Plans for a Johannesbau (Johannes Building)—named after the artist character in Steiner's plays—had already been under way in Munich, but there were drawbacks; the proposed building would be surrounded by residential structures, and because of this, deference to local zoning laws would have to be made. Steiner was unhappy with this constraint, and although he believed the authorities would reject his proposal, he allowed it to go ahead anyway. As with other crucial turns in his career, Steiner trusted in destiny to show the way.

In September 1912, Steiner had given a lecture series in Basel, Switzerland, and afterward was invited to the country home of Dr. Emil Grossheintz, a successful dentist and longtime theosophist. Dr. Grossheintz owned considerable land on the foothills of the Jura Mountains, near the town of Dornach, and while there, Steiner showed an unexpected interest in the countryside, exploring the whole district. Later, he asked Dr. Grossheintz what he intended to do with the land. The dentist replied that he didn't know, but that he expected the future to reveal why he had bought it. Dr. Grossheintz's wife commented that she had thought of building a boarding school, so children could receive a proper upbringing. Steiner, knowing that the proceedings in Munich would amount to nothing, then remarked that "we have been thinking about a kind of Bayreuth." Dr. Grossheintz, who was aware of the difficulties Steiner was having with the Munich authorities, added that Dornach had no building restrictions, to which Steiner commented, "And Basel has a favourable theosophical karma," which suggests that even at the start of his new anthroposophical enterprise, Steiner was not averse to linking it, if appropriate, to its predecessor.

Steiner was right about Munich. The authorities rejected his plans, and in February 1913, soon after the first annual meeting of the Anthroposophical Society, Steiner turned to Dr. Grossheintz and accepted his generous offer. Years later, Marie von Sivers recorded that during his first visit to what would become the site of his most concrete achievement—literally—Steiner had displayed an uncharacteristic depression. He was "bewildered, crushed, gloomy," something she had never seen in him before. Steiner's clairvoyance was usually focused on events far in the past or in the distant future, but it's possible that on this occasion he had foreseen a tragedy that would come to pass in the short span of merely a decade.

8. ANTHROPOSOPHIA

On the evening of September 20, 1913, a group of about forty of Steiner's followers gathered on the hill near Dornach that would become the site of the Goetheanum, the building that Steiner saw as the temple of his new spiritual teaching. Once the thought of erecting the Johannesbau in Munich had been abandoned, Steiner's ideas about the structure expanded, and again it seemed that destiny had looked upon the Doctor's plans with approval. In deference to the constraints of local government and popular acceptance, if it had been built in Munich, the Johannesbau would have looked conventional enough on the surface, and only within it would the full fruit of Steiner's architectural vision be allowed to blossom.[1] Now, no longer hampered by these considerations, Steiner saw an opportunity to send a message to the world, a clear sign of anthroposophy's purpose and aims. For years Steiner had felt that art had to speak to the world in a new way, a way that would help bring the spiritual closer to people's lives. The Goetheanum was intended to be the first step in this process. In a lecture given a year later, Steiner explained that while previous works of art used color and form to give expression to space, in the Goetheanum, the space itself would be the most important thing. It would act, he said, like "a jelly mould," giving shape and form to what was put inside it. What would be put inside this particular jelly mold were people's souls. The work of art, then, would be what these souls experienced. What Steiner hoped they would experience would be the voice of the gods. The Goetheanum, he believed, would act as a kind of cosmic larynx, through which the gods would once again communicate directly to humankind.

Yet on the evening when Steiner placed the foundation stone of his new building in the earth, it seemed as if the powers of darkness had decided to announce their opposition to his plans. As the stone, a double pentagonal dodecahedron of hammered copper, was laid into the soil, the sky grew dark, distant thunder rumbled, the wind rose, lightning crackled, and the landscape, which Steiner had so enjoyed on his first visit, became strange and threatening. Steiner turned to the four points of the compass and announced to his small band of onlookers that the stone represented the "striving human soul immersed as a microcosm in the macrocosm."[2] Through the rain, driving wind, and growing darkness—Steiner's followers had to light torches to carry on— Steiner called on the spiritual hierarchies to help them in their task. Then Steiner spoke ominously of Ahriman, the spiritual being who worked to draw humankind away from its lawful evolution. Ahriman sought to cloud our vision, to spread chaos, and to obscure our spiritual sight. Steiner called on the hierarchies to help him and his followers find the strength to resist Ahriman's designs, and closed the ceremony with an ancient prayer that, he said, the young Jesus had learned during the celebration of an ancient mystery. Through this he hoped that his listeners could come to recognize the true darkness in which the world was enveloped.

Steiner seemed to have forebodings of evil, a return of the gloom he had experienced on his first visit to Dornach. The stone, which was for them "a symbol of knowledge, love and strong courage," would for their "enemies" be "a stumbling block and will arouse their anger." "We are," he said, "only at the beginning of our difficulties."[3] Years later, Steiner would tell his followers that "it was the construction of the building which first created the opportunity for our opponents to find an audience."[4] Steiner seemed to realize that in constructing the Goetheanum, he was not only creating something more than a concert hall, something much more like a sacred site, from which the teachings of anthroposophy would emanate. He was also setting up a target.

The building itself, however, whatever opposition it aroused, was a tremendous accomplishment. Although never actually completed and requiring nearly a decade's work, it was one of the most remarkable structures of the twentieth century, and photographs of it appear in many histories of architecture, as an example of one of the few works of Expressionist architecture ever erected. (Although anthroposophists resist the association, the structure is clearly reminiscent of the Art Nouveau and Expressionist styles popular in Europe in the first decades of the century.) Steiner's aim was to create an organic form, in keeping with the ideas about nature and metamorphosis held by the building's inspiration, Goethe. Steiner believed that if one understood the connection in the human form between thinking, feeling, and willing, then one would be able to create new organic forms, using nature's laws themselves, the "hidden secrets" that Goethe believed it was the artist's business to discover. The building then had a minimum of straight lines and right angles, and was designed to give the impression that it had *grown*. Curves, swirling and flowing lines, and wavelike shapes would convey the sense that it had been molded by the same etheric forces that gave form to living beings. (Readers familiar with Steiner's lectures will note that his own rhetoric mirrors this theme; he frequently uses terms like "flowing," "stream," "current," "surging," "coursing.") Stairways resembled tree trunks. Stained-glass windows bathed the interior with rich, warm color and light. In the huge auditorium, which could seat a thousand people, seven pairs of columns seemed to reprise Steiner's decorations for the 1907 Munich Congress, and their carved capitals illustrated Goethe's ideas on plant metamorphosis. The most immediately impressive feature, however, was the two interlocking domes of unequal size, one larger than that of St. Peter's in Rome. Constructed of the same wood used to make violins—the better, one suspects, to vibrate to the music of the spheres—the domes presented a considerable engineering challenge. Much of the Goetheanum was constructed of wood, a material that allowed for a greater sense of living forces; as one writer commented "the lumber demanded for this gigantic building project affected the timber market all over Europe."[5] The auditorium's columns, for example, were each made from a different tree: beech, ash, cherry, oak, elm, maple, and birch. The choice of wood certainly made much Goethean sense, yet sadly, it later became the cause for much regret.

Covered in Norwegian slate, which reflected the shifting light of the sky, one dome faced east and the other west, a gesture of the role Steiner felt both anthroposophy and Central Europe were to play in coming years, as a meeting ground between the growing superpowers of the West and East. Like many others, Steiner believed that some kind of struggle between these two giants was imminent. Given his words of warning, it seems he may have felt that it would happen sooner than expected.

It was providential in more ways than one that Dr. Grossheintz had offered Steiner the use of his land. Steiner's followers quickly responded to his call, and money for the building was collected. Steiner hoped to complete construction by August 1914, as he intended to stage a fifth Mystery Drama then; as mentioned, this was never completed, and other events would make the idea impossible. Although many of his wealthy followers had contributed generously, it soon became clear that the funds collected wouldn't be enough, and Steiner was forced to give a series of fund-raising lectures. Work seemed to move in fits and starts, and often Steiner had to take time away from other responsibilities to oversee construction. By April 1914, the groundwork was complete, and the framework was up, the two massive domes jutting out of the hillside like some weird science fiction landscape. Land adjoining Dr. Grossheintz's had also been acquired; here, structures following the same design were built, adding to the otherworldly effect. Members from all walks of life gave up their time and energy to devote themselves to the task. Many of them had never picked up a hammer before, and they worked beside the few skilled builders who were hired to help. Steiner himself seemed tireless, always on hand to give advice or instruction, or to roll up his sleeves, striding from this part of the site to another in his workman's smock and high-top leather boots. Then on June 28, 1914, Archduke Franz Ferdinand was assassinated in Sarajevo, and the world was suddenly very different.

When World War I broke out, Steiner and Marie von Sivers were on their way to Bayreuth. Rushing to return to Dornach,

Steiner saw the work of Ahriman: chaos had arrived in the form of the madness that was spreading across Europe. Soldiers were everywhere, guards were closing borders, crowds filled the railway stations, trying to escape. As Marie was still a Russian citizen, she stood a chance of being arrested, but luckily an anthroposophist who was also a railway official helped her and Steiner board a train in Stuttgart. (This was one reason why Steiner decided it was time he and Marie were married, so she could receive Austrian citizenship; on Christmas Eve that year they did marry.) Hours later, when they had finally crossed into Switzerland, just before the borders closed, Steiner may have felt that he had perhaps been tempting fate by making so bold a gesture as building the Goetheanum. But the fact that he had chosen Swiss soil on which to do it at least allowed him to carry on his work relatively unimpaired. Although he believed in the mission of the German people and was patriotic—but not nationalistic—it would have been a mistake for anthroposophy to be seen as a German effort. Here, on neutral soil, he could carry on his work and hope that Ahriman was not as powerful as he seemed.

In fact, the Goetheanum itself became a gesture against the madness. Russians, Poles, Germans, Austrians, French—seventeen nationalities in all—came together in an effort that transcended their own personal or national interests. When the guns of August started blazing—and Steiner could clearly hear them at times in the distance—volunteers of opposing sides worked hand in hand on the construction. Many knew that at some point they might be called by their governments to enter the madness, perhaps to fire on a fellow anthroposophist. Andrei Belyi tells us that Steiner himself organized the group to help care for the wounded, instructing everyone in a course in first aid. Switzerland believed the war might extend into its territory and took precautions: artillery was positioned directly above the Goetheanum. Seeing this, Belyi tells us, Steiner was "taciturn, calm and sad," and looked "infinitely tired." At one point, Belyi became concerned about the groups of soldiers, many of them drunk, who took to loitering around the worksite. He was worried that their cigarettes might ignite the huge piles of wood shavings that stood near the fence. Once a group of about forty demanded to see the site and to know "what was going on." The men guarding the entrance were unsure what to do; fearing a riot, Belyi quickly found Steiner. The Doctor recognized the situation and graciously invited the men in. After a half-hour tour, during which he happily answered their questions, he climbed a scaffold to give them a demonstration of how they worked, grabbing a hammer and chisel and showing them his carving technique. The men were won over by the Doctor's sincerity and Austrian charm. He arranged for regular tours for anyone interested, and good relations with the army were secured.

Steiner himself, however, couldn't escape being held responsible for the bad turn the German war effort quickly took. Germany's generals were convinced that Germany couldn't lose the war, and they banked their convictions on what was known as the von Schlieffen plan. This called for the army to throw everything it had at the French in one massive blow; then, having knocked them out, to quickly turn and hurl themselves at the Russians. But the commander in chief, Helmuth von Moltke, was undecided; even the Kaiser, who had spent the last few years rattling his sabre, had hesitated about declaring war. Von Moltke's wife was a follower of Steiner, and it's some tribute to his reputation that he was asked to give von Moltke advice.[6] A meeting, however, couldn't be arranged immediately, and before Steiner could speak with him, von Moltke had decided against the von Schlieffen plan and so split his forces. The result was that for the next four years Europe collapsed into the horror of trench warfare. Steiner finally saw von Moltke, but only three weeks after his decision, and it is unclear what, if any, advice he would have given him had they met sooner. Nevertheless, when it became known that von Moltke had seen Steiner, the rumor started that the Doctor was responsible for the mistake. Von Moltke himself was relieved of his command and died two years later. The hostility toward Steiner that would characterize his last decade had begun.

The war forced Steiner to curtail his lecturing, and anyone who takes even a casual look at Guenther Wachsmuth's exhaustive *The Life and Work of Rudolf Steiner*, which gives a detailed account of the thousands of lectures Steiner gave in his lifetime, can't be blamed for thinking that for all his dedication to work, Steiner must have enjoyed the respite. He still spoke in Austria, Germany, and Switzerland, but the war allowed him to concentrate on the Goetheanum and to write books like *The Riddles of Man* and *The Riddles of the Soul* and to give a lecture course in Dornach on eurythmy as "visible speech." The war, of course, was on everyone's mind, and Steiner lectured on its spiritual meaning. On the surface, economic and political reasons may have seemed the factors involved in its outbreak, but Steiner told his followers that the statesmen of Europe had been lulled into a kind of sleep by the spiritual forces working against mankind's evolution.

Like many others at the time, Steiner, at least in the beginning, felt that it was still possible for something good to come out of the carnage—he shared the hope of the German Expressionists who believed a new world would emerge from the ruins of the old. Yet he had no illusions about the bloodshed, and after 1917, when the German military played its trump card by shipping Lenin to the Finland Station, thereby setting in motion the collapse of Russia and the rise of the Bolsheviks, Steiner's lectures took on a darker tone. The Ahrimanic spirits had been set loose on earth, and Steiner told some of his closest followers that certain occult orders had made a kind of pact with them, in return for power over their fellow humans. The violence and death had disrupted the balance between the spiritual and earthly realms, and this had allowed these dark brotherhoods to make use of the dead for their own purposes.

The dead had, we've seen, always been a concern of Steiner's, but now he called for his followers to be especially attentive to them. Before the war, Steiner had instructed his followers on how they could help their departed loved ones in the spiritual world; he even suggested that simply reading to them about anthroposophy would benefit them.[7] Now he returned to this idea, and in 1918, he delivered a lecture, "The Living and the Dead," in which he informed his listeners that the best time to communicate with the dead was in that curious state of consciousness that falls in between sleeping and waking.[8] Then, briefly, the spiritual worlds are open to us, and we can send the departed words of comfort. One suspects that Steiner had something of this kind in mind when he opened the lectures he gave at this time—mostly on world history—with a prayer, and closed them with a meditative verse in which he hoped that "from the courage of the fighters" and "the grief of the bereaved," "the fruit of spirit" might arise.

Although Steiner was glad that his position in Switzerland allowed him to avoid taking sides, he was criticized by some anthroposophists because of this. Others, like the Frenchman

Edouard Schuré, who had left the Theosophical Society to follow Steiner, felt he expressed too much Germanic nationalism and broke off relations (they were later reconciled after the war). That Steiner had abandoned plans for a fifth Mystery Drama and was instead focusing his efforts on a production of Goethe's *Faust* may have had something to do with this. But Steiner's Germany—like Goethe's and Nietzsche's—wasn't the militarism of the hysterical Kaiser Wilhelm, but the great humanist and Idealist tradition, the spiritual wealth of German culture. Steiner rejected the Allied propaganda that Germany was solely responsible for the war and that German soldiers had a monopoly on committing atrocities. He maintained, like other respected figures such as the novelist Thomas Mann, that Germany had a mission to transmit its high culture to the world, and in many public lectures in places like Berlin, Steiner tried to instill a new confidence in the German people. Today, lectures with titles like "The Enduring and Creative Power of the German Spirit" and "The Rejuvenating Power of the German Folk-Soul" may strike us as dubious presages of the darker Germany to come. But Steiner's vision had nothing in common with the forces of fascism that would emerge with Germany's defeat (he would, as mentioned, become one of its targets). Steiner linked his thoughts about the German folk-soul to his ideas on the evolution of consciousness. Within this, it was the task of the German folk-soul to develop the I, and the history of German philosophy, Steiner said, was evidence of this. On the more immediate scene, Steiner felt that Central Europe—an area covering Germany, Austria, and what is now the Czech Republic—should work as a balancing factor between the growing megapowers of Russia and the United States. This notion of balance became increasingly important to Steiner, and one of the projects that occupied him now was a towering wooden sculpture depicting "the Representative of Humanity," a Christ-like figure that occupied the middle space between the evil spirits of Ahriman and Lucifer. Left to themselves, the energies represented by Ahriman and Lucifer lead mankind astray, but if their influence can be absorbed and reconciled through the mediating work of the Christ, they can lead to spiritual freedom.

It was clear to Steiner that whatever its outcome, the war would leave a vastly changed Europe. Since the start of his mission, Steiner was convinced that anthroposophy had to play a larger role in the world's affairs, and with the Munich Congress of 1907, he had started to take the first steps toward fulfilling this obligation. What was needed now, he saw, was to rethink society as a whole.

Steiner was not alone in these thoughts. In May 1917, Otto von Lerchenfeld, a German diplomat in Berlin who was also an anthroposophist, approached Steiner, asking him for his ideas on how a true peace could be reached, once the war was finally over. It still seemed possible then that the war leaders could arrive at an acceptable end to the fighting. This, sadly, was not to be, and the horror continued, with the United States soon to enter the fray. But Steiner felt Lerchenfeld's need and listened to his concerns and despair over how Germany had been led into the abyss. Then, over the next three weeks, Steiner and Lerchenfeld collaborated on two memoranda in which Steiner laid out his criticisms of the decisions that led to Germany's entering the war and his ideas on how a true peace could be achieved. Most important, though, were Steiner's thoughts on the need for a fundamental restructuring of society.

In a footnote in his book *The Riddles of the Soul*, Steiner, almost offhandedly, speaks of an idea that was to become the central theme of his social philosophy, as well as of the anthropo-sophical medicine that would develop after his death. Steiner linked the soul's powers of thinking, feeling, and willing to what he saw as three autonomous but interrelated aspects of the human organism. Thinking Steiner saw as linked to our head and nervous system; feeling to what he called the rhythmic system, which included breathing, circulation, and heartbeat; and willing to our metabolic system, with which Steiner included our limbs. For Steiner, in our thoughts we are awake, in our feelings half asleep—or dreaming—and in our will unconscious, and if we reflect on this, it seems to make sense. I can choose what I think about, but not what I feel, which, although I am aware of it, seems to happen to me. And while I can gain some minimal control over my breathing and even heartbeat (although these are best left undis-turbed), processes like digestion are completely involuntary. Steiner saw that if it was to function in accord with the realities of the human organism, society needed to restructure itself to reflect this "threefold order."

Steiner and Lerchenfeld's memoranda reached some figures in the upper branches of the German and Austro-Hungarian govern-ments, but, as could be expected, they made little if any impact and quickly sank out of sight. But they were the first draft of what would become one of Steiner's most powerful ideas, one that for a time made him something of a major player on the European stage. Steiner argued that society itself must be ordered to embody the three functions of thinking, feeling, and willing, in accord with the "threefold order" of the human organism. Society, too, he said, has a head, a circulatory system, and a metabolic system, and to these Steiner linked the ideals of the French Revolution, liberty, equality, and fraternity. The head is the world of culture and human creativity, in which the freedom of the individual must be paramount. The political sphere, that of rights, is the circulatory/ feeling aspect of society, and its central concern is to ensure that all members of society receive a just and equitable recognition of their rights. Society's metabolic system is the economic sphere; here our common fraternity must be recognized, and wealth must be produced for the good of the community, not for individual gain. The centralized role of the state must be minimized to allow these three separate but interdependent social functions to oper- ate freely, and the functions themselves must not interfere with one another. Steiner was especially concerned about the state's involvement with education, which, for him, was the responsibility of the cultural/creative head. (State education, he argued, pro- duces an individual useful merely to the state, not to himself.) The result, Steiner believed, was that a society would emerge in which the freedom of the individual and his opportunities for spiritual growth would be the central concern.

Practical-minded politicians, like those who more than likely scanned Steiner's memoranda then deposited them in the trash, would understandably find these ideas utopian. Yet when the war ended and Europe found itself looking for a new direction, his idealism struck a chord in the common mind. Steiner's little book *The Threefold Social Order,* published in 1919 and translated into many languages, became a kind of bestseller, with eighty thou- sand copies sold in its first year. For a time "threefoldness" became something of a popular idea, the way that certain "green" or "organic" ways of thinking catch on for a time today. Yet Steiner's appearance on the political/social stage also attracted less welcome notice. His predictions about the opposition that anthroposophy would generate with the construction of the Goetheanum would soon appear disturbingly accurate.

W ith the end of the war, Steiner was once again free to travel, and his lecturing returned to its older, frantic pace. (Anyone interested in getting an idea of what a Steiner lecture was like should see the collection *Rudolf Steiner: Blackboard Drawings 1919–1924* [Forest Row, England: Rudolf Steiner Press, 2003], which gathers many of the illustrations Steiner used in his talks; regardless of what you might think of his ideas, the drawings are beautiful in themselves and give a strong sense of what Steiner must have meant when he spoke of "picture thinking."[9]) He was, however, especially focused on Germany at this time, and while returning soldiers grumbled about the "stab in the back" that lost them the war, and the tensions between right-wing nationalists and internationalist Communists grew, as did anti-Semitism, Steiner tried to communicate the ideals of his threefold restructuring. Steiner wasn't alone in trying to turn a defeated Germany's soul away from bitterness and self-pity. In 1919 the novelist Hermann Hesse, a German who had emigrated, like Steiner, to Switzerland, and who during the war wrote denunciations of militarism and nationalism, published an essay, "Zarathustra's Return," in which Nietzsche's prophet calls upon the returning soldiers to rise above their anger to work toward creating a better Germany. Although some heeded Hesse's message, most criticized him for his lack of patriotism, and along with other noted figures, Hesse's name appeared among the many who had signed Steiner's *Appeal to the German People and the Civilized*

World, which preceded the publication of *The Threefold Common-wealth.* Steiner was troubled by the turn the peace negotiations were taking, and he was especially critical of Woodrow Wilson's famous Fourteen Points, the most well-known of which was his insistence on the right of a nation to its "self-determination." Steiner saw Wilson's "professorial," "schoolmasterly," and "abstract" thinking as a sign that he was under the influence of Ahriman, and his remarks about the American president are uncharacteristi-cally hard. With his appeal, Steiner hoped that Germany would have a voice in the proceedings, but he also hoped it would be a Germany that recognized the need for change.

The war, however, had made the world a harsher place, and nowhere was more harsh than defeated Germany. Inflation was astronomical, unemployment levels skyrocketed, there was wide-spread hunger and unrest. The Kaiser had abdicated, and a weak Socialist government was trying to restore order, and had already put down a rebellion by more extreme leftist factions. A Socialist leader in Bavaria had been assassinated, and in Munich a Soviet government had been announced, only to be quashed by the forces in Berlin. The Freikorps, bands of disgruntled soldiers, roamed the streets looking for trouble, disgusted with the Weimar Constitution and the Treaty of Versailles. Anarchy reigned, more or less, and some of Steiner's followers, if not Steiner himself, believed the chaos presented them with an opportunity to make "threefoldness" a reality. This wasn't to be, but Steiner's ideas impressed some important businessmen. Emil Molt, owner and director of the Waldorf-Astoria cigarette company in Stuttgart, along with the industrialist Carl Unger and the political econo-mist Roman Boos, wanted to put Steiner's ideas into practice and formed an association. They asked Steiner to meet with them, and although he already had more than enough on his plate, he did, delivering a lecture to a group of enthusiasts the three had organized. In August a public lecture on social renewal was a success, and Steiner was asked to speak to other groups. Steiner was becoming a name on the political scene, and it's curious to think that if he had decided to enter politics, he could have done very well. Steiner spoke with workers in their taverns and also at their factories. A Union for the Threefold Social Order was created, followed by a similar one in Switzerland.

But all the attention attracted opposition, and Steiner found himself the target of vicious attacks. Marxists who wanted a revolution saw him as an obstacle, drawing the workers away from the real battle, and ordered their followers not to attend his lectures. Right-wing nationalists hated him for his antiwar sentiments and his belief in the abolition of national borders. The anti-Steiner sentiment reached a dangerous level in 1921, when Steiner saw an opportunity for his ideas to take practical shape in a referendum held by the people of Silesia, in northeastern Germany, who were voting on whether they should be a part of Germany or Poland. Followers of Steiner's threefold scheme saw a chance to offer an alternative, and Steiner helped them by training them in public speaking and organizing a campaign. The effort, however, was hopeless, and a member of one of the groups sent out to address the voters remarked that they often just nearly escaped being arrested or shot. Steiner himself was branded a "traitor" by a nationalist political group, who later backed Hitler's Munich putsch. A year later, Steiner was almost assassinated in Munich, when a group of proto-Nazis broke up his lecture and then attacked him. Steiner was saved by his own presence of mind, and the presence also of his young followers, who outnumbered the thugs and who, after forming a ring around him, escorted him out the back door.

This wasn't the only hostility. Theosophists still held a grudge against him, and early on had spread the rumor that he was secretly a Jesuit. When Steiner was asked by the Protestant pastor Friedrich Rittelmeyer to provide a sacrament for his newly formed Christian Community, Protestants and Catholics alike were outraged and attacked him in the press; they had already raised objections to his teachings, seeing in them the makings of a new sect. Occultists believed he had betrayed the mysteries by making esoteric teachings public, and he spoke darkly of "black brotherhoods," who would use their power against him. Labor unions distrusted his social and economic ideas and harangued those who followed them. Steiner was accused of German nationalism by non-Germans, and of not being German enough by Germans. He was also said to be a Jew and a key player in an internationalist conspiracy involving French secret societies, the Communists, Irish Republicanism, and the Fabians.[10] At the height of interest in the Threefold Social Order, Steiner was being booked into the largest halls in Germany—at one engagement, the crowds were so large they stopped traffic and hundreds had to be turned away. So it isn't surprising that groups eager to gain power would keep an eye on his activities and, when possible, do what they could to disrupt them. Steiner had to get used to being heckled and threatened, and to performances of eurythmy being laughed at. He endured all this with dignity and calm, although personal slurs sometimes affected him. Even though he drew large crowds, the nastiness at Steiner's lectures began to take its toll, and his booking agent told him that until things calmed down, he wouldn't be speaking in Germany. Hearing of Hitler's failed putsch in 1923,

Steiner himself remarked that if "those people" ever came to power, he would never see Germany again. In contrast to his reception in Germany, at the East-West Congress held in Vienna in June 1922, the Viennese welcomed him as one of their own, the audience of two thousand cheered his lectures, the eurythmy performances held at the Vienna State Opera House were a success, and Steiner's hotel room was the site of a nonstop stream of visitors and followers seeking his advice.

But if "threefoldness" never became the serious social alternative that Steiner had envisioned—and he himself said that it could never be imposed on people, but must arise from them voluntarily—it did provide the inspiration for Steiner's most well-known initiative.

Emil Molt, one of the most enthusiastic of Steiner's followers, asked Steiner for advice on setting up a school for his employees' children. This, of course, was Steiner's forte—he was a born teacher—and he responded brilliantly. As early as 1907, Steiner had lectured on "The Education of the Child in the Light of Theosophy," but hadn't yet had an opportunity to put his ideas into practice. Now that Molt had asked, he could. Molt supplied the funds, and an old restaurant in downtown Stuttgart was purchased and refitted as a school. In September 1919, the Stuttgart Waldorf School, the first of its kind, opened with twelve teachers and 253 children. Most of the children came from the workers' families, with about fifty coming from the local anthroposophists. Molt paid the fees for his employees' children, and the initial student body was made up of both working- and middle-class children—a mix that, for economic reasons, wouldn't occur in later schools. (One drawback to Steiner Waldorf schools today is that, like most private schools, they tend to be expensive.) A few of the

Stuttgart anthroposophists were teachers and could help make up the faculty; the rest Steiner handpicked from volunteers, who gave up their regular work to help. The school had no management other than Steiner, who assumed the role of "guide and spiritual adviser," and the teachers had to learn how to work together and to organize the curriculum efficiently. Steiner gave a series of courses on the spiritual basis of education, and on the strength of a single memorandum, the state authorities granted Steiner three years in which to make the school work.

By the end of that time the number of students had grown to eleven hundred, and hundreds more had to be turned away. There was a widespread hunger for something new in education, and Steiner's belief that the most important thing a teacher had to teach was a *love* of learning was fresh and inspiring. Steiner's insights into education came from his spiritual research, and, as can be expected, some of his ideas seem rather odd. Probably the most well-known of these is the idea that children shouldn't be taught to read until they lose their first set of teeth, which generally occurs around the age of seven. What losing teeth and reading have in common isn't immediately obvious, but Steiner's insight is based on his understanding of human development, and on the importance he placed in seven-year cycles. The loss of milk teeth is a physical indication of a spiritual change that takes place around the seventh year. Until then, Steiner says, children live entirely in their senses, but with the seventh year, the senses "separate off," leaving the child's soul and spirit to develop independently. Then, up until puberty, which marks another seven-year cycle, the child's soul lives "pictorially." Or to put it another way, before the age of seven, a child's relation to the world is imitative; children at this stage are drawn to imitate whatever is around them. But with the change of teeth, this also changes, and the child is now drawn not to what he sees with his eyes, but by what is revealed to his growing soul by the moods and feelings of the teacher. Given that Steiner education—or Waldorf education, as it came to be called—is based on the developing spiritual life of the student, teachers remain with their classes throughout the process, rather than acquiring new students each year (this means, of course, that the students also do not acquire new teachers).

Steiner believed that conventional education stifled spiritual growth and led to the dead, abstract thinking and stunted lives that characterize a society based on materialism. Steiner saw a link between his ideas on imagination, inspiration, and intuition, the seven-year cycles, and the development of the etheric body, the astral body, and the I. Seven- to fourteen-year-olds, who are developing their etheric bodies, are taught in a way that will nurture their imaginations, through pictures, stories, and other imaginative experiences. With puberty, the shift is to inspiration and the astral body, when the ideas which were at first introduced in images can now be grasped directly. Then, with the age of twenty-one—recognized by many as the point of maturity, although, to be sure, maturation can and should continue throughout life—the I fully "incarnates," and the possibility of free self-education arrives, which is the work of intuition. The central idea is to create a learning environment which can motivate live thinking and active imagination, and not the mere mechanical parroting of the lesson at hand, with the aim of finding a place for oneself in the economic and social hierarchy.

In 1921, Steiner hosted a conference on education at the Goetheanum, which attracted many foreign educators. One result of this was that Steiner was asked to lecture on his educational ideas at other cities in Europe. England in particular proved very receptive, and in April 1922, Steiner was asked to speak at an education festival in Stratford-on-Avon, the birthplace of Shakespeare. Steiner spoke on his ideas, but (predictably) also gave a lecture on Shakespeare and attended performances of several of his plays. (Steiner apparently approved of the way the comedies were presented but had his own ideas about the tragedies.) Steiner's lectures impressed a journalist from the *Manchester Guardian,* who wrote that "the entire congress finds its central point in the personality and teaching of Dr. Rudolf Steiner." Because of this, Steiner was asked to give a course of lectures on education at Manchester College, part of Oxford University, where he sat on the same panel as other highly respected educators. Steiner's reputation grew in English educational circles, and in the following years (1923 and 1924), he was invited to give lectures in other English cities. Finally, a Steiner school like the one in Stuttgart was proposed, and in 1925, the year of Steiner's death, a school was established in Streatham, a suburb of South London. This later became Michael Hall, which still exists today, although it has relocated to Forest Row in Sussex, an area of England that has become a kind of center for anthroposophical activity in the UK (among other things, it's the home of Emerson College, a Waldorf adult education school). Around the same time, a school was opened in Holland, and a few years later the Rudolf Steiner School in New York, the first in the United States, was opened in 1928. Today Steiner is most well known for his educational ideas, and it's not unusual for many parents sending their children to Steiner schools to be unaware of his occult philosophy; indeed, many of the first Steiner teachers were not particularly well versed in anthroposophy, to the dismay of many of Steiner's older followers. The Nazis, as could be expected, closed the German Steiner schools, on the grounds that their founder was insufficiently nationalistic, and for the more threatening reason that they were aimed at producing free individuals, something for which Hitler and his henchmen had no need.

It's unclear when Steiner first began to feel the effects of the illness that would eventually kill him, but the impression one gets of his last years is of a man determined to sow as many seeds as possible, with the hope that a few at least might take root and grow. In the same year as he established Steiner education and was active in promoting the Threefold Social Order, Steiner gave lecture courses on a variety of practical subjects. He spoke on science for the many scientists who were becoming attracted to his ideas and gave as well his first series of lectures for physicians. There was a course on Thomas Aquinas, more lectures on education and the Threefold Social Order, and a new series of lectures on the curative properties of color; 1921 saw courses on curative eurythmy, astronomy, and public speaking. There were also courses on medicine and therapy, and the first series of lectures on theology. In 1916 the Protestant minister Friedrich Rittelmeyer, whom we met earlier, became a follower of Steiner when he had to admit that Steiner's knowledge and insight into Christianity was greater than his own. Rittelmeyer himself was an important and popular figure in the Protestant world, and he hoped that something of the new vision he received from Steiner might find his way into mainstream Protestantism. In June 1921, Steiner gave a series of lectures on theology to a small group of young Protestant ministers in Stuttgart. These then spoke to other ministers and invited them to attend a series of theological lectures that Steiner proposed to give in Dornach. More than a hundred did, and toward the end of the series Steiner voiced his belief that it was important to devise a new sacrament, one that would be suitable for what he termed the "consciousness soul," the form of consciousness it was the task of the present age to actualize. Those who heard him recognized that the kind of religious renewal necessary for the age wouldn't be possible within the established church and would have to come from a new source. The outcome was the Christian Community, for which Steiner provided a new sacrament, the Act of the Consecration of Man. Steiner knew that he was often accused of wanting to start a new religion, and so he remained apart from the Christian Community itself, acting only as an adviser and "guide." It's clear, though, that Steiner recognized that the intellectual approach of much of anthroposophy couldn't fill the need many had for a form of daily ritual and that he hoped that the sacraments of the Christian Community could provide this. Sadly, although many ministers gave up their pulpits to take part in the new movement—whose forty-five priests included three women and a Buddhist—Steiner's efforts were misunderstood, and the Christian Community became another target for the rising anti-Steiner hostility.

The culmination of that hostility was marked by the fire that broke out in the Goetheanum on the night of December 31, 1922, completely destroying the building. Several sources seem to indicate that Steiner had a premonition that something like this would happen. The unusual gloom Steiner experienced during his first visit to Dornach, and the unexpected storm which darkened the foundation stone ceremony, seemed to many an ill omen. Steiner himself is reported to have remarked more than once that the Goetheanum would not "last long," and we have seen how he spoke of the building as a "stumbling block" that would arouse his enemies' anger. There's also a story that on the day the Goetheanum burned, Steiner almost broke his neck, falling through a pit on a stage.[11] A coincidence, surely, if true, but for a group who believed that the evil forces of Ahriman were ranged against them, little, I suspect, would fall under that category. Others, too, had premonitions. In 1922, a woman who had never seen the Goetheanum expressed a strong desire to visit it for the Christmas conference and asked Steiner for help. He couldn't help her then, he said, but perhaps something could be done for Easter? She insisted that if she didn't see it at Christmas, she would never see it. "We are going to lose it," she told Steiner. "It will burn to the ground and will no longer exist at Easter." Steiner only repeated that he couldn't help her now, but would do what he could for Easter. But the woman was determined and somehow made it to Dornach at the end of December. When she arrived she told some friends of her premonition, one of whom replied that she "was not normal." That evening the Goetheanum burned.[12]

Although opened in 1920, the Goetheanum was never really completed, and for most of the time, the Schreinerei, the massive workshop adjoining the main building where Steiner worked on his great wooden statue, was the real center for anthroposophic activity. Since the start of construction, Steiner was faced with the constant need to raise funds and to recruit people for the labor. During the war years this proved a real problem, as many of the men had been called to service, and so much of the workforce then were women. But perhaps Steiner's biggest challenge was to convince anthroposophists in other cities of the Goetheanum's importance. Many of his German followers resented the fact that the center of anthroposophic activities had shifted from Berlin (or Stuttgart or Munich) to Switzerland, where there were far fewer anthroposophists, and that the followers who could relocate there had acquired a cachet that others couldn't share, rather like the Wagnerians who resided at Bayreuth. And although the building had been a symbol of international cooperation during the war, it wasn't without its own squabbles. National pride broke out occasionally, artists bickered over the designs and execution, and younger members fired with idealism were often frustrated by what they saw as the older followers' lack of enthusiasm and resistance to change.

Dr. Grossheintz, whose land it was anyway, expressed the wish to erect a house of his own near the Goetheanum, to which the younger idealistic members reacted violently. Andrei Belyi recalls that the artists among them (who had little faith in a dentist's aesthetic taste) wouldn't allow "Citizen Grossheintz" to locate his "middle-class, one-family dwelling in front of our Goetheanum," understandably concerned that the sight of a clothesline might detract from the building's effect. Steiner, straddling the fence between artistic purpose and the need to respect the wishes of the person who was making the building possible, chided the younger members for their impatience, and remarked that "a wash-line was by no means a desecration of the Goetheanum," reminding his followers that their mission was to strive for the new life "in all its facets." Separating "the temple," as they called it, from the concerns of ordinary life, would be mere sentimentality. "Here particularly," he said, pointing to a spot on the hill, "diapers should flap on the washline in the wind."[13]

Steiner's remark about diapers may have been at least partially tongue in cheek, but on other occasions he expressed an unshakable seriousness about "the temple." Performances of *Faust* or the Mystery Dramas were preceded by solemn music, often a mass or symphony by Anton Bruckner. Women were not allowed to wear slacks when inside, and men had to wear jackets. On one occasion he reprimanded one of his women followers for setting her wristwatch temporarily on one of the columns. This, he said, was a gesture of disrespect, not only to the work they were all involved in, but to the spirits who guided their activities. When Steiner discovered a woman eating a bun in the auditorium, he very firmly asked her to leave, and when he found a young couple sitting on the balustrade of the terrace, he scolded them for their bad manners. Even royalty was subject to Steiner's stern code of conduct. When the Dutch prince consort visited the Goetheanum, he was told by Steiner that he would have to leave his cigar outside (he did). Many who came to work on the building found a new life there. Belyi himself worked on the carvings with his wife, Aasya Turgenieff, grandniece of the famous writer. When Belyi left Dornach in 1916, called back by the war to Russia, Aasya Turgenieff stayed behind. Their marriage soon collapsed, and Belyi's attempts to revive it failed. Aasya herself remained at Dornach for the rest of her life. Belyi was a labile personality, and his own relationship with Steiner went through many changes; at one point he repudiated him publicly, but later changed his mind, and again spoke highly of the Doctor. Steiner, too, had to contend with the many anthroposophists who wished, like Dr. Grossheintz, to build their own homes near the temple. Although Steiner promoted individuality, he was concerned that the colonists eager to build would be patient, and that their ideas would harmonize with the style and effect of the central building. He had to emphasize often that they were not a sect, clearly concerned that what he saw as a developing system of knowledge should not gain a reputation as simply another cult.

What effect the building did have is debatable and, since its destruction, can only be surmised. It's understandable that the followers who worked on the temple would be sensitive to its influence; others, however, seemed to have been disturbed by it. When the people at Dornach pressed Steiner to set a date for when the building would truly become the center for anthroposophy it was intended to be, he consented, and announced a conference that would last three weeks. The conference was "officially" known as a "collegiate course," and would not, Steiner warned, be the formal opening of the building. Steiner invited many nonanthroposophists to attend, including many university students from all over western Europe. Lectures by nonanthroposophists would be welcome, and they would be expected to take part in discussions. There would also be the first public performances of eurythmy.

The result wasn't what most had hoped for. More than a thousand people took part, but to the uninitiated, the strangely flowing interior proved unsettling, and to the anthroposophists, most of what the nonanthroposophical speakers had to say seemed out of place, even hostile. And even some anthroposophists found the setting slightly upsetting. A sense of uneasiness colored the proceedings, which was lifted only when Steiner himself addressed the gathering. It may be, as has been said, that the Goetheanum itself was sensitive to what took place within it, and that it rejected the critical tone of some of the nonanthroposophical speakers. But it's also possible that people who hadn't spent several years working on creating a spiritual space receptive to etheric forces may have found Steiner's architectural ideas too extreme.

Steiner himself came away from the conference feeling that the anthroposophical movement wasn't yet strong enough to have the kind of impact on the outside world that it should have. It was perhaps the first sign of a need for a change that would soon become pressing.

On New Year's Eve, 1922, Steiner delivered the concluding lecture of a series on the "Spiritual Communion of Mankind." At around ten o'clock, when those attending had just returned home, the night watchman at the Goetheanum noticed smoke in the White Room, which had recently been the site of the first performance of the *Act of the Consecration of Man.* The alarm was sounded, but no fire could be found. Then, when a wall in the west wing was broken into, it was clear; it was blazing inside. Guenther Wachsmuth quotes from an occult magazine a warning given to Steiner of "spiritual sparks hissing" against the Goetheanum, and that he would "have need of some of his cleverness . . . if a real spark of fire is not one day to bring about an end to the magnificence of Dornach." Similar sentiments from other sources, combined with the very real hostility Steiner experienced, led to the belief that arson was to blame. Others point out that as the fire was discovered inside a wall, it could have been an electrical fault. More than likely we will never know. By midnight the flames shot through the massive domes and illuminated the sky. Local firefighters and anthroposophists joined to battle the blaze, but the wood was too plentiful a fuel, and eventually Steiner instructed them to leave the building to its fate. Many risked their lives, rescuing what they could, and the lawn surrounding the ruin was soon littered with the figures of the elemental beings that Steiner had intended to use in a performance of *Faust,* a darkly apt sight. The Schreinerei, which housed Steiner's great sculpture of the Representative of Humanity, was saved, as were the other adjoining buildings. Steiner himself, with some others, stayed at the site until dawn, when the last timbers were consumed, and acrid smoke rose up to greet the morning light. All that was left was the concrete foundations. "Much work and many years," Steiner was reported to have said. We can, I think, forgive him if at that moment he also wondered what karmic debt had been repaid with the loss of what he and so many others had sacrificed so much to achieve.

9. LAST DAYS AND LEGACY

S teiner bore the destruction of the Goetheanum with almost superhuman equanimity, but the loss of ten years' effort was a massive blow, and it was clear that the movement to which he had dedicated his life had reached a major crisis. It was evident that it couldn't continue in the way it had, yet Steiner was in no way inclined to give up. While the structure burned, he walked around the blaze in silence. Then, when New Year's Day, 1923, came, he announced to those who had remained with him that their work would go on. "We will continue to do our self-imposed duty in the premises that are still left to us,"[1] he told his followers. Shortly afterward, the Christmas conference continued as scheduled in the Schreinerei and that evening even a play that had been planned was performed. Many of the performers were heartbroken and understandably had difficulties with their lines. But Steiner proved a true leader, encouraging them to go on, refusing to let their loss stop the work they had begun. Almost immediately he began plans to rebuild. The second Goetheanum (he refused to call it the new one) would be very different from the first. It would be made of concrete, and its design would be less inviting and much more austere, defiant even,

reflecting the siege sensibility that many anthroposophists understandably shared. Like its predecessor, it would be a remarkable
visionary work, being one of the first structures to employ re-
inforced concrete, and today it is included in many books on
modern architecture.[2] But unlike the first Goetheanum, whose
organic shape blended with the countryside, the second's sculpted
form stands out starkly against the Jura foothills, announcing
unequivocally that the movement it houses had no intention of
fading away, a fact that visitors to Dornach today can attest to. It's
also much larger than the first, a necessary expansion, due to the
large increase in members of the Anthroposophical Society. Yet it
was the very success of the society in attracting new members
that, even before the destruction of the first Goetheanum, led
Steiner to rethink its meaning and aims.

After World War I, Steiner's message reached a different and
mostly young audience, eager to build a new world on the ruins of
the old. Many who came to anthroposophy then did so through
the movement for the Threefold Social Order, and their motives
differed from those of the older members. Many of the newer
members were students and, like the students of a later generation, they were impatient with what they saw as their elders' complacency. Although as early as 1907, Steiner had made clear that
anthroposophy's role in the world would be different from that of
the Theosophical Society, which focused on individual spiritual
development, many of those who had been with him from the
start resented the urgency of youth. To the older members, the
young knew little but wanted to do much, while for the younger
ones, the situation was reversed. For them, the older members
knew quite a bit, but did nothing. Tensions between the two
groups were high, and Steiner found himself having to agree to

the founding of a Free Anthroposophical Society, to meet the demands of the younger members. Members of the older group were shocked at this and, feeling threatened, retaliated by entrenching themselves in dogma and authoritarianism. Other members, also enthusiastic about the idea of social and cultural renewal, focused on this to the detriment of the basics of anthroposophy. And although he repeated the injunction that clear thinking was the first and absolutely necessary step on the path of esoteric knowledge, Steiner still found himself having to weed out much sentimentality and fuzzy mysticism.

Steiner was facing the problems that all leaders of movements, spiritual or otherwise, eventually confront: dissension and revisionism. From a rigorous method of attaining knowledge of the spirit world, Steiner's ideas had turned into a battleground. Had he been content to write his books—accepting that, more than likely, his readership would remain small—he could have avoided this, and focused on getting his message across with as much clarity and force as possible. Taking the path of a spiritual leader made it possible to reach a larger number of people more immediately, but it also meant re-creating microcosmically the same muddle that he hoped his insights would unravel.

Steiner's own polymath talents are partially to blame for this. With Steiner education, the Threefold movement, the Christian Community, and other new areas like farming and medicine, the original aim of anthroposophy was being lost. The tributaries branching off from anthroposophy were worthy and valuable, but they were in danger of losing contact with their source. Many anthroposophists found that the Christian Community answered their needs more directly than anthroposophy did itself and had more or less transferred their attentions to it. Waldorf education also siphoned off much vital energy. Steiner, who was never a member of the Anthroposophical Society, was aware of this, and however crushing a blow, the destruction of the first Goetheanum must have seemed to him an appropriate cue to make some changes. Possibly it was a sign from fate or karma that he had made a wrong turn somewhere and had to start anew. At one point he even thought of abandoning the society altogether and making a fresh start with just a few of his closest followers. But time was running short, and to start all over again may have proved too taxing, even for his phenomenal powers.

External problems were also a consideration. Business enterprises the society had engaged in, like Futurum AG in Switzerland and Der Kommende Tag (The Coming Day) AG in Germany, had, like many others, been drained by postwar inflation and had to liquidate many of their assets. Early in January, French troops occupied Germany's Ruhr Valley, demanding war reparations. The path toward World War II was being cleared, and later that year Hitler would make his failed Munich putsch; arrested, he spent his time in prison writing perhaps the century's most dangerous book, *Mein Kampf.* Clearly, at the beginning of 1923, this was yet to come, but Steiner must have felt the psychic pressures, and realized that to withdraw now would only leave the field open to the influence of Ahriman.

Yet although he was determined that a second Goetheanum would rise from the ashes of the first, Steiner was also determined that a new Anthroposophical Society must likewise emerge from the scattering of energies and bickering he saw around him. Steiner was the gentlest of men, but he didn't avoid the responsibility he felt to the future, and the lectures from this time are full of stern admonitions and warnings to his audience that they must rethink their motivations and get "back to basics." In June 1923, he gave a series of lectures on the history of the Anthroposophical Movement, tracing his own path, and trying to instill in his followers a feeling for the destiny of the movement, hoping to heal the splintering that had turned the society into a collection of competing initiatives. He told them of "the homeless ones" he encountered in his early days in Vienna, those individuals who felt out of touch with the "chaos of contemporary life," and who sought some spiritual sustenance in the music of Wagner and later in the writings of Madame Blavatsky. Now his listeners were also "homeless," in a more immediate sense, having lost the Goetheanum, but also their sense of direction. It was necessary now, he told them, for all who had come to anthroposophy from other fields—from science, medicine, education—to recall the basic truths about the spirit, otherwise the real significance of the movement would be lost. From Steiner's remarks it's difficult to avoid the feeling that for all the accomplishments and progress he had made in the last twenty years, he was disappointed, not only with anthroposophy's affect on the world, but with the anthroposophists themselves. They lacked, he felt, a real feeling of Anthroposophia as a true spiritual being, "a living, supersensory, invisible being who moves among anthroposophists."[3] Without this, he told his listeners, they might as well choose a different path, and form cliques and groups who enjoy tea parties and the occasional lecture. Every individual must reflect and ask himself if his actions derive from the heart of anthroposophy. If they do not, he said, then anthroposophy was in danger of falling into what Steiner called a "latent state," a kind of hibernation, and this could only bode ill for mankind.

What effect Steiner's words had on his listeners is unknown, but Steiner himself had made up his mind. In July he again warned his audience that "we must not turn into a circle of teachers, a circle for religious renewal, a circle of scientists, or a circle of young people. . . . Specialization has become too great among us . . . it has grown so great that the mother has been forgotten."[4] Five months later he took steps to change this.

At the Christmas Conference of 1923, Steiner made his decision clear. To the eight hundred or so members who came to a chilly Dornach that December 25 he announced that he had founded a new society, the General Anthroposophical Society, and that, unlike his previous relation to the old society as "spiritual adviser," he was appointing himself its president. Steiner also announced the creation of a College for Spiritual Science, of which he was also head, and that in his work for the college, he would be joined by his appointed collaborators. These included the poet Albert Steffen, who was deputy chairman and head of the literature section; Marie Steiner,[5] head of speech and music; Dr. Ita Wegman (Steiner's own physician), head of the medical section; Dr. Elizabeth Vreede, head of mathematics and astronomy; and Guenther Wachsmuth, Steiner's then secretary (and later biographer), who was treasurer. The tutor who had begun with a few students many years ago was now establishing his own university. The aim of the General Anthroposophical Society was to promote spiritual research, and the aim of the college was to carry it out. Among some of the other changes Steiner announced in his inaugural lecture was that as "the spirit of the present age demands full publicity for everything," he was authorizing the publication of his lectures, which until then had been available only to members. So when readers interested in knowing more about Steiner are today daunted by the rows and rows of books on display at a Steiner bookshop, they have the 1923 Christmas Conference to thank. Until then only Steiner's written works were available to the public.

Readers curious about the details of the new society should look once again to Stewart C. Easton's account. Steiner's belief in the importance of his decision, however, was absolute. Aside from the spiritual import of founding the new society, Steiner took his responsibilities as president very seriously. To give one mundane example, it was decided that all members of the various national or local branches of the old Anthroposophical Society should be issued with membership cards for the new society. Steiner took this to heart and personally signed and issued all twelve thousand cards.

A more esoteric founding ceremony occurred on New Year's Day, 1924, one year after the destruction of the first Goetheanum. Then Steiner laid a second "foundation stone," to initiate construction of the second Goetheanum. The original foundation stone of 1914 still lay beneath the ruins, and this second "stone" was of a different nature. It was, he said, laid not in the earth, but in the hearts of all members of the new society, present *and* future. The resonance between this symbolic "stone" and others, like the philosophical stone of the alchemists and the "rock," Peter, upon whom Christ's church would be built, seems evident. More immediately, the new "stone" was a meditative verse that Steiner gave to those attending, and it was his hope that through working with this meditation, the spiritual reality of the "stone" would be revealed over time. It's understandable that many who were at the ceremony considered it to be the most solemn occasion of their lives. Steiner told them that they were in fact preparing to erect two new buildings: one of concrete, the other formed of "the individual work done by us severally, in all our groups, as we go out into the wide world."[6] Through this Steiner hoped to fuse the different streams of anthroposophical activity into one living unity, to heal the conflicts and make Anthroposophia whole once more. Again, for all his comments to the contrary, Steiner's language has a distinct religious tone, and it's difficult to avoid the feeling that his aim was, after all, to inaugurate a new religion.

Today the practical application of Steiner's ideas, which he felt threatened anthroposophy as a whole, have had the most impact. Along with Steiner education, two other important areas opened up in the years just before the destruction of the Goetheanum, anthroposophical medicine and what became known as biodynamic farming.

As early as 1911, Steiner had given a lecture series in Prague on "Occult Physiology," and over the years he had given his followers advice on diet and health. He was, however, never dogmatic about this. Although he himself was a teetotaler and had given up smoking (but was, apparently, still fond of snuff), he never demanded that his followers do the same. It's often assumed that a vegetarian diet aids spiritual development, and, true or not, many anthroposophists gave up meat. Yet when one of his followers told Steiner that although he had given up eating ham, he still often thought about it, Steiner told him to go ahead and eat it. "Better to eat ham than to think ham," he said, emphasizing again that thinking was still, for him, the royal road to the spirit.

In the spring of 1920, Steiner gave a series of lectures to physicians and medical students; later published as *Spiritual Science and Medicine,* these talks became the basis of anthroposophical medicine. In the audience then was Ita Wegman, who became Steiner's own physician and, as mentioned, later the head of the medical section of the College for Spiritual Science. Steiner had met Ita years before in Berlin, when she attended one of his early theosophical lectures. Then she was interested in Swedish massage and hydrotherapy, but Steiner advised her to study medicine. She did, and in 1911 received her qualification in Zurich, where she opened a small private clinic. After hearing Steiner's medical lecture, she decided to move her clinic to Basel, and not long after, with a few other anthroposophical physicians, she moved again to Arlesheim, near Dornach, and set up the Clinical-Therapeutical Institute. A laboratory was established, which Ita named Weleda, after the Celtic goddess of health. Today many people who have never heard of anthroposophy are familiar with the Weleda brand of anthroposophical health and well-being products. At the same time, another clinic and Weleda laboratory was set up near Stuttgart.[7] In Arlesheim, a research institute for the study of cancer, as well as a small cancer clinic, was later established; both make use of a preparation, Iscador, based on mistletoe, that Steiner suggested would be useful for cancer therapy.

Like Steiner's social theories, anthroposophical medicine is based on his insights into the threefold human nature. In many ways similar to the more familiar homeopathy—using highly potentized tinctures and preparations—anthroposophical medicine also takes into consideration the body's nervous, rhythmic, and metabolic organization, as well as the etheric and astral forces active in it. The nature of an illness and its location in the body is also important, and as anthroposophical medicine treats the individual, and not the disease, Steiner believed that standardized treatment was useless and could even be harmful. What could work as a remedy for one person could be a poison for another. Steiner also incorporated music, color, art, and dance—in the form of "curative eurythmy"—as part of anthroposophical therapy.

As in much holistic medicine, Steiner saw illnesses as a result of an imbalance, specifically between two tendencies that are directly related to the work of the spiritual beings Ahriman and Lucifer. Ahriman is present in the organism in its tendency to sclerosis, or hardening, and Lucifer is associated with fever and inflammation. As in Chinese ideas about yin and yang, both are necessary for well-being, but they must be kept in the proper balance; rather than attack a symptom head on, Steiner believed that treatment should be aimed at stimulating the weaker tendency. So, if the sclerotic forces were growing too strong, the body's Luciferic energies should be made to compensate for this. Steiner also believed that certain illness and ailments were the result of a loosening of the etheric body.[8]

Steiner never intended for anthroposophical medicine to be a substitute for orthodox treatment, just as he never saw his spiritual science taking the place of the mainstream variety. It should, however, complement it. And, like his approach to science, his medical research and that of his followers was rooted in Goethean "active imagination," the ability to perceive the living reality of the patient and not merely an abstract symptom. Where, for all its success, modern medicine regards the organism as more or less a machine made up of different parts, which can be treated separately as one can fix, say, a faulty valve in a car, Steiner, like many other thinkers, looked at the whole person. Even further, he considered his or her life as a unity, and based his approach on that. The value of Steiner's ideas is probably most evident in the remarkable success of what he called "curative education," based on his early work with the severely handicapped Otto Specht. Although the highly successful Camphill schools and communities for special-needs children, which are based on Steiner's insights, wouldn't emerge until after World War II, the core ideas had been established decades earlier. Steiner argued that the care of severely mentally or physically handicapped children required a very different approach from that used with normal children. In the case of handicapped children it was, he said, essential to work with their *souls*. Such children Steiner called "children in need of special care of the soul," and what characterizes the success of the Camphill schools is the great patience and affection the carers have for their charges. Steiner's belief that karma and reincarnation are responsible for these unfortunates will strike some of us as glib; he maintained that for karmic reasons, the souls of these children had been housed in diseased or misshapen bodies, but given sufficient love and care, they had a possibility of development, something the success of the Camphill projects has corroborated. Many of us will find it difficult to accept that a child born with hydrocephaly is working out his karmic destiny, but if we remember Steiner's success with Otto Specht, the results of this belief can be close to miraculous.

Along with Steiner/Waldorf education, the movement most associated with Steiner today is biodynamic farming and agriculture. Steiner himself didn't use the term "biodynamic," although it does reflect his belief that farming and gardening should be practiced "biologically" and "dynamically." This means that the soil used on a farm or in a garden should be seen as a living, organic system, and not merely as an inert collection of minerals and chemicals like potassium, nitrogen, and other plant nutrients. And for the soil to produce the best results, it needs to be "dynamized" through methods that can direct the flow of the etheric and cosmic forces related to the seasons, the phases of the moon, the stars, and the planets. While many organic farmers find much value in Steiner's "biological" ideas—which predate the interest in organic farming by decades—his ideas about the spiritual and cosmic influences on plant growth are often misunderstood or discarded. This has led some anthroposophists to complain that many farms advertising themselves as biodynamic are making something of a false claim.

In 1922, Steiner was asked by some of his followers to give some suggestions on how they could improve their farm production. Steiner had already spoken often about the influence of the formative etheric forces on plant growth, and it should be remembered that the kernel of anthroposophy rests in Goethe's ideas about the *Urpflanze,* the archetypal plant whose presence Goethe discovered through his practice of "active imagination." The farmers approached Steiner for advice because in recent years they had recognized a problem. They saw an increasing sickness of the land itself, and also what they considered a degeneracy in modern seeds, resulting, they felt, in a loss of nutritional value in produce. Others asked him for advice on animal diseases, while Count Keyserlingk, owner of a large estate in Koberwitz, near Breslau, wanted suggestions about how to treat certain plant diseases. Steiner's replies made it clear that he had much to say on the matter. His central idea was that the soil itself was sick, and so the produce grown on it suffered. This in turn affected the animals and people who ate it.

Steiner gave one of his followers, Ehrenfried Pfeiffer, a scientist interested in studying the etheric forces, some very practical advice. Certain natural preparations, he said, used in combination with compost and manure, could help restore vitality to depleted soil. These preparations, however, would need to be subject to "cosmic rhythms" and the "terrestrial forces" of the seasons. This would help concentrate their beneficial energies. Guenther Wachsmuth explains that certain substances were mixed together according to Steiner's directions; the resulting mixture was then placed in some unusual receptacles: cattle horns. These were buried and then left to receive the influence of the sun, moon, and earth. When these were later dug up in the spring—apparently there was some difficulty remembering where they had been buried—Steiner emptied the horns into a bucket of water. This he stirred, using Pfeiffer's walking stick, and then instructed his somewhat baffled student in the proper means of application, before abruptly leaving for another appointment. The results proved impressive enough for Pfeiffer and others to want to hear more.

Although asked repeatedly for more formal instruction, it wasn't until June 1924 that Steiner found time to give a lecture course on his agricultural ideas. Sixty people, many of them farmers and landowners, gathered on Count Keyserlingk's estate, to hear the eight lectures forming the basis of what would become biodynamic farming.[9] Along with somewhat more esoteric information about the human being's relation to the cosmos, most of the talks were dedicated to very practical matters—Steiner, we should remember, grew up in a rural setting and as a young boy helped maintain his family's garden, where they grew a great deal of their own food. Steiner instructed his audience in how to make a "dynamic" compost, how to control pests without the use of pesticides (a key concern for today's environmentalists), how to inhibit weed growth, and also on how many plants considered mere weeds could be cultivated to much profit. Steiner maintained that a farm or garden should be "self-sufficient"; so, for example, livestock should be fed on the plants grown on the farm, and the animal's manure should be recycled as fertilizer (after it had been properly "dynamized"). Steiner also spoke on how the plant is a kind of "upside-down" human, with its roots in the earth as its "head," its stalks and leaves its "rhythmic system," and its flower and seeds its "metabolic system," thus applying his principle of threefoldness to the plant world. He also pointed out that each of our own "systems" is nourished by eating the corresponding part of the plant. Today, Weleda homeopathic products are prepared using plants grown according to biodynamic principles, and like the once famous results at Findhorn, the general conclusion is that, whatever may be responsible, fruit and vegetables grown biodynamically are appreciably more nutritious and flavorful than those grown using more "modern," mass agricultural methods.[10]

Stewart Easton calls 1924 Steiner's *annus mirabilis*, his "miraculous year," and for a man who was already suffering from the disease that would kill him, to say that the amount of work he accomplished then is remarkable is an understatement.[11] His travels and lectures continued as always: he spoke in Prague, Paris, Stuttgart, Arnhem (Holland), and several other cities, not to mention his lectures at Dornach. In 1923, Steiner had visited England and Wales; at the stone circle at Penmaenmawr, Wales, he spoke of the ancient Druids and their mysteries, and threw out a suggestion about the stones that has by now become a standard theme: that they were basically astronomical calendars. In August 1924, Steiner again visited England, where he attended a summer school in Torquay, Devon. During a two-and-a-half-week stay he delivered some seventy lectures—a crushing workload, even for a man in the best of health. Some of these formed part of a series of lectures he had begun in Dornach on *Karmic Relationships,* and had given in several cities across Europe. These dealt with the influence of karma on history, and the links between different historical figures in their different incarnations. Some of these have been mentioned earlier, and the interested reader who follows the series through its eight published volumes (there are eighty-two lectures in all) will find fascinating if often baffling insights into the karmic life of figures like Ralph Waldo Emerson, Karl Marx, the nineteenth-century French occultist Eliphas Levi, Victor Hugo, Franz Schubert, Voltaire, and many others. To give some example of Steiner's approach: Karl Marx's hatred of the bourgeoisie is a result, he says, of Marx's former life as a landowner whose property had been taken from him; Friedrich Engels, with whom Marx wrote *The Communist Manifesto,* was, in his former life, the person who appropriated Marx's land. Friedrich Nietzsche's madness, Steiner claims, can be accounted for by the fact that in a former life he had been a Franciscan friar who so mortified his flesh that he was in constant pain. Nietzsche's "karmic memory" of this led to his unconsciously trying to free himself of his body. Yet his body's vitality (an odd remark to make about Nietzsche, whose life *was* one of almost constant pain, as he suffered from a variety of ailments) prevented this. The result of this tug-of-war was that Nietzsche's mind snapped. (Steiner either was unaware of or disregarded the most probable cause of Nietzsche's madness: syphilis.)

Whatever we may think of these and other revelations, *Karmic Relationships,* one of the most "esoteric" of Steiner's lecture series, can be a rewarding study; if nothing else it shows the scope of Steiner's knowledge and feeling for history; often, what at first seem baffling connections between different historical personalities begin, after a time, to reveal a striking intuition. What's also interesting about these lectures is that in them Steiner includes people from his own past. He speaks of Karl Julius Schröer, the man who introduced him to Goethe and who helped Steiner get his first big break, editing Goethe's scientific writings. He also talks about his geometry teacher, who he doesn't name, but who had a powerful influence on Steiner's own pedagogic style. Steiner had by this time begun his autobiography, which, as mentioned, was serialized in the society's "in house" magazine, and it's possible he felt an instinctive need to review his life and to possibly gain some insight into his own karma.

Whatever Steiner's motivations, it was clear to those closest to him that when he returned to Dornach in September from his demanding stay in England (after Torquay he had gone on to London to give still more lectures), something was wrong. His followers more than likely would find it hard to believe, but the Doctor was a dying man. Photographs of Steiner from this time show an exhausted, gaunt face, his already deep-set eyes receding even deeper into their hollows. Under Ita Wegman's orders he allowed himself a few days' rest in Stuttgart, but he soon slipped the harness on again. He then returned to Dornach and continued to lecture. More than a thousand students had gathered there in anticipation of the courses and lectures that had been scheduled. Steiner managed to give the first of these on September 5. He also continued to give his series of talks to the workmen who had started construction of the second Goetheanum.[12] (One such lecture series, on bees, has become something of a classic in beekeeping, and it later became a central influence on the work of the German artist Joseph Beuys.[13]) He carried on as usual until the twenty-third, giving lectures each day, especially enjoying a course on speech and drama, in which he recited and acted out whole scenes (there's a good possibility, I think, that Steiner was a dramatist in a past life). Although sick, weary, and saddled with a failing body, when lecturing, Steiner could somehow tap otherwise dormant energies, and display his old vitality; it was only when he wasn't speaking that his condition was evident to others. Ita Wegman and others had continued to urge Steiner to rest. But he felt compelled to carry on, although in a later letter to Marie Steiner, he admitted that it might have been better had he listened to their advice. He felt, however, that he owed it to "the higher powers" to continue. We might see this as presumption, or the inflexible habit of an extraordinary workaholic. Or we may take Steiner at his word. But for all his insights, Steiner apparently refused to recognize, or was unaware of, the seriousness of his situation, and continued to speak in terms of a quick recovery and resumption of his duties. But here, for once, the Doctor was wrong.

Ita Wegman was finally able to convince him to stop work and rest, and on September 27, followers who had come to hear his lecture on Saint John the Evangelist and the Mystery of Lazarus were astounded to find a note on the Schreinerei bulletin board announcing that it was canceled because the speaker was ill, something that most of them would have considered unthinkable. It had simply never happened before. Although some knew that the Doctor had recently begun a strict diet, few knew that he was ailing and, aside from those closest to him, no one had any idea how serious his condition was. The next day was the start of the Michaelmas Festival, and many were cheered when, punctual as usual, Steiner was there to give the opening lecture. But few could fail to see that he was frail and that his voice had lost some of its power. And shortly after he had begun, Steiner excused himself and told those present that he couldn't continue. His strength, he said, was not sufficient. He spoke a few more brief words, then, in closing, gave his listeners a verse meditation on the archangel Michael, whose importance for Steiner we will return to shortly. Work had only just begun on the second Goetheanum; the anthroposophical phoenix was slowly rising from its ashes. But the impossible had happened. The unstoppable Dr. Steiner had given his last lecture. He left the podium for the last time and slowly walked from the lecture hall to his studio in the Schreinerei, which also served as his bedroom. There stood the unfinished carving of Lucifer, Ahriman, and the Christ. At the foot of this was his bed, and here Steiner would remain for the last six months of his life.

At first Steiner could leave his bed occasionally and sit in his easy chair, but soon even this minimal effort proved too much. For a man who had spent so much of his career on the move, this must have been difficult. He still continued to do what work he could. Guenther Wachsmuth reports that Steiner expected his correspondence to be delivered every morning at eleven o'clock. He would read through it and dictate appropriate replies. He would also go through the books Wachsmuth brought him, choosing at a glance which he would read and rejecting the others; by the time another batch was delivered, Steiner had gleaned what was of value from the first. At the time he was still writing his *Autobiography* by hand. Practical business concerning the new society occupied some of his time; it was necessary, according to Swiss law, that a formal constitution for the new society be drafted, and Steiner also composed a new ritual for the Christian Community. His visitors were few: Marie Steiner, Ita Wegman, Albert Steffen, Wachsmuth, and Dr. Ludwig Noll, who Ita Wegman had asked to help her in caring for Steiner. But on occasion he still saw a few others. One such was a eurythmist whose work interpreting a poem he was especially interested in seeing. He took a personal concern in her efforts and arranged her colored veil with his own hands. Steiner still believed that he would soon make a complete recovery. He seemed to have some insight into his illness, and he prescribed certain preparations which he believed would help. But it became increasingly clear to Ita Wegman that these accomplished little, if anything, and that Steiner's body was not absorbing sufficient nutrition to keep him alive. Significantly, on New Year's Eve, 1924, on the second anniversary of the destruction of the first Goetheanum, his health took an unmistakable turn for the worse. Ita Wegman, who had shared Steiner's optimism, now felt it had been premature. It was only a matter of time, she saw, before his vitality gave out. Again, while his immediate ailment was his body's inability to retain nourishment, many who knew him believed that the real cause of his death was his inability to refuse the many who came to him for help. As Andrei Belyi recounts, "In his kindness, the demands he made upon himself were unending." "Compassion has its limits," one of his followers said. "No," the Doctor replied, "compassion has no limits. . . . The more one gives, the more one has to give."[14] Steiner gave without qualm, although, when his illness began to trouble him, he did occasionally mutter a word to Marie about the lack of consideration of some of his followers. But in the end he was always there. Few things can be more draining than listening to the problems of others, and Steiner did this regularly, for hours at a time, often having to advise on matters such as relationships, careers, and, ironically, health, after already spending a full day on other important and demanding tasks. Thousands walked away from these consultations with a little piece of the Doctor. Finally, although he would be the last to admit it, there was nothing left to give.

A long with his *Autobiography,* Steiner had spent the months prior to his illness composing a series of letters to the members of the society. Published in *What Is Happening in the Anthroposophical Society,* a news sheet for members, these were, as mentioned earlier, later collected in book form as *Anthroposophical Leading Thoughts.*[15] Written in a highly condensed, aphoristic style, these "leading thoughts" form a kind of distilled essence of anthroposophy and can be taken as Steiner's final word on the insights at the core of his life's work. Unlike the *Autobiography* which, whatever its reservations about Steiner's personal life, is still chatty and probably his most readable book, the gnomic "leading thoughts" assume a knowledge of anthroposophy and a familiarity with Steiner's worldview most beginning readers lack; this makes them a difficult study. The first "leading thought" contains perhaps the best known definition of anthroposophy, and has already been quoted in this book: "Anthroposophy is a path of knowledge, to guide the spiritual in the human being to the spiritual in the universe." In the third "leading thought," Steiner returns to the problem that obsessed him in his early days: "There are those who believe that with the limits of knowledge derived from sense-perception the limits of all insight are given. Yet if they would carefully observe *how* they become conscious of these limits, they would find in the very consciousness of the limits the faculties to transcend them."[16] Steiner is reiterating the insight that informed his entire pursuit of supersensible reality: that thought itself provides the means to transcend itself and go beyond its so-called limitations. He remarks that although a fish may swim only to the limits of water, the medium in which it lives, because it lacks the organs necessary to exist beyond it, human beings do possess the organs needed to enter the world beyond the senses. We are, in a sense, a kind of amphibian, able to exist in two realms. The problem is that we don't realize that we possess these organs. We can see Steiner's life's work as an attempt to get human beings to recognize who they really are. And readers of Steiner who are attracted to him because of his "ecologically correct" atti-tude toward nature may be surprised at the decidedly *anti*-natural tone of some of his last pronouncements. Human beings, he writes, need "a knowledge of the spiritual world." For "however widely [we] may feel the greatness, beauty and wisdom of the nat-ural world, this world gives no answer to the question of [our] own being." "Great, beautiful, wisdom-filled Nature does indeed answer the question, How is the human form dissolved and destroyed? (meaning that once dead and bereft of our etheric body, our physical bodies decay) but not the other question, How is it maintained and held together?"[17] Obviously this isn't to say that Steiner is "against nature" in some rapacious, exploitive way; clearly a man concerned with "cosmic rhythms" and "terrestrial forces" and who gave detailed instructions on how to "dynamize" farming and who was aware of the spiritual beings behind it has a powerful feel for the natural world and our responsibility toward it. But Steiner is intent on reminding his followers that what is truly *human* about us isn't what is "natural." The "natural" is often another way of saying the "material," and Steiner's whole life was a forceful attempt at making clear that any "explanation" of human existence in terms of "natural" or "material" forces is woefully inadequate, as they leave out what is truly human about us: the spiritual. In Europe, Steiner's ideas have rightly found a new responsive audience among the Greens; yet Steiner himself, I think, would be dismayed if his loving and responsible attitude toward the natural world overshadowed his central insight into the *spiritual reality* at the core of human being. For all his feeling for the natural world, any philosophy that would subsume the human into the strictly natural, for whatever worthy reasons, would, for Steiner, be misguided.

The remaining "leading thoughts" (there are some 185 of them, the last composed two weeks before Steiner's death) touch on the whole field of anthroposophical work, but a central figure throughout is the archangel Michael, who in Steiner's last years had taken on a crucial significance. Steiner believed that in the evolution of consciousness, which was his fundamental concern, certain historical periods were guided by the work of powerful spiritual beings. For Steiner, the archangel Michael became the ruling spirit in 1879—notably, the same year that Steiner went to Vienna. In the earliest times, mankind had direct participation in the divine, but, in order for humanity to approach the spirit worlds in full freedom, this initial immersion in the higher worlds had to be abandoned. This process was gradual, and Steiner's occult history is an account of the steady withdrawal of human consciousness from the spiritual worlds.[18] Yet this necessary process also carried the danger that mankind would completely sever its connection with the higher worlds, and so be left open to the influence of Lucifer and, more crucially for our own time, Ahriman. For this to be avoided, the Christ being descended to earth and, with his incarnation, ensured that humanity would have the possibility of returning to its original participation in the divine, without losing its own hard-won independence. Steiner charts this process over centuries and makes the curious announcement that 1899 marked the end of the Kali Yuga, the "dark age" of Hindu belief. It was now possible for humankind to move closer to the divine, and it was Michael's task to guide us in doing this.

The work, however, is not easy and there are no guarantees of success. Steiner was especially concerned about the rise of technology, the abuse of which he saw as a manifestation of Ahriman, and which he characterized as "Sub-Nature." (One element of the modern world that Steiner was especially troubled by was popular culture; one follower recounts that he often spoke of the "Ahrimanic-mechanical effects of the cinema."[19] Whether his concern was justified or not is debatable.) In the technological age, Steiner writes, "the possibility of finding a true relationship to the Ahrimanic . . . has escaped man. He must find the strength, the inner force of knowledge, in order not to be overcome by Ahriman in this technological civilization. He must understand Sub-Nature for what it really is. This he can only do if he rises, in spiritual knowledge, at least as far into extra-earthly Super-Nature as he has descended, in technical sciences, into Sub-Nature. The age requires a knowledge transcending Nature, because in its inner life it must come to grips with a life-content which has sunk far beneath Nature."[20] And if any readers think that an answer to this challenge is some form of "archaic revival," a return of some kind to a pristine, pretechnological world, Steiner has some sobering reflections. "Needless to say, there can be no question here of advocating a return to earlier stages of civilization. The point is that man shall find the way to bring the conditions of modern civilization into their true relationship—to himself and to the Cosmos."[21] It is necessary to do this, Steiner said, so that we can create within ourselves "the inner strength *not to go under.*"[22]

On March 29, Steiner's condition worsened. The last few months had brought him much pain, but now it seemed to have lifted and a kind of calm expectancy came over him. Marie Steiner, who had spent much of the time away from Dornach with her eurythmy troupe—Steiner had insisted that she carry on with her work—received a message that she should return. She did the next day, but too late to see her husband alive a final time. On the morning of March 30, 1925, Rudolf Steiner died. When Marie arrived he had already passed over into those realms we inhabit between "death and rebirth." According to Guenther Wachsmuth, his face at the end bore an almost radiant peacefulness and serenity, and his death mask, at least to the present writer, seems to bear some resemblance to the figure of the Representative of Humanity, the great reconciler of opposing forces, whose unfinished form stands today in the second Goetheanum.

At the time of writing, it is eighty years since Steiner's death, and although his name is no longer quite as familiar and respected as it was in post–World War I Europe, his work and his influence carry on in ways that he himself may have found surprising. In his last letter to the teachers of the first Waldorf school in Stuttgart, Steiner called the school "a child that needs special care" and a "visible sign of the fruitfulness of anthroposophy within the spiritual life of humankind."[23] Today thousands of students around the world receive the benefits of Steiner education; in many places it has become the most popular form of alternative schooling, drawing more applicants than other alternative approaches like the Montessori schools. As John Barnes writes, "Waldorf education . . . is the largest non-parochial, independent educational movement in the world."[24] Thousands of farms on different continents operate along biodynamic principles, and fruit and vegetables "dynamized" through Steiner's methods find a place on more dinner tables today than ever before. The Camphill schools and villages dedicated to providing the kind of special care required by handicapped children have helped numerous individuals enjoy rewarding and fulfilling lives they would otherwise have missed. Weleda and Demeter (another anthroposophical brand) products prepared according to Steiner's principles are popular health and well-being items, and like other forms of holistic medicine, anthroposophical medicine is increasingly seen as a viable alternative to orthodox treatment. Steiner's architectural ideas, although still outside the mainstream, have influenced a generation of architects dissatisfied with cold, impersonal modernism as well as with the frivolity of the postmodern. Steiner's belief in our responsibility to the natural world has influenced a generation of environmentalists and ecologically minded individuals. His ideas on art have been a source of inspiration for many practicing artists, as well as those working in various forms of art therapy; and although it hasn't become a widely accepted art form in itself, eurythmy has also found many champions, especially in its curative application. Goethean science, once considered the embarrassing aberration of a great poet, is today receiving more serious consideration as a viable alternative to the dominant mechanistic model than it ever has, finding applications in chaos theory, complexity theory, and other nonreductive approaches. Steiner's College for Spiritual Science is still enrolling students, the second Goetheanum is still the center of anthroposophical activity, and the General Anthroposophical Society has branches and members around the world. More than any other spiritual or esoteric thinker, the practical application of Steiner's ideas has had a remarkable success, and there is little evidence that this will change in the near future. Indeed the opposite is more likely.

Steiner, I think, could only be pleased to see this. And, if he is still occupying those transitional realms between "death and rebirth" and is at all aware of what he has made possible, he could not be blamed for experiencing a sense of satisfaction, however briefly he would let himself enjoy it. Yet I wonder what he would feel about his other work, his basic insights into consciousness and the reality of human freedom. Mainstream philosophy has as much use for Steiner today as it did a century ago, but his work has been picked up by more alternative thinkers, like William Irwin Thompson and Richard Tarnas. Where his presence was once ignored, histories of modern art and literature today devote respectable space to Steiner's influence on artists like Kandinsky and writers like Andrei Belyi, and the influence of the occult—an unfortunately overloaded term—in general and Steiner in particular on modern culture receives more academic attention now than at any previous time. "The best-kept secret of the twentieth century," as Owen Barfield is said to have called Steiner, is increasingly seen to have been one of its major thinkers, at least to those disinclined to disregard him as a crank. Yet the Ahrimanic sensibility that Steiner strove so hard to counter has, it seems to the present writer, only grown more dominant in recent years, and materialist models of the mind and consciousness have, with few exceptions, become firmly entrenched.

Clearly, the work of one man, however brilliant and industrious, can hardly be expected to overthrow the intellectual sediment of centuries single-handedly, and *The Philosophy of Freedom,* in my opinion Steiner's most important book, shares shelf space with the work of other philosophers and thinkers who recognized the dangers of the materialist view—Henri Bergson, Alfred North Whitehead, Michael Polyani, David Bohm, Edmund Husserl, Jean Gebser, Maurice Merleau-Ponty, Karl Popper, to name a few. Yet even the combined work of these and many others is still seen as a curious but ultimately unfruitful adjunct to the main thrust of modern thought. All the evidence suggests that that thrust is toward the final and satisfactory "explanation" of the universe and everything in it, including ourselves, in terms of some physical, material, and hence meaningless process. With many scientists eagerly anticipating putting the final touches on a theory of every-thing, and the union of human beings and machines—or, to use the preferred euphemism, computers—seemingly inevitable, the idea that humankind is at heart spiritual, free and evolving into a new state of consciousness may seem somewhat quaint. To point to the practical success of Steiner's ideas is no argument against their conclusions, the materialists would say. That Waldorf educa-tion achieves remarkable results, they would point out, is no proof that a spiritual world exists, even though that success is based on that belief. If it ever was discovered that an apple never fell on Isaac Newton's head, this would not displace the law of gravity.

In some ways, the very success of anthroposophical ideas in education, farming, health care, and other areas may work against Steiner's philosophical insights ever gaining a greater foothold in the zeitgeist. Ours is an age of specialization; the polymath is frowned upon, and for the professionals, a man with his fingers in as many pies as Steiner had could only be a dilettante. That he also spoke about disreputable subjects like Atlantis, life after death, reincarnation, astral bodies, and so on only confirms this suspicion. Likewise his insistence that what he was doing was a science, a distinction that most contemporary scientists would deny him. Hurdles like these make it unlikely that his important insights into consciousness, epistemology, and the relation between the mind and the world will receive the study they deserve, outside, that is, of individuals who recognize the need for this. And even in anthroposophical circles, this aspect of Steiner's work, fundamental as it is, often receives more respectful rhetoric than real engagement.

For anthroposophists and others convinced of Steiner's importance, these considerations are negligible. But for readers like me, sympathetic but not believers, complete commitment to the anthroposophical life—or any other spiritual belief system—is more often a deterrent than an attraction. For all Steiner's attempts to prevent this, for the average person, anthroposophy too often comes across as a cult. Many have found a rewarding, spiritually fulfilling home within it. For others, equally seeking spirit, the inclusiveness—what foods to eat, what medicines to take, how our children should be taught, how our living spaces should be built—is off-putting. Yet it would be a loss if Steiner's insights into our most immediate contact with spirit—our inner world— should be thrown out with the bathwater. Personally, I have been familiar with Steiner's work for more than two decades, and while I still find enormously suggestive insights in his lectures, and am always surprised to discover something new in them, it is his early work on Goethe and consciousness rather than the major occult books to which I find it most rewarding to return. The importance of Steiner's fundamental insight: that the human I is an irreducible reality; that it is free; that consciousness, spirit, is at the core of existence itself; and that we, for so long alienated from the world around us, are really the solution to its riddle, is impossible to overestimate. If it were ever to take the central position it should occupy in our ideas about ourselves and the cosmos, it would, quite literally, inaugurate the start of a new age. But when, or if, this might happen is still anybody's guess.

These considerations, however, shouldn't prevent anyone from discovering Steiner's importance for themselves, in whatever form that might take. And people already engaged in the many fruitful practical activities to arise from Steiner's insights will more than likely not give this a second thought. Recognizing the unquestionable goodness of this almost saintly man makes any reservations about his work or life seem churlish. But it should also be pointed out that although he is more often than not presented as an infallible, indeed holy, man, Steiner was, after all, a human being. He could be stern and demanding, reprimanding a student who had forgotten to prepare for her lesson, insisting that one's hands should be washed before meditation, and that one's arms or legs should never be crossed. But he also had a sense of humor and could inform some eurythmists that their "Lucifers [were] like noodles" and their "Ahrimans like pocket knives." That Austrian *Gemütlichkeit* never left him. He was a great fan of Strauss, and once complained that he didn't have a decent tie to wear to the theater. He would crack jokes on the train, on route to a lecture in Cologne, Berlin, or some other city, and when he informed his companions that Wagner was the magician Merlin in a former life, it was not always clear if this was meant seriously or not. On car journeys he would pour some of his coffee onto the ground, so that the earth "could participate in the enlivening substance," and he always broke the first sandwich handed to him, and shared it with his neighbor. He enjoyed eating with others and socializing and forbade any talk of higher matters around the table. He was also, as probably hardly needs saying, a religious man, and every afternoon at three o'clock, he would recite the Lord's Prayer in Latin, a habit acquired no doubt in his early years.[25] As with all those who come into contact with a remarkable human being, the many who knew him shared an experience we who come later can only imagine.

And Steiner the seer? Depending on how you look at it, this, I think, still remains either a stumbling block or a challenge. We may take some, perhaps most, of his occult insights with a grain or two of salt, and even dismiss many of them as products of his imagination. This hardly matters. Steiner himself would encourage us to subject his work to the greatest scrutiny and would encourage any who could to correct him. His devotion to the human spirit, however, and the good that came of it—this remains undeniable, and in our troubled times, something to aspire to.

NOTES

INTRODUCTION: RUDOLF STEINER'S ROSE

1. For my involvement in the Gurdjieff work, see my *In Search of P. D. Ouspensky* (Wheaton, IL: Quest Books, 2004).

2. Colin Wilson, *Rudolf Steiner: The Man and His Vision* (Wellingborough, England: Aquarian Press, 1985).

3. Maurice Maeterlinck, *The Great Secret* (London: Methuen, 1922), p. 212.

4. Gary Lachman, *A Secret History of Consciousness* (Great Barrington, MA: Lindisfarne, 2003).

5. Rudolf Steiner, *Man in the Past, the Present and the Future* (London: Rudolf Steiner Press, 1982), p. 25.

6. "Rudolf Steiner and the Fate of the Earth," *Gnosis,* Spring 1994.

1. THE DWELLER ON THE THRESHOLD

1. Rudolf Steiner, *An Autobiography* (Blauvelt, NY: Rudolf Steiner Publications, 1977), p. 17.

2. Wilson, *Rudolf Steiner: The Man and His Vision*, p. 61.

3. Steiner, *An Autobiography,* p. 401.

4. Stewart C. Easton, *Rudolf Steiner: Herald of a New Epoch* (Spring Valley, NY: Anthroposophic Press, 1980), p. 158.

5. In conversation with Christopher Bamford, a Steiner scholar and author of respected works on the history of Western esotericism,

I asked about Steiner's sex life. He replied that to the best of his knowledge, Steiner was celibate.

6. Rudolf Steiner, *Knowledge of the Higher Worlds and Its Attainment* (Blauvelt, NY: Anthroposophic Press, 1947), p. 232.

7. Steiner adapted the idea of the Guardian of the Threshold from the Rosicrucian novel *Zanoni* (1842) by Edward Bulwer-Lytton, a writer, occultist, and paranormal investigator in the mid–nineteenth century. Bulwer-Lytton is remembered today, if at all, for his historical novel *The Last Days of Pompeii* (1834) and for writing what many considered one of the worst opening lines in literature, "It was a dark and stormy night" (*Paul Clifford*, 1830). For more on Bulwer-Lytton, see *A Dark Muse* (New York: Thunder's Mouth Press, 2005), pp. 99–105.

8. Steiner, *An Autobiography*, p. 23.

9. See Ouspensky's introduction to *A New Model of the Universe* (New York: Alfred A. Knopf, 1969).

10. Steiner, *An Autobiography*, p. 28.

11. Ibid.

12. See Anthony Storr's *Feet of Clay* (New York: Free Press, 1996), pp. 69–70.

2. THE RUSTIC SCHOLAR

1. In this context it is interesting to refer again to Anthony Storr's notion of "schizotypy," one of the characteristics of which is often an inability to assimilate incoming stimuli, and a sensation of being overloaded by impressions. Another characteristic, one that seems appropriate in Steiner's case, is the need to clarify thoughts. Steiner's youthful need to answer deep, existential questions, and his later emphasis on the absolute importance of lucid, clear thinking may stem from a feeling that his mind was overcrowded with ideas. It is also important to point out that Storr argues that many "schizotypic" characteristics are also those involved in creativity and should not be seen as purely aberrant traits. For more on the psychology of creativity, see his important study *The Dynamics of Creation* (New York: Atheneum, 1972).

2. Again, the resemblance between Steiner's and P. D. Ouspensky's exploits in school bears comparison. In Ouspensky's case it was a book about physics. See his introduction to *A New Model of the Universe*, mentioned above.

3. Steiner, *An Autobiography*, p. 43.

4. Ibid.

5. Readers unhappy with epistemology may reflect on the old chestnut "If a tree falls in a forest and there's no one there, does it make a sound?" which presents the same dilemma in concrete terms. To know whether or not it makes a sound, either we, or someone else, or a machine that mimics the human ear, would have to be there, and if this is so, then the conditions are compromised. The sound is a product of the tree's falling *and* our being there to hear it. For Kant, the world is a product of a something *and* our perceptual apparatus.

6. Robert McDermott, ed., *The Essential Steiner* (New York: Harper & Row, 1984), p. 13.

7. Steiner, *An Autobiography*, p. 47.

8. Again, there is an interesting similarity here to a remark of P. D. Ouspensky in his account of his time with Gurdjieff, *In Search of the Miraculous*. Ouspensky comments that in teaching what he had learned from Gurdjieff to others, his insights into material he felt he *already knew* were refreshed and made deeper. Until teaching it to others, he saw that he didn't *really* know it. See *In Search of the Miraculous* (London: Routledge & Kegan Paul, 1983), p. 277.

9. Some of Steiner's astonishing erudition got him into a bit of trouble with his instructor in German. Along with other subjects, Steiner tutored his fellow pupils in composition, and often he would sacrifice to them his own best and briefest ideas for essays, leaving his own to end up somewhat longer than desired. (The source of Steiner's somewhat prolix style?) One day the instructor informed Steiner that the length of his essays annoyed him. But there was something about this instructor that made Steiner curious; he then discovered that he was a disciple of the philosopher Johann Friedrich Herbart, unknown today. Steiner bought Herbart's books, and then

in his essays he inserted ideas from his philosophy. At the close of one essay, however, Steiner ended with the words, "And such a person is free, psychologically." This instructor remarked on this and informed him there was no such thing as "psychological freedom." To which Steiner replied that there is; it is just that "there is no 'transcendental freedom' in ordinary consciousness." The instructor then replied that his essays gave the impression that he had a "philosophical library," and he advised him not to use it, "as it only confuses your thoughts." Steiner profited by this instructor, though, as his lessons included selections from Greek and Latin poetry in translation. Attending the Realschule rather than the Gymnasium meant that Steiner had had no instruction in either language. Steiner felt that the German translations didn't convey the true beauty of the original, so he bought the Gymnasium textbooks and taught himself Greek and Latin. Later he would tutor in these as well.

10. Steiner, *An Autobiography,* p. 53.

11. Francis Crick, *The Astonishing Hypothesis: The Scientific Search for the Soul* (London: Simon & Schuster, 1994), p. 3. For more on the urge to explain consciousness, see the introduction to *A Secret History of Consciousness.*

12. Steiner, *An Autobiography,* p. 80.

13. It's ironic that neither Goethe nor Blake, both of whom were great readers in the Western hermetic tradition, was aware that Newton himself wrote more about alchemy and hermeticism than he did about gravity; Newton's hermetic writings were not discovered until the early twentieth century.

14. For an excellent essay on Goethe's methods of observation, see Erich Heller's "Goethe and the Scientific Truth," in *The Disinherited Mind* (New York: Farrar, Straus and Cudahy, 1957).

15. Quoted in McDermott, *The Essential Steiner,* p. 39.

16. Quoted in Heller, *The Disinherited Mind,* p. 31.

17. John Barnes, *Nature's Open Secret* (New York: Steiner Books, 2000), p. 274.

3. AT THE MEGALOMANIA CAFÉ

1. Steiner, *An Autobiography,* p. 60.
2. McDermott, *The Essential Steiner,* p. 13.
3. Ibid., p.14.
4. Steiner, *An Autobiography,* p. 60.
5. Quoted in Johannes Hemleben, *Rudolf Steiner: A Documentary Biography* (East Grinstead, England: Henry Goulden, 1975), p. 26.
6. Ouspensky, *A New Model of the Universe,* p. 30.
7. Quoted in Hemleben, *Rudolf Steiner: A Documentary Biography,* p. 26.
8. Schopenhauer, incidentally, developed some ideas of Kant. He argued that the reality of existence was a blind, striving, unconscious will which, however, we never perceive directly; we can only see its representations, the appearances the will takes on through our means of perception. Human life is made of suffering because this will is never satisfied; any satisfaction we achieve is automatically replaced with new cravings. Schopenhauer's solution to this problem was a philosophy of profound detachment and world rejection; in this many see the influence of Eastern, specifically Buddhist thought.
9. Steiner, *An Autobiography,* p. 75.
10. Ibid., p. 111.
11. Wilson, *Rudolf Steiner: The Man and His Vision,* p. 44.
12. Ibid.
13. Steiner, *An Autobiography,* p. 119.
14. Ibid., p. 170.
15. Easton, *Rudolf Steiner: Herald of a New Epoch,* p. 37.
16. The Café Griensteidl was for Steiner the equivalent of the Stray Dog Café that the young P. D. Ouspensky frequented in St. Petersburg in his years before meeting Gurdjieff. For more on the Russian occult revival of the early twentieth century, see my books *In Search of P. D. Ouspensky* and *A Dark Muse.*

    In his article "Schoenberg and the Occult: Some Reflections on the 'Musical Idea'" (*Theory and Practice: Journal of the Music Society of*

New York State no. 17 [1992], pp. 103–18), the musicologist John Covach speculates that some of the people influenced by Steiner's work on Goethe, and who may even have heard of his café conversations, were the composers Arnold Schoenberg and Anton Webern, members of the so-called Second Viennese school, responsible for modern developments in music like the twelve-tone system and serial composition. Both Schoenberg and his friend Wassily Kandinsky were later clearly influenced by Steiner's occult ideas, as is apparent from Kandinsky's essay "On the Spiritual in Art," and in his correspondence with Schoenberg; Kandinsky attended some of Steiner's lectures as well. (Another central occult influence on Schoenberg was Emanuel Swedenborg.) Covach points out that by the time Schoenberg was himself a frequenter of Vienna's cafés, the occult scene in Vienna was at its height, and that although Steiner himself had by this time—the 1890s—moved on to Weimar and Berlin, his ideas about Goethe's worldview were still part of café discussion. Webern's radically compressed compositions are a musical expression of Goethe's *Urphänomen,* the most vocal and visible advocate of which at that time was Steiner.

17. In *God Is My Adventure* (pp. 58–59), Rom Landau makes the curious statement that Steiner "indulged for a short time in an excessive consumption of wine, and at the end of this period any possibility of hereditary clairvoyance was destroyed." Landau doesn't give a date for Steiner's alleged binge-drinking, but if it did happen, his student years seem a likely possibility. I haven't come across this reference in any other work on Steiner, but it is true that Steiner saw what Landau calls "hereditary clairvoyance," the native clairvoyance of mediums like Madame Blavatsky, as a remnant of an earlier stage in the evolution of human consciousness. As such, it was something to be transcended in order for contemporary human beings to achieve their appropriate level of development which, Steiner argued, can only be attained through rigorous practice of the disciplines he puts forth in his work. That Steiner himself was blessed with "hereditary clairvoyance" is clear

from his early experiences; it is also clear that, given his ideas about the evolution of consciousness, he would want to avoid any suspicion that his own supersensible perception was rooted in what he saw as an atavism.

18. In this context Steiner in some ways resembles the Austrian composer Anton Bruckner, another rustic genius who was known for his social faux pas and who was Steiner's older contemporary. Like Steiner, Bruckner had an unshakable belief in spiritual reality; he once remarked that his symphonies were all dedicated to God.

19. Quoted in Hemleben, *Rudolf Steiner: A Documentary Biography*, p. 33.

20. Steiner, *An Autobiography*, p. 143.

4. IN THE GOETHE ARCHIVES

1. Quoted in Hemleben, *Rudolf Steiner: A Documentary Biography*, p. 43.

2. Barfield's classic work on this idea is his *History in English Words* (London: Faber and Faber, 1953), but see also his last book, *History, Guild and Habit* (Middletown, CT: Wesleyan University Press, 1981).

3. Quoted in Hemleben, *Rudolf Steiner: A Documentary Biography*, p. 47.

4. Quoted in Wilson, *Rudolf Steiner: The Man and His Vision*, p. 62.

5. Quoted in Hemleben, *Rudolf Steiner: A Documentary Biography*, p. 47.

6. For a fascinating study of Elisabeth Förster-Nietzsche, and a more detailed account of her relations with Rudolf Steiner, see H. F. Peters, *Zarathustra's Sister* (New York: Marcus Weiner, 1985).

7. Ibid., p. 151.

8. Steiner, *An Autobiography*, pp. 222–23.

9. Rudi Lissau, *Rudolf Steiner: Life, Work, Inner Path and Social Initiatives* (Stroud, England: Hawthorn Press, 1987), p. 10.

10. Steiner, *An Autobiography*, p. 206.

11. McDermott, *The Essential Steiner*, p. 15.

5. BERLIN AND THE TURNING POINT

1. Steiner, *An Autobiography*, p. 277.
2. Ibid.
3. This insight is, of course, at the heart of the Chinese symbol of the yin yang.
4. Steiner, *An Autobiography*, p. 78.
5. Readers familiar with Jungian psychology will recognize in this an expression of what Jung called "the transcendent function," the realization that a psychological problem confronting an individual is never solved in the usual sense of the word, but *outgrown*. Between the individual and the insurmountable problem arises an unexpected third element—thrown up, Jung argues, by the unconscious—which is precisely what is needed for the individual to move on. Life carries the individual beyond the problem, which strikes me as very close to what Steiner is saying here.
6. From *Goethe's Conception of the World*, quoted in McDermott, *The Essential Steiner*, p. 49.
7. Steiner, *An Autobiography*, p. 303.
8. Ibid., p. 310.
9. As Steiner was writing theater reviews at a time when Maeterlinck enjoyed great popularity, one wonders if a review by Steiner of one of Maeterlinck's plays had anything to do with Maeterlinck's remarks about Steiner quoted in the introduction.
10. Stirner is little read today, but readers interested in him can find a contemporary expression of his ideas in the work of the German novelist Ernst Jünger (1898–1999), whose philosophy of the anarch is influenced by Stirner's work. It is curious to wonder how much Steiner knew of Mackay's life as a homosexual; under the pseudonym "Sagitta," Mackay wrote novels such as *Der Puppenjunge*, depicting the life of Berlin boy-bars in the early 1920s. Like Bernard Suphan, Steiner's associate in Weimar, Mackay would commit suicide. Ten days after the Nazi book burnings at the Institut für Sexualwissenschaft in 1933, Mackay took his own life. See http://en.wikipedia.org/w/index.php?title=John_Henry_Mackay&oldid+74228351.

11. Hemleben, *Rudolf Steiner: A Documentary Biography*, p. 73.

12. Steiner, *An Autobiography*, p. 326.

13. Rudolf Steiner, *From Symptom to Reality in Modern History* (London: Rudolf Steiner Press, 1976), p. 144.

14. Ibid.

15. Ibid., p. 155.

16. Fräulein Muecke, present at the lecture, quoted in Easton, *Rudolf Steiner: Herald of a New Epoch,* p. 100.

17. Ibid., p. 101.

18. Ibid., p. 102.

19. See lecture 6 in Steiner, *From Symptom to Reality in Modern History.*

20. Ibid., p. 150.

21. Ibid., p. 104.

6. THEOSOPHY AND COSMIC MEMORIES

1. Fritz Seiler went on to become an important member of the Anthroposophical Society and one of Steiner's stenographers, transcribing more than one thousand of his lectures.

2. See my chapter on A. R. Orage and his lecture to the Leeds branch of the Theosophical Society, "Consciousness: Animal, Human and Superman," in *A Secret History of Consciousness*.

3. Some sources give the date as August 22.

4. For more on Goethe's fairy tale and his general interest in alchemy and other forms of occultism, see *A Dark Muse*. For a recent, updated translation of "The Green Snake and the Beautiful Lily," see my *Dedalus Occult Reader: The Garden of Hermetic Dreams* (London: Dedalus, 2005).

5. Rudolf Steiner, *Mystics After Modernism* (Great Barrington, MA: Anthroposophic Press, 2000), p. 197.

6. Newly translated as *Mystics After Modernism*.

7. Marie Savitch, *Marie Steiner–von Sivers* (London: Rudolf Steiner Press, 1967), p. 31.

8. Rudolf Steiner, *The Occult Movement in the Nineteenth Century* (London: Rudolf Steiner Press, 1973), p. 47.

9. Henri F. Ellenberger, *The Discovery of the Unconscious* (London: Fontana Press, 1994), pp. 684–87.

10. Steiner, *An Autobiography,* p. 319.

11. Although *The Grand Initiates* would not be translated into German until 1909, seeing that it was a famous work by a good friend, Marie von Sivers no doubt spoke with Steiner about its ideas.

12. Easton, *Rudolf Steiner: Herald of a New Epoch,* p. 113.

13. Ibid., p. 130.

14. Ibid.

15. James Webb, *The Occult Establishment* (LaSalle, IL: Open Court, 1976), p. 65.

16. At the Eighth Ecumenical Council, held in Constantinople in 869.

17. There is evidence for a kind of electrical field associated with living organisms, which we can see as an etheric body. See Harold Burr, *Blueprint for Immortality: The Electric Patterns of Life* (London: Neville Spearman, 1972). Rupert Sheldrake has also made the idea of an etheric body more respectable, through his notion of "morphic resonance." See his *A New Science of Life: the Hypothesis of Formative Causation* (London: Blond & Briggs, 1981) and *The Presence of the Past: Morphic Resonance and the Habits of Nature* (London: Collins, 1988).

18. Steiner actually posits a ninefold system as well, but for the sake of clarity and brevity I have decided to stick to seven. Steiner's breakdown of human nature is, to say the least, complex and, as his able interpreter Robert A. McDermott admits, at times confusing. Along with the body/soul/spirit ensemble, and the occult arrangement of physical body, etheric body, astral body, and I, Steiner goes into fascinating but challenging detail about the specific structure of the separate bodies. So, as I discuss in chapter 8, the physical organism is composed of a three-part system of head and sensory system, rhythmic system (heart and lungs), and metabolic system (limbs). These in turn parallel the system of the body politic: the economic sphere corresponding to the head, the sphere of rights to the rhythmic system, and the cultural sphere to the metabolic system. The soul is the

seat of three activities: thinking, feeling, and willing, which correspond to three different states of consciousness: waking, dreaming, and dreamless sleep. These, too, correspond to human life, animal life, and plant life—sheer physical or mineral existence is a kind of death (and indeed, one of Steiner's strangest contentions was that each day we are engaged in a constant battle against the forces of death, and that the earth itself was dying).

The seven/three connection is also evident in Steiner's occult history. As I explain further on, prior to our present earth incarnation, Steiner argued that human beings and the world existed in three earlier forms, and will evolve into three further stages. Here we have three different stages of cosmic evolution on either side of our current stage, which occupies the middle, 3/1/3. This is recapitulated in Steiner's breakdown of occult history during our earth incarnation. There are seven post-Atlantean epochs: we are currently in the fifth, with two more to follow. The descent and incarnation of the Christ—*the* event in human and earthly history—occurred in the fourth epoch, that is, in the middle, 3/1/3 again.

Although at first daunting—if not positively off-putting—if one stays with Steiner's system it gradually begins to make an enlightening, if strange, sense, and even to display a kind of beauty. It's also interesting to wonder how much the influence of Hegel and Haeckel informs Steiner's scheme. Hegel's philosophy is famous for its celebrated dialectic, which posits a threefold structure to the progression of thought, as well as the evolution of consciousness. Although often misapplied, the formula *thesis, antithesis,* and *synthesis* is generally seen as Hegel's philosophy. This describes the motor of thought and history (for Hegel the two were synonymous): A thesis is put forth; this prompts its contradiction, and the ensuing stalemate is overcome by a third proposition that reconciles the two. This synthesis then brings forth its opposite, which is overcome by another synthesis, and so on. The idea of three forces or influences is also present in Hindu thought and is a key element in the equally challenging esoteric system of Steiner's brief contemporary G. I. Gurdjieff. The Hegelian character of Steiner's thought is perhaps best seen in his central threesome, the two negative spiritual beings Ahriman and Lucifer, who are overcome and absorbed in the reconciling presence of the Christ. Haeckel's influence is evident in Steiner's use of recapitulation, the idea that an earlier stage of development is returned to and experienced again, but at a higher level, a theme Haeckel made popular in his writings. Expressed in the formula "Ontogeny recapitulates phylogeny," this means that in its development, an organism goes through the stages that its species as a whole experienced at an earlier time, i.e., prior to birth, the human organism passes through the entire evolutionary cycle.

19. Rudolf Steiner, *Rosicrucian Wisdom* (London: Rudolf Steiner Press, 2000), p. 87.

20. Readers familiar with the ancient idea of the elements will recognize that Steiner's occult prehistory follows the pattern of fire, air, water, and earth. Prior to these there existed only nonmanifest spirit, an idea common to many spiritual teachings (it is the Pleroma of the Gnostics, for example, or the Ain Soph of the Kabbalah), which in alchemy was called the quintessence, or fifth element, the title, incidentally, of a relatively recent science fiction film.

21. Sadly, space permits me to only mention this fascinating idea. Interested readers may find my article "Rudolf Steiner and the Fate of the Earth," *Gnosis* (Spring 1994), a good starting point for further study.

22. See *The Story of Atlantis and Lost Lemuria* (London: Theosophical Publishing House, 1968).

23. A number linked, incidentally, to the "precession of the equinoxes," the apparent backward journey of the sun through the zodiac, giving rise to the notion of various ages like the Age of Aquarius, the dawning of which occultists and astrologers have been expecting for more than a century now.

24. See my article "Rudolf Steiner, Jean Gebser and the Evolution of Consciousness," *Journal for Anthroposophy*, Fall 1995; also *A Secret History of Consciousness*, pp. 217–67.

25. Rudolf Steiner, *Cosmic History* (New York: Harper & Row, 1981), p. 40.

26. The idea of an Akashic Record, by now a commonplace of occult and new age thought, has an interesting history. Although most associated with Steiner and before him Madame Blavatsky, Blavatsky herself adopted it from the work of the ex-socialist turned magician and kabbalist Alphonse Louis Constant, better known as Eliphas Levi. In his highly influential book *Transcendental Magic* (1865), Levi posits what he calls the astral light, a kind of infinitely fine and subtle material that possesses qualities like that of the animal magnetism of Anton Mesmer (see *A Dark Muse*). Levi is important in the history of Western occultism because, along with many other things, he was one of the first to relate magic to the imagination, thereby creating a strong link between occultism and the arts. Rejecting the traditional apparatus of magic spells, conjurations, and so on, Levi asserted that the true power of magic resided in the magician's own imagination, fuelled by his will, which, when sufficiently powerful, can impress itself upon the astral light, an idea in keeping with Romantic notions of the artist. This astral light, like the Akashic Record, retained impressions of all that has happened in history and, provided the magician's powers of imagination were strong enough, he could see these impressions. Blavatsky borrowed heavily from Levi (as did Aleister Crowley), and also from Levi's friend, the Victorian novelist Edward Bulwer-Lytton, from whom Steiner, too, adopted some ideas. Given her predilection for Eastern themes, Blavatsky transmuted Levi's astral light into the Akashic Record, *akasha* being Sanskrit for "ether," which at that time was believed to be an infinitely fine material substance permeating the universe. The nonexistence of the scientific ether was proven by the Michelson–Morley experiment of 1905; the theosophical ether has enjoyed a longer life span.

27. Steiner, *Cosmic Memory*, pp. 38–40.

28. Wilson *Rudolf Steiner: The Man and His Vision*, p. 164. See also Wilson's writings on what he calls "Faculty X," the ability to perceive the *reality* of "other times and places," and the many examples he gives of this in literature. One example which seems cogent here is that of the historian Arnold Toynbee's sudden vision of the whole of history on

the steps of the British Museum. See Wilson's *The Occult* (New York: Random House, 1971), pp. 60–61.

29. See Lachman, *A Secret History of Consciousness*, pp. 85–94.

30. From this Penfield discovered that the brain retains the memory of *everything* it has experienced, giving rise to a possible source of the phenomena of instantaneous life recall at the point of death (which Steiner would locate in the astral body) and also of the kind of involuntary memory that the novelist Proust made the subject of his *Remembrance of Things Past*.

31. See the account of Steiner's visit to Tintagel in Cornwall, England, in Wilson, *Rudolf Steiner: The Man and His Vision*, pp. 114–16.

32. See my article "Dreaming Ahead," *Quest*, Winter 1997.

33. See Lachman, *A Secret History of Consciousness*.

7. THE RISE OF DR. STEINER

1. Webb, *The Occult Establishment*, p. 66.

2. Quoted in Stewart C. Easton, *Rudolf Steiner: Herald of a New Epoch*, p. 169.

3. Rudolf Steiner, *The Way of Initiation* (London: Theosophical Publishing House, 1908), p. ii.

4. Ibid., pp. 33–34.

5. For an interesting perspective on Steiner's involvement with the OTO, see Francis King's highly entertaining *Modern Ritual Magic* (Dorset, England: Prism Press, 1989), pp. 99–108 and 205–7. Also A. E. Waite's *Shadows of Life and Thought* (London: Selwyn & Blount, 1938). Waite, a prominent occult scholar of the time, was leader of an offshoot of the Golden Dawn and provides some details about Steiner's involvement with some of its members. How long Steiner was involved in the OTO proper is unclear, although he does say that the use of rituals continued until the outbreak of World War I. And although the group involved in these rituals was not secret, it was a private group, set apart from the main body of the society.

6. Introduction to Steiner, *The Way of Initiation*, p. 10.

7. For more on Steiner's part in the Russian occult revival, see *A Dark Muse*, pp. 210–16. See also Bernice Glatzer Rosenthal, ed., *The Occult in Russian and Soviet Culture* (Ithaca, NY, and London: Cornell University Press, 1997), pp. 99–133.

Not all, however, were quite taken with Steiner. In his remarkable autobiography, *Dream and Reality* (London: Geoffrey Bless, 1950), the Russian existentialist thinker Nicolai Berdyaev records his impressions on attending the Helsinki lectures. Berdyaev writes:

> Steiner himself made an extremely painful impression, although he did not strike me at all as an impostor. He was a man who convinced and hypnotized not only others but himself. He seemed to possess a number of characters which he changed like masks as the need arose: now he was a benevolent pastor . . . now a magician holding sway over human souls. Seldom have I met anyone so completely devoid of grace as Steiner. Not one ray of light seemed to fall on him from above. His sole purpose and aspiration was to obtain possession of all things from below, by his own titanic devices, and to break through by a passionate effort to the realm of the spirit. . . .
>
> He may have possessed oratorical gifts, but he lacked the true gift and feelings for words. His speech was a kind of magical act, aimed at obtaining control over his hearers by means of gestures, by raising and lowering his voice, and by changes in the expression of his face. He hypnotized his disciples, some of whom even fell asleep. (pp. 192–93)

8. This wasn't true of one of Russia's most important theosophists, the composer Aleksandr Scriabin, who sought to convey the reality of spiritual experience through his music. Scriabin was involved in many occult themes of the time, most famously synesthesia, the phenomenon of sensory correspondence, in which, for example, certain colors are associated with certain tones, a theme that Steiner himself was deeply interested in. Scriabin at one point devised a color organ, a device that projected different colored lights associated with different

keys. His most ambitious project, a huge choral work entitled *Mystery*, was to have incorporated music, dance, painting, singing, even incense, and its performance would, he believed, have inaugurated a new spiritual age. Unfortunately, he died before completing it. See *A Dark Muse*, p. 143.

9. The Futurists, Cubo-Futurists, Dadaists, and Surrealists, as well as novelists like James Joyce and philosophers like Ludwig Wittgenstein, all shared Steiner's interest in a translogical speech, which we can see as a part of a general crisis of the word experienced by Western culture in the late nineteenth and early twentieth centuries. For more on this, see George Steiner's *Language and Silence* (New York: Atheneum, 1967) and *Extraterritorial* (New York: Atheneum, 1972).

10. As the century progressed, other esoteric teachers would recognize the value of art. G. I. Gurdjieff came to notoriety in the West as a teacher of sacred dance—the impresario Serge Diaghilev was at one point interested in his work—and even the dark magician Aleister Crowley presented his own version of the Mysteries of Eleusis, and was for a time the manager of a song-and-dance troupe, the Ragged Ragtime Girls.

11. There were, according to Steiner, actually two Christs: one a reincarnation of the Persian prophet Zarathustra, the other a simple-minded individual who had never incarnated before. When the Zarathustra Jesus died, his mother adopted the other Christ. Steiner also makes a distinction between the man Jesus and the spiritual being Christ, who had been awaiting incarnation since the beginning of human evolution. In the last three years of the man Jesus' life, the Christ being descended into the physical form of Jesus, in order to thwart the efforts of the beings Ahriman and Lucifer to deter human evolution. See Rudolf Steiner, *The Fifth Gospel* (New York: Rudolf Steiner Press, 1985).

12. The father later thought better of his decision and asked for the boys' return. When Leadbeater refused, the father went to the courts. In his highly entertaining if critical history of the Theosophical Society,

Madame Blavatsky's Baboon (London: Secker & Warburg, 1993), Peter Washington reports that the case, which the father lost, was unique in the annals of the Raj, being the only time when both sodomy and Godhood in relation to the same person appeared in the judge's notes.

13. See Easton, *Rudolf Steiner: Herald of a New Epoch,* chapter 7.

14. Quoted in Henry Barnes, *A Life for the Spirit* (Hudson, NY: Anthroposophic Press, 1997), p. 100.

15. Ibid., p. 103.

16. For more on Steiner's influence on modern art, see *The Spiritual in Art: Abstract Painting 1890–1985* (New York: Abbeville Press, 1986).

17. Krishnamurti himself later rejected the idea that he was the new Messiah, or any kind of spiritual teacher at all. On August 2, 1929, in front of an audience of three thousand people, he publicly repudiated theosophy and formerly dissolved the Order of the Star in the East. See Washington, *Madame Blavatsky's Baboon,* pp. 278–79.

18. Like Steiner, Leadbeater had pedagogical interests, although unlike Steiner, his commitment to educating the young—especially boys— was often guided by ulterior motives. In 1906, Leadbeater's passion for the psychic education of children took a sordid turn when it was revealed that, along with other lessons, he had given intimate instruction to a chosen few on the subtleties of masturbation. Evidence suggests that Leadbeater clothed this practice in theosophical dress and intimated that it was merely the first step toward a more satisfying release. In the face of the accusations against him, Leadbeater resigned from the Theosophical Society. See Washington, *Madame Blavatsky's Baboon,* pp. 121–23. It has to be said in Leadbeater's defense that at the time the idea of sexual education was promoted in several progressive camps, and Annie Besant herself had earned some calumny for her advocacy of birth control.

19. The title of the lecture series was "The History of Mankind's Evolution, as Shown in the World Conceptions from the Earliest Oriental Ages down to the Present Time: Or Anthroposophy."

20. Henri F. Ellenberg, *The Discovery of the Unconscious,* p. 685.

8. ANTHROPOSOPHIA

1. For a few years the construction at Dornach continued to be referred to as the Johannesbau, and became the Goetheanum only in 1917.

2. Quoted in Easton, *Rudolf Steiner: Herald of a New Epoch,* p. 195.

3. Ibid., p. 197.

4. Rudolf Steiner, *The Anthroposophic Movement* (Bristol, England: Rudolf Steiner Press, 1993), p. 63.

5. Barnes, *A Life for the Spirit,* p. 118.

6. Although Steiner clearly was not a confidant of the royal family and had no influence on the course of things, it is interesting to recall that the Russian powers had their own spiritual adviser, in the form of the ambivalent figure of Rasputin.

7. See "Reading to the Deceased," in Richard Seddon, ed., *Rudolf Steiner: Essential Readings* (Wellingborough, England: Aquarian Press, 1988), pp. 44–45.

8. Rudolf Steiner, *Earthly Death and Cosmic Life* (London: Rudolf Steiner Press, 1964), pp. 54–72. In this lecture Steiner makes the curious statement that when, as we fall asleep and enter the hypnagogic state, we ask the dead a question, it is really the dead themselves who give the question to us, just as when we rise out of sleep, the answer we receive actually comes from ourselves. Another explorer of inner worlds, the Scandinavian sage Emanuel Swedenborg, also spoke of the hypnagogic state as the best suited for entering the spiritual realms. See Wilson van Dusen's *Presence of Other Worlds* (London: Wildwood House, 1981).

9. Steiner's blackboard drawings have since been recognized as artworks in themselves, and have been the subject of several exhibitions. See Lawrence Rinder, ed., *Knowledge of Higher Worlds: Rudolf Steiner's Blackboard Drawings* (Berkeley: University of California, Berkeley Art Museum and Pacific Film Archive, 1997).

10. See Steiner, *The Anthroposophic Movement,* pp. 93–94.

11. Ilona Schubert, *Reminiscences of Rudolf Steiner* (London: Temple Lodge, 1991), pp. 45–46.

12. Lissau, *Rudolf Steiner: Life, Work, Inner Path and Social Initiatives,* pp. 46–47.

13. Belyi, Turgenieff, Voloschin, *Reminiscences of Rudolf Steiner* (Ghent, NY: Adonis Press, 1987), p. 60.

9. LAST DAYS AND LEGACY

1. Hemleben, *Rudolf Steiner: A Documentary Biography*, p.141.
2. At the time of Steiner's death in 1925, only the foundations of the second Goetheanum had been completed. The building itself was only opened in 1929, and today visitors are welcome. For an excellent study of Steiner's architectural ideas and their influence, see Hagen Biesantz and Arne Klingborg, eds., *The Goetheanum: Rudolf Steiner's Architectural Impulse* (London: Rudolf Steiner Press, 1979).
3. Steiner, *The Anthroposophic Movement*, p. 121.
4. Rudolf Steiner, *What Is Anthroposophy?* (Great Barrington, MA: Anthroposophic Press, 2002), p. 27.
5. Along with the attacks on anthroposophy and himself, and the destruction of the Goetheanum, in the years just after World War I, Steiner had had to assimilate great personal misfortune too. Because of an accident, by the end of the war Marie Steiner had been confined to a wheelchair. Soon after, her legs had to be encased in splints, and would remain so for the last thirty years of her life. For the co-developer of eurythmy, this must have been a tremendous tragedy.
6. Easton, *Rudolf Steiner: Herald of a New Epoch*, p. 329.
7. Today there are several Weleda centers in different countries, and a few years ago I had the opportunity to visit one in Ilkey, England, one of the places Steiner himself had visited in Great Britain. On the same trip I also visited a biodynamic farm associated with the Weleda center. Both were thriving.
8. A good introduction to anthroposophical medicine in the context of homeopathy is Francis X. King, *Rudolf Steiner and Holistic Medicine* (London: Rider, 1986).
9. These lectures are collected in Rudolf Steiner, *Agriculture Course: The Birth of the Bio-Dynamic Method* (London: Rudolf Steiner Press, 2004).
10. In his book *The Spear of Destiny* (Sphere Books: London, 1990)—a doubtful account of Hitler's involvement with the occult and how

this brought him into conflict with Steiner—Trevor Ravenscroft relates a story of how Steiner helped Count Keyserlingk deal with a rabbit infestation. Steiner asked for one of the rabbits to be shot. A preparation was made from the dead animal and this Steiner mixed with water. The resulting concoction was then sprayed over the count's estate. At first there seemed to be no effect, but a few days later, Ravenscroft informs us, those present were witnesses to a rabbit exodus, as the animals were seen leaving the area en masse.

11. One uncorroborated suggestion for the cause of Steiner's illness is that he was poisoned. See Schubert, *Reminiscences of Rudolf Steiner,* p. 53.

12. These have subsequently been published in a kind of "A to Z" series. Titles such as *From Elephants to Einstein* (London: Rudolf Steiner Press, 1998) and *From Beetroot to Buddhism* (London: Rudolf Steiner Press, 1999), as well as many others, give an idea of the topics covered.

13. See Rudolf Steiner, *Bees* (New York: Steiner Books, 1998). This edition also includes an essay on Joseph Beuys relating Steiner's influence on his work.

14. Belyi, *Reminiscences of Rudolf Steiner,* p. 17.

15. Rudolf Steiner, *Anthroposophical Leading Thoughts* (London: Rudolf Steiner Press, 1985).

16. Ibid., p. 14.

17. Ibid.

18. As mentioned earlier, readers interested in Steiner's account of the evolution of consciousness can find much to ponder on in the work of Owen Barfield, one of Steiner's most able interpreters, and a literary critic and philosopher of great insight in his own right. *Romanticism Comes of Age* (Middletown, CT: Wesleyan University Press, 1986) is Barfield's most "anthroposophical" work, but readers will also be interested in *Saving the Appearances* (New York: Harcourt, Brace & World, n.d.), which deals as well with the evolution of consciousness. A summary of some of Barfield's ideas can be found in my *A Secret History of Consciousness.*

19. Schubert, *Reminiscences of Rudolf Steiner,* p. 78.

20. Steiner, *Anthroposophical Leading Thoughts,* p. 218.

21. Ibid. Steiner's ideas on technology bear comparison with those of other influential thinkers on the subject, such as Martin Heidegger's *The Question of Technology* and Jacques Ellul's *The Technological Society,* for example. To be sure, Steiner's approach is more esoteric, and much of his thought is guided by his belief that the earth itself is dying. Although many ecologists would say the same, Steiner's attitude toward this idea is not negative. Earth's death is a necessary part of our ongoing cosmic evolution and will lead to a new incarnation as Jupiter—not the planetary body we are familiar with, but a new stage of consciousness. Symptomatic of earth's death is, Steiner says, the phenomena of electricity, which Steiner called dying light. For more on Steiner's ideas on the dying earth, see my article "Rudolf Steiner and the Fate of the Earth," *Gnosis,* Fall 1994. While we may find the notion of dying light odd, Steiner's concern that electricity leads down from Nature to Sub-Nature, and his warning that we must "beware lest [we] slide down with it" (*Anthroposophical Leading Thoughts,* p. 218), can find some resonance in contemporary worries about the abuses of our information age. We can only surmise what Steiner may have felt about computers. It is also interesting in this context to reflect on Steiner's remarks about Sub-Nature. He remarks that "since about the middle of the nineteenth century, the civilized activities of mankind are gradually sliding downward, not only into the lowest regions of Nature, but even *beneath Nature*" (ibid., p. 219). Quantum physics was still in its infancy at the time Steiner wrote this and it's unclear how aware he was of it, but this strikes me as a remarkable intuition about the direction that science would take in the twentieth century, with its increasing fascination with smaller and smaller elementary and *sub*atomic particles. See the article mentioned above for Steiner's other apparent intuitions about atomic energy and black holes.

22. Steiner, *Anthroposophical Leading Thoughts,* p. 219.

23. Quoted in Barnes, *A Life for the Spirit,* p. 254.

24. Barnes, *Nature's Open Secret,* p. 289.

25. See Schubert, *Reminiscences of Rudolf Steiner,* and Lissau, *Rudolf Steiner: Life, Work, Inner Path and Social Initiatives.*

BASIC BOOKS

Although the collections of lectures that crowd Steiner bookshops might suggest otherwise, Steiner was not a prolific writer, and his main ideas can be found in a handful of titles. Readers interested in following up this book with some of Steiner's own work may wish to start with the autobiography, the most readable of Steiner's writings. In recent years new editions of this, as well as some of Steiner's other books and many of the lectures, have become available.

Autobiography: Chapters in the Course of My Life 1861–1907 (Hudson, NY: Anthroposophic Press, 2000).

Intuitive Thinking as a Spiritual Path: A Philosophy of Freedom (Hudson, NY: Anthroposophic Press, 1995).

How to Know Higher Worlds: A Modern Path of Initiation (Hudson, NY: Anthroposophic Press, 1994).

Theosophy: An Introduction to the Spiritual Processes in Human Life and in the Cosmos (Hudson, NY: Anthroposophic Press, 1997).

An Outline of Esoteric Science (Hudson, NY: Anthroposophic Press, 1997).

Nature's Open Secret: Introduction to Goethe's Scientific Writings (Hudson, NY: Anthroposophic Press, 2000).

FOR FURTHER STUDY

In addition to some of the titles mentioned in the text and notes, a reader wanting to know more about Rudolf Steiner and his ideas may find the following suggestions helpful.

Websites
There are many Rudolf Steiner, anthroposophical, or related websites available on the Internet. A Google search under "Rudolf Steiner" will produce a large number of entries, more than I could possibly list here. Below I've provided addresses of some websites that I've used, along with others that seem promising.

www.rsarchive.org
www.goetheanum.org
www.waldorfanswers.org
www.steinercollege.org
www.steinerwaldorf.org.uk
www.steiner.edu
www.biodynamics.com/steiner.html
www.bamfa.berkeley.edu/exhibits/steiner/weblinks.html
www.goetheanscience.org
www.kheper.net/metamorphosis/Goethean.html
www.awakenings.com/goetheanscience/

Lectures

A daunting number of Steiner's lectures are available in book form in English translations, covering a sometimes bewildering range of topics, only some of which I've been able to touch on in this book. An enterprising reader may wish to plunge in at the deep end and start at random, diving into titles that attract his or her curiosity. Less courageous souls, however, would profit by some kind of catalogue, according to subject. In recent years, Sophia Books has produced a series of handy anthologies, the Pocket Library of Spiritual Wisdom, bringing together many of Steiner's lectures on central topics like agriculture (biodynamic farming), architecture, Christian Rosenkreutz (supposed founder of the Rosicrucians), the Holy Grail, social and political science, religion, education, science, alchemy, and art. Readers wanting to get a feel for Steiner's lectures would find a good starting place here.

Again, I strongly recommend any reader to begin with Robert McDermott's *Essential Steiner*. Along with the selections included in the anthology, McDermott also provides an extensive study guide and bibliography—nearly 100 pages—which the interested reader will find indispensable. A slimmer volume is Richard Seddon's *Rudolf Steiner: Essential Readings* (Wellingborough, England: Aquarian Press, 1988). This lacks McDermott's exhaustive guide, but is a good representative collection of short extracts covering Steiner's central concerns.

INDEX

Olden, Hans and Grete, 86–87
Opposites, life as union of, 102–3
Order of the Star in the East, 169, 170, 253n17
Order of the Temple of the Orient (Ordo Templi Orientis; OTO), 155, 250n5
Organic farming, 217–18
OTO. See Order of the Temple of the Orient
Ouspensky, P. D.
    on masters, 50
    and physics, 16–17, 239n2
    on teacher's knowledge, 239n8
Outline of Occult Science, An (Steiner), xvii, 93, 137–38, 143, 149

Pain, after death, 142, 143
Paracelsus, 128
Peace
    Steiner's thoughts on, 187
    after World War I, 191
Penfield, Wilder, 150
Perception
    of aura, 138–39, 141, 162–63
    awareness for, 96–97, 239n5
    Benn on, 100
    clairvoyance and, 242–43n17, 249–50n28
    consciousness and, 95
    of eternity, 148
    fallibility of, 148
    of Goethe, 43
    of history, 249–50n28
    transformation in, 100–102, 138
Perception, spiritual
    for art, 134
    of Christianity's evolution, 132–33
    fallibility of, 148
    handbook on, 138
Personality
    after death, 64, 97
    of Steiner, 168–69, 235–36, 251n7
Pessimism
    of culture, 52
    of delle Grazie's poetry, 53
    inner being versus, 55
Petersburg (Belyi), 167

Pfeiffer, Ehrenfried, 218–19
Phenomenology, 95
    and objectivity, 101–2
Philosophers, 233. See also specific names
Philosophy
    on consciousness, 36–38
    of detachment, 241n8
    of life, 135
    See also Anthroposophical Society; Knowledge; Materialism; Theosophical Society; Threefold Social Order
Philosophy of Freedom, The (Steiner), 70, 76, 88, 92, 94, 97, 105, 138
Philosophy of Spiritual Activity, The. See Philosophy of Freedom, The (Steiner)
Philosophy of the Unconscious, The (Hartmann), 65
Physical body, 139, 140
    after death, 227
    in incarnations, 141, 143, 144, 145, 246n18
Physical health, mental state for, 59, 60
Physical world, spiritual versus, 27
Physics, 16–17, 239n2
"Picture consciousness," 150
    in Old Moon consciousness, 145, 149
    origins of, 9–10
    See also "Picture thinking"
"Picture thinking," 190
Plants, 144
    etheric forces on, 218
    Goethe on, 43
    meditation on, 138
    for Weleda products, 220, 255n7
Plato, 77, 146
Platonism, 76–77
Poetry
    of delle Grazie, 53–54, 55, 56
    in Greek and Latin, Steiner's reading of, 240n9
Politics
    esoteric insight versus exoteric theory for, 112
    Steiner's lectures on, 191–93
Portal of Initiation, The (Steiner), 164
Pralaya (rest period), 144

276 INDEX

Soul's Probation, The (Steiner), 167
Specht, Ladislaus, 58, 61
Specht, Otto, 57–60
Specht, Pauline, 57–60
Specht, Richard, 60
Specht, Robert, 73
Speech
    eurythmy as, 129, 160, 167, 184
    of Steiner, 251n7
    translogical, 252n9
Spirit
    Christianity versus, 139
    as core of existence, 234–35
    nature's balance with, 40–41
    as nonmanifest, 248n20
    soul versus, 139–40
    spirit-self, 141
Spirit, human
    belief in, 139, 246n16
    Steiner's devotion to, 236
Spirit world
    access to, 99–100
    approach to, 91, 96
    denial of, 64
    discrimination for, 91
    exploration of, 62, 63
    need for, 227
Spirits, 91
    Ahrimanic, 185
    respect for, 202
"Spiritual Communion of Mankind"
        (Steiner), 204
Spiritual knowledge, waking conscious-
        ness for, 135
"Spiritual science"
    adult education and, 212, 231–32
    body of knowledge as, 172
    for life review, 2
Spiritual space, 18–19
Spiritualism
    materialism versus, 106
    Steiner versus, 47–48, 134
Spiritualists, 47–48
Spirituality, 64. See also Anthroposophy;
        Religion; Theosophy
Steffen, Albert, 165, 212
Stein, Heinrich von, 76–77
Steiner, Anna. See Eunicke, Anna

Steiner, Franziska. See Blie, Franziska
Steiner, Johann, 6–7, 8, 9, 10, 11
Steiner, Marie
    handicap of, 255n5
    Steiner's death and, 230
    See also Sivers, Marie von
Stirner, Max, 111–12, 244n10
Stockmeyer, Karl, 161
Stone circle, in Wales, 220
Storr, Anthony, 15, 92, 238n1
"Structures of consciousness," 147
Subjectivity
    Goethe and, 44
    introversion and, 101
    reality versus, 95–96
Sub-Nature
    Ahriman and, 229
    mankind's activities and, 257n21
Super-Nature, 229
Suphan, Bernard, 73, 79
Swedenborg, Emanuel, 94, 150,
        241–42n16, 254n8

Tabula rasa, xxi, 94–95
Tantric yoga, 138–39
Teachers, 120
    love of learning from, 195
    tutor as, 33–34, 57–58, 59–60
Teaching
    and knowledge, 33, 239n8
    method of, for spiritual experience, 172
    self-teaching, of languages, 239–40n9
    See also Teachers
Technology, 229
Teeth, and reading policy, 195–96
Tesla, Nikola, 150
Theater
    criticisms of, 110–11, 244n9
    Steiner and, 110–11
*Theory of Knowledge in Light of Goethe's
        Worldview* (Steiner), 60, 93
Theosophical Congress, 133–34, 156,
        159, 163, 164
Theosophical Society, 67. See also Besant,
        Annie; Blavatsky, Madame
        (Helena Petrovna); Krishnamurti
        (Jiddu)
    religion and, 131

ABOUT THE AUTHOR

Gary Lachman is the author of *Into the Interior: Discovering Swedenborg* (2006), *The Dedalus Occult Reader: The Garden of Hermetic Dreams* (2005), *A Dark Muse* (2005), *In Search of P. D. Ouspensky* (2004), *A Secret History of Consciousness* (2003), and *Turn Off Your Mind* (2001). As Gary Valentine, he was a founding member of the rock group Blondie and wrote some of their early hits; *New York Rocker: My Life in the Blank Generation* (2002) is his memoir of his years as a musician. He writes for *The Guardian, The Independent on Sunday, Fortean Times,* and other periodicals in the United States and the United Kingdom. In 2006 he was elected to the Rock and Roll Hall of Fame. He lives in London.